KNOWLEDGE UNPLUGGED

The McKinsey&Company

global survey on knowledge management

KNOWLEDGE
UNPLUGGED

JÜRGEN KLUGE • WOLFRAM STEIN • THOMAS LICHT

CO-AUTHORS

ALEXANDRA BENDLER

JENS ELZENHEIMER

SUSANNE HAUSCHILD

UWE HECKERT

JAN KRÖNIG

ANDRÉ STOFFELS

palgrave

First published 2001 by
PALGRAVE
Houndmills, Basingstoke, Hampshire RG21 6XS and
175 Fifth Avenue, New York, N.Y. 10010
Companies and representatives throughout the world

PALGRAVE is the new global academic imprint of
St. Martin's Press LLC Scholarly and Reference Division and
Palgrave Publishers Ltd (formerly Macmillan Press Ltd).

ISBN 0–333–96376–8 hardback

This book is printed on paper suitable for recycling and
made from fully managed and sustained forest sources.

A catalogue record for this book is available
from the British Library.

Library of Congress Cataloging-in-Publication Data
Kluge, Jürgen.
   Knowledge unplugged : the McKinsey & Company global
survey on knowledge management / by Jürgen Kluge, Wolfram
Stein, Thomas Licht.
      p. cm.
   Includes bibliographical references and index.
   ISBN 0–333–96376–8
   1. Knowledge management. I. Stein, Wolfram. II. Licht,
Thomas. III. Title.

   HD30.2 .K625 2001
   658.4'038—dc21   2001034819

Editing and origination by
Aardvark Editorial, Mendham, Suffolk

Original artwork by
Ulrich Scholz Design, Düsseldorf, Germany

10   9   8   7   6   5   4   3   2   1
10 09 08 07 06 05 04 03 02 01

Printed in Great Britain by Bath Press, Bath

contents

v

list of figures

acknowledgements

Almost $2^{1}/_{2}$ years ago, an engineer and a physicist sat together in the garden of an Italian restaurant on the outskirts of Darmstadt. As they relaxed over an espresso, they started to wonder about all the hype surrounding knowledge management. The engineer was Prof. Dr.-Ing. Herbert Schulz, Director of the Institute of Production Engineering and Machine Tools (PTW) at Darmstadt University of Technology, and I was the physicist, at least by training. Professionally at the time I was head of McKinsey & Company's global Automotive & Assembly sector. Much had been published in the academic world about knowledge management, and there were case studies that seemed to support the belief, however vague, that knowledge management might be the key to success in managing businesses. The mysteries still surrounding the topic defied our backgrounds in the hard sciences: knowledge was difficult to measure, hard to explain, but it was clearly becoming increasingly important. Our conclusion was obvious. We decided to try to demystify the topic and transfer proven analytic tools to the field of knowledge management. We wanted to identify success patterns and develop a pragmatic approach for managers to improve the utilization of their companies' knowledge base. This book is one result of that effort.

A joint team of doctoral students at the PTW and McKinsey consultants set out with an ambitious work plan and the even more ambitious goal of blowing the smoke away from the knowledge management discourse and shattering the mirrors. In January 2001, the third generation of team members met with Prof. Schulz and me for the final project review meeting.

Joachim Metternich, a doctoral student at the PTW was invaluable during the first year of this research project in setting up the interview guides, contacting the companies and finally conducting the interviews. He left a tremendous database of

ACKNOWLEDGEMENTS

knowledge for his colleague Jens Elzenheimer. Whatever hypotheses the team developed, Jens, with all the data at his fingertips, was there to give these punts an authoritative thumbs up or down. And then there is Alexandra Bendler, the rock-solid foundation of the team. Whatever could not be codified into our database was embedded in her mind and quickly retrieved. Except for the originators, Alex is the only team member on board from the first to the last day. Whenever a particularly prickly question arose during the writing of *Knowledge Unplugged* all eyes turned to Alex – and she never disappointed.

On the McKinsey side, Wolfram Stein and Stefan Spang joined as senior advisers early on in the process, just as the first hypotheses were being raised and discarded. Wolfram held things together during the evaluation phase and was the driving force as the results were being finalized.

Several McKinsey consultants rolled on and off the team, with some leaving the effort to complete doctoral theses centering on knowledge management. Maike Braun (alumnus), Martin Eyl, Ralph Fries, Philipp Lewinsky (alumnus), Stina Nordeng (alumnus), Olga Rabrenović, and Manuel Rehkopf all helped to lay the foundations for this book. Haruko Nishida, head of McKinsey's research team in Tokyo, was helpful in numerous ways during our visits to Japanese companies.

We are particularly indebted to the 40 companies that opened their doors and their businesses to us as part of our survey. Because of our confidentiality agreements, most will have to remain unnamed, but each contributed to the quality of our findings. A few took a step further when we approached them to ask whether we could discuss them openly as case examples for this book, and we offer an extra expression of thanks to Aisin AW, Buckman Labs, FujiXerox, Intel, John Deere, Oticon, Outokumpu, and SAP for this added support.

After the fog around knowledge management was lifted by the research team, Wolfram and I gathered a core group together to harvest the fruit of their efforts. To help us to prepare this manuscript, Alex and Jens were joined by McKinsey consultants Susanne Hauschild, Uwe Heckert, Jan Krönig, and André Stoffels. Thomas Licht of McKinsey's Munich office took the lead in this important final phase. He urged the team forward time and time again, pushing all obstacles out of the way and contributing substantially to the concepts that are the foundations of this book. As a team, this group tackled the mammoth job of compiling the results of our survey into a cohesive manuscript, acting as sparring partners for one another and fine-tuning the analysis.

Axel Born, a director in McKinsey's Düsseldorf office, was also invaluable in taking the time to help evaluate early drafts of this manuscript.

Furthermore, we were very fortunate to have access to the substantial McKinsey knowledge base. Not only did we draw from the Firm's vast databases and other repositories, but – far more importantly – we were able to tap into the experiences and ideas of some of our most provocative, inspiring, helpful and talented colleagues. Thanks are due in particular to Sebastian Ahrens, Matthias Beck, Michael Jung, Detlev Hoch, George Kerschbaumer, Jane Kirkland (alumnus), Michael Kloss, Peter Kraljic, Andreas Krinninger, Martin Lösch, Brook Manville (alumnus), Wolfgang Neubert, Günter Rommel, and Carsten Schildknecht (alumnus).

Besides these internal knowledge sources, we also benefited from a group of knowledge management specialists. Special thanks are offered to Professor Georg von Krogh and the "Knowledge Source" of the University of St. Gallen.

To research the case studies, Paul Reichmann, Sebastian Moffett, and Carolyn Whelan revisited some of the survey participants and contributed the boxed articles included in this book.

Roger Malone and Jonathan Turton – our in-house editors – were our devil's advocates, almost driving us crazy by repeatedly asking questions such as: What does this really mean? By challenging most of our thoughts, they lifted the conceptual thoroughness and pried us out of the narrow focus of our knowledge management shell. They also undertook the enormous and unenviable effort of rewriting our manuscript, turning our ideas into enjoyable prose.

We are also grateful to McKinsey's Communications Services department in Germany for creating the visual concepts for this book, as well as for essential support in bring this book to publication, and to Ulrich Scholz Design for creating the artwork. Rolf Scherer, of our Visual Aids department, also contributed to the effort. Additionally we would like to thank all the McKinsey support staff who helped over the past two years to prepare the questionnaires, program the analyses, take care of the logistics and conferences and optimize the company-specific feedback.

And last but not least, we would like to thank Stephen Rutt and his team at Palgrave for their support and encouragement.

Although all these friends and colleagues contributed to bring value to this project, any errors of fact or logic are solely the fault of the authors.

JÜRGEN KLUGE
Düsseldorf

chapter one

Why knowledge is important

As industrialization swept through most of the world, individual entrepreneurs and global corporations have had to grapple constantly with the ebb and flow of factors of production. At various stages over the past few hundred years, a succession of factors have formed bottlenecks to efficiency, threatening to strangle growth or asphyxiate industries entirely.

At the end of the 1800s, limits on the amount of available arable land caused problems as populations were growing and there were simply more mouths to feed. Then, as large-scale manufacturing reached its peak, urban labor became the most valuable asset to the emerging class of industrialists. Following a string of pivotal technological breakthroughs, machinery began to improve and automation reduced industry's dependence on such hordes of tired workers. But machinery costs money, and access to capital became all-important. Controlling flows of capital was the foremost problem for the factory owners.

As we plunge headlong into the 21st Century, further waves of technological innovation continue to affect the way we live and work. At least in the more developed countries, we no longer think about businesses on a local or regional scale, and we no longer think about land, labor, or capital in the same way. At this stage on the globalization curve we have unlocked vast amounts of land – both literally and through improved agricultural techniques. Excess labor can be tapped more readily, and companies have the option of running factories where labor is cheap. Meanwhile capital flashes around the world instantaneously to all manner of projects and institutions – both worthy and unworthy.

But while the traditional three factors of production – land, labor, and capital – have become easier to handle, a fourth is increasingly showing its head above the parapet. To say that it is "new" is misleading. It has always existed and has always been crucial. But with the three concrete production factors so abundant and accessible, it is this more transient factor that is starting to differentiate clearly one company's success from another company's failure. Knowledge is at the heart of much of today's global economy, and managing knowledge has become vital to companies' success. While the importance of knowledge is, at the very least, widely acknowledged, we are still missing a comprehensive approach to managing knowledge in order to maximize returns.

Knowledge is very different in many ways from the traditional critical assets, particularly because the way it operates within your company is difficult to track and the value it adds is not readily quantifiable. Although companies are able to use ever-more sophisticated accounting techniques, these are only really applicable for dealing with a company's measurable assets. But simply sitting down with a spreadsheet and crunching some numbers will not keep you up with your market or your customers. Nor will it help you to assess effectively the necessary risks your business must take. As intangibles – predominantly knowledge based – are an ever-increasing part of a company's differentiation, an understanding of knowledge and an ability to manage it are vital parts of assessing your company's position and making those all-important predictions in order to allow your company to continue to grow, compete, and become more profitable.

KNOWLEDGE MANAGEMENT MAKES THE DIFFERENCE

Managing knowledge may be widely recognized as crucial to ensuring growth and creating shareholder value, but to many it is still unclear what "knowledge management" really is and how the challenges it presents can best be tackled. Following a McKinsey survey, we can demonstrate that more-successful firms generally have a firmer understanding of knowledge management. They grasp that it requires a holistic approach that goes beyond changes in infrastructure and touches every aspect of a business, transcending divisions, functions, and hierarchies. In many companies the need for active knowledge management is accepted, but all too often in practice this boils down to a belief that waving a sophisticated and expensive information technology (IT) wand is all that is needed for good knowledge management.

The media is filled with reports of managers working harder just to keep pace with the competition and working even harder still to push their companies ahead of the pack. As globalization creates increasingly large gaps between the winners and the also-rans, the stakes at play are much higher than ever before. In such a fast-paced, high-pressure environment, managers are tempted to use traditional management techniques without taking the time to think about the knowledge dimension. This leads them to seize IT solutions as a quick fix to their knowledge management problems. But such a blinkered approach can at best be misguided and costly, and at worst damaging. While infrastructure is a vital foundation, knowledge management will bring sustainable results only with a systematic approach that reaches beyond IT solutions. This book offers insights into how companies are overcoming this hurdle and are pushing each employee and manager to unplug themselves from an overemphasis on infrastructure and a focus on traditional assets and to become adept knowledge practitioners.

In looking at how good knowledge management influences a company's long-term prospects, we considered success as a firm's ability to generate sustainable growth and profits. Moving a level deeper and trying to define success in terms of knowledge management is more difficult because common metrics for success – profit, market capitalization, market share, and others – are generally indirect results of good knowledge management and are affected by many other factors. This understanding does not diminish the role of knowledge management, but rather shows that it simply requires a greater effort to see the linkages.

Looking at market capitalization, we can get a better illustration of how some of these linkages work. Market capitalization generally reflects investors' expectations of a company's ability to generate future earnings. These expectations can swing sharply – for instance, as the enthusiasm surrounding Internet shares runs hot and cold – but overall they offer a common, neutral, and external verdict of a company's potential for long-term success. In today's economy, traditional, tangible assets such as factories, inventories and property account for a smaller and smaller portion of market capitalization. Long-time denizens of the Dow Jones Industrial Average such as General Electric and IBM have only 14 percent and 23 percent, respectively, of their market capitalization covered by tangible assets. At Microsoft, just I percent of market capitalization can be tied to tangible assets.

The remainder of corporate worth, the difference between book value and market value, is attributed to intangible assets. But what are these intangibles, and can they be properly managed? Intangible assets include, among other things, customer relationships, patents, brands, special skills, superior supply chains and so on. Think for a moment, and you will see that all these are closely related to knowledge – knowledge of customers, of products, of technologies, of how to make a company work. Knowledge contributes significantly to these intangibles that investors now hold dear. Managing the under-current of knowledge that feeds these intangibles works effec-tively to support and bolster market capitalization. But it goes beyond simply managing intangibles, it also helps you to run your business better – be that through process optimization or successfully building new businesses. Understanding how know-ledge works throughout your organization therefore allows you to reap the highest rewards from knowledge management: the ability to adapt successfully through constant reinvention and optimization, to tap into new market opportunities, to jump on the latest trend earlier and more decisively than others, and to innovate.

Launching a dynamic knowledge management program can also trigger a sea change in a corporation's overall perspective of its business and the challenges it faces. By going beyond the stan-dard, one-dimensional tracks – faster, better, cheaper – and shut-tling your efforts onto the multidimensional track of doing things smarter, managers can inject a fresh sense of creativity and purpose into their operations. This can offer a rarely afforded chance of tackling old problems from completely new angles.

A HANDLE ON KNOWLEDGE MANAGEMENT

Knowledge has become the preeminent production factor, and it needs as much careful, conscious management as its traditional counterparts. Land, labor and capital each have their own well-established set of structures that help executives to manage them effectively, but knowledge is often treated as a poor relation. It is given the spare room when available and thought about only if a visit is imminent. But to treat knowledge as a side issue or special project is risky. Knowledge has a set of unique characteristics that must be consciously addressed for maximal impact. Of course, in some cases knowledge might be well managed as a by-product of good management elsewhere, for example good human resources management helps a company to retain essential knowledge held by satisfied employees. But such accidental knowledge management is neither coordinated nor comprehensive and is not a model for sustained success.

Corporate history is littered with examples of companies that have fallen by the wayside because they were not able to adapt to shifting markets or simply were not able to stay on top of their day-to-day operations. We have seen airlines lose their wings, watched prestigious manufacturers become little more than coveted brand names, and witnessed the fall of national conglomerates. The knowledge needed to overcome the obstacles these companies faced was probably available – somewhere. Someone probably understood the new markets, the potential impact of globalization, and how to improve processes. Effective knowledge management could have made a real difference in the fortunes of many. This is speculation, of course, but the possibility is tantalizing and cannot be brushed aside.

Whether by design or by default, every company has a storehouse of accumulated knowledge. This holds true for the successful and the unsuccessful, the rising and the falling, the stars and the bit players. The key questions that all managers face is how to apply and distribute this knowledge, and also how to cultivate new knowledge. In other words, how to manage it and make it work for you. The task is made more difficult since the links to profits and losses are indirect and blurred by countless other factors ranging from market cycles to natural disasters. "Knowledge is one of those concepts that is extremely meaningful, positive, promising and hard to pin down," write leading knowledge management academics Georg von Krogh, Kazuo Ichijo and Ikujiro Nonaka.[1] "Knowledge itself is mutable … and can take on many faces in an organization." Those faces can appear in almost every corner of a company from R&D to sales. No area is devoid of knowledge, but whatever shape this knowledge takes, it cannot readily be entered into a ledger or placed on an inventory sheet. Such measurement problems make many business leaders reluctant to use it in any kind of fact-based decision-making.

As a result, many firms have denigrated knowledge to the level of information management. But information is facts and figures. For example, reading that a company's annual turnover is $400 million is nothing more than a piece of information. Knowledge is understanding the significance of that figure. For instance, it is knowing how $400 million compares with past turnover or with turnover posted by the company's rivals or, more importantly, what decisions, good or bad, led to that number. That is knowledge. Knowledge management is using a company's understanding of these relationships – whether to improve products, processes, or customer relations – to increase profitability.

For a more formal definition of knowledge, we have been guided by the following:

> Knowledge is the understanding of relations and causalities, and is therefore essential in making operations effective, building business processes, or predicting the outcomes of business models.

Our brief definition of management is also helpful in clearing the confusion that often surrounds this topic:

> Management is conscious and systematic decision-making about the best use of scarce resources under uncertainty to achieve lasting improvements in an organization's performance.

Knowledge management can be a slippery subject, but, in seeking straight-forward business solutions to the challenges, we found that it is not helpful to get distracted by its nebulous nature. Our definitions may not be perfect. They cut a broad swathe around the topic. But we feel they also throw into stark relief some of the key findings of our survey.

Another point must be made here. Most work on knowledge management discusses at length the distinction between explicit knowledge (knowledge that can be structured and documented) and tacit knowledge (knowledge that is linked to human senses and experience). This may be a handy way to dissect the field, but the situation is really more complicated. These two categories are so heavily interlinked that such a bipolar map is not easy to draw in practice. For example, to understand completely a written document (explicit knowledge) often requires a significant amount of experience (tacit knowledge). A sophisticated recipe is meaningless to someone who has never stood in a kitchen, and legal texts can be all but incomprehensible without some legal training.

Following these basic definitions and remarks, we see knowledge in terms of relationships rather than databases. This understanding greatly expands the role that knowledge management plays within an organization. Thomas H. Davenport and Laurence Prusak observe:

> Knowledge management coexists well with business strategy, with process management, with staying close to your customer and so forth. It can help you do a variety of things you are already doing better. Ultimately, knowledge management work needs to be blended in with these other activities or it's unlikely to be effective.[2]

Getting knowledge management right brings substantial benefits to a company. But there are also downside risks of not doing it all or not doing it well. The most obvious, of course, are the likelihood of neglecting areas of potential improvement, missing promising opportunities, or wasting money on ill-conceived schemes. In the extreme, your company could be left in the dust by competitors who have managed to steal a march on you by deploying their knowledge faster and more effectively.

Bearing this in mind, it is clear that dedicated techniques must consciously be used to make knowledge management happen. Many of these techniques are well known – forming cross-functional teams or introducing appropriate incentive schemes, for example – but their application, coordination and alignment, as well as their detailed design, make the difference between successful knowledge management and an expensive project that not only fails, but is counterproductive. The price of failure is not only the cost in resources outlaid on the program, but also the damage to the internal reputation of knowledge-building efforts. Staff may quickly grow to resent programs that rob time from other activities and bear little fruit.

Embracing knowledge management means creating a new corporate mindset while still being able to make trade-off decisions with this extended scope. The challenge is to engender a new way of thinking about all aspects of your company's operations that includes weighing knowledge into the decisions. For example, in a traditional environment one way to cut costs is to cut staff. But if you approach the problem from a knowledge management perspective, you see that knowledge is walking out of the door for the last time along with those departing employees. This could be the brilliant idea needed to solve next week's problem on the production line or the know-how needed to handle a tricky but important customer. But if that knowledge was never extricated, it is lost for your company forever. Job cuts are often a corporate reality, but, with the right management, companies can minimize the loss of knowledge that accompanies the loss of employees. In the same way, by thinking about knowledge management as part of the day-to-day operations throughout your business, you can maximize the returns garnered from the available knowledge.

IN SEARCH OF LEADING-EDGE KNOWLEDGE MANAGEMENT

To drive our understanding of knowledge management much further and to reveal links between knowledge management techniques and corporate success, we conducted a global field survey with 40 leading companies in Europe, the US, and Japan. From questionnaires and interviews with a broad range of managers and knowledge management authorities, we gathered insights into a range of techniques for successful knowledge management and found many best-practice examples.

The survey

No one disputes that knowledge management is a good thing. More specifically, it is widely accepted that it contributes to corporate success. But to date there has been a notable absence of compelling evidence that this is actually true. Some ground-breaking and solid theoretical work has been produced, mostly by academics such as Ikujiro Nonaka, Georg von Krogh, Dorothy Leonard and Gilbert Probst. In addition, there have been several bouts of field research and case study analysis carried out by practitioners such as Karl Erik Sveiby, Thomas H. Davenport and Laurence Prusak, and Carla O'Dell. But both sets of researchers were more focused on certain subjects or tied to particular forms of analysis. We felt there was a missing link between the highly conceptual academic work and the experiences from the field.

McKinsey's knowledge management survey was set up to unearth how knowledge management actually makes a positive contribution to corporate success and to understand what best-practice companies do in this field, in order to give companies useful, practical, and clear advice on how to improve their knowledge management efforts.

To create a framework, before beginning the survey we examined the existing literature, spoke to knowledge management specialists, and conducted detailed interviews with practitioners and process specialists. These sources provided us with a basic set of 139 knowledge management techniques. As the product development process and the order generation and fulfillment process are the core components of most companies' business, we focused our attention on knowledge management techniques that worked toward improving the performance of one or both processes.

For each of these techniques, we identified five different methods of application. For example, if the technique were "incorporating knowledge from different functions across a company in the product development process," the five different methods varied from regular video conferencing to full-time co-location of cross-functional teams. For every technique the methods were listed in a logical order. This did not necessarily range from bad to good, but followed along a relevant scale, such as least intensive to most intensive or deterministic to self-organizing (see Figure 1.1).

In the survey we analyzed 40 companies distributed roughly equally throughout Europe, the US, and Japan. We tended toward manufacturing companies to provide a homogenous sample with relatively comparable product development and order generation and fulfillment processes. Within that sector, our sample covered a

FIGURE 1.1

Knowledge management techniques and methods of application

Knowledge management technique	Method of application				
	A	**B**	**C**	**D**	**E**
1. Incorporating knowledge from different functions by ...	... regular video conference	... irregular meetings	... weekly meetings	... common team room	... full-time co-location of cross-functional team
2. Recognition of innovative ideas ...	... not institution-alized	... person-ally by the superior only	... in front of the entire department	... in front of the entire unit/ company	... in public
3. ...	...	...	...	...	...
139. ...	...	...	...	...	...

Source: McKinsey knowledge management survey

broad spectrum ranging from traditional machinery companies such as John Deere, Ingersoll, and Trumpf via automotive makers including Renault, and Toyota to high-tech players such as Intel. To broaden our perspective, we also included a small selection of companies listed in "The Most Admired Knowledge Enterprises (MAKE)",[3] including such knowledge management stalwarts as Microsoft, Buckman Laboratories and Skandia.[4] Altogether, our interviews and detailed research into corporate fundamentals generated a database with almost 50,000 entries, which became the foundation for our analysis.

At each company we conducted at least eight interviews, talking with functional managers from R&D, procurement, production, and marketing/sales, plus the chief executive or chief manager of a specific business unit, the person responsible for knowledge management, and two managers with expertise for product development process and order generation and fulfillment process running across the functions. These interviewees allocated 100 points to each of the five design options for techniques relevant to their position. These expressed the extent to which these methods are applied in their area. They could allocate the points as they wanted, but the tendency was to focus on just one or two of the methods.

We also wanted to establish which of the surveyed companies were more successful by looking at their performance. Our performance indicator reflects a company's process performance, as well as its overall financial success (see Figure 1.2). Including both financial and process figures in the indicator has several advantages. First, the process component balances out any extraordinary financial results. Second, management action tends to have a faster and more direct impact on process indicators than on the financial indicators. However, some financial component is required to account for the fact that the approach to process performance has an impact on the bottom line. It is easy to imagine a situation where perfect

FIGURE 1.2

Components of performance indicator

Percentage

* Share of sales from products
  on the market for two years or less

Source: McKinsey knowledge management survey

process performance is achieved at exorbitant expense, negating any positive impact on the bottom line.

We used this indicator to rank all companies according to their performance and then categorized the top 15 companies as more successful, the next 10 as average, and the bottom 15 as less successful. To illustrate some of the differences, on average, development time at more-successful companies was reduced each year by 4.6 percent, compared with a 0.7 percent annual reduction at the less-successful companies between 1995 and 1998. The more-successful companies cut throughput time by almost 11 percent annually, compared with an average 1.6 percent cut at the less-successful companies. Looking at the financial and growth performance of the sample reveals that even the less-successful companies in our survey are generally solid companies. On average, the less-successful companies increased sales by 7 percent a year in the study period and earned about 4 percent return on sales (ROS). This performance is below the average posted by the more-successful companies (about 19 percent annual sales increase and almost 14 percent return on sales), but still respectable. So, when we talk about more- and less-successful companies, bear in mind that these are all premier league corporations (see Figure 1.3).

After interviewing the eight managers in each of the 40 companies about the initial set of knowledge management techniques, we analyzed the allocation of the 100 points. To get clear results we compared the answers of only the 15 more-successful and 15 less-successful companies. For each technique, we conducted a cluster analysis of the point allocation, and wherever the cluster of the

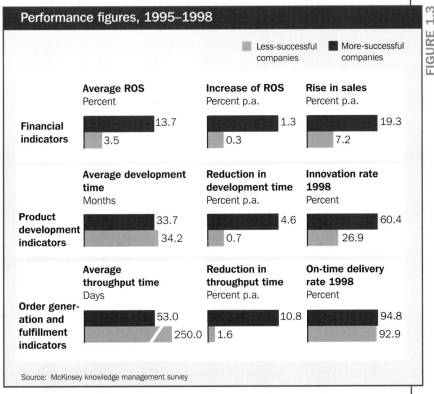

Performance figures, 1995–1998

FIGURE 1.3

Less-successful companies / More-successful companies

	Average ROS Percent	Increase of ROS Percent p.a.	Rise in sales Percent p.a.
Financial indicators	13.7 3.5	1.3 0.3	19.3 7.2
	Average development time Months	**Reduction in development time** Percent p.a.	**Innovation rate 1998** Percent
Product development indicators	33.7 34.2	4.6 0.7	60.4 26.9
	Average throughput time Days	**Reduction in throughput time** Percent p.a.	**On-time delivery rate 1998** Percent
Order generation and fulfillment indicators	53.0 250.0	10.8 1.6	94.8 92.9

Source: McKinsey knowledge management survey

more-successful companies differed significantly from the cluster of the less-successful companies we concluded that this particular way of applying the technique contributes to making a difference in the company's process – and eventually financial – perform-ance. This assumption builds on our conviction that good know-ledge management improves process performance, which in turn must have a positive impact on the company's financial result. The more-successful companies showed a significant difference in how they applied 73 of the 139 knowledge management techniques compared with the less successful companies (see Figure 1.4). We called these the "differentiating techniques." Interestingly, there are no differences across industries or across geographies.

To structure the results and make life easier for us and you, we grouped the differentiating techniques with the six characteristics that distinguish knowledge from traditional assets. By plotting a

FIGURE 1.4

Example: Analysis of knowledge management technique

Percentage of participants in each category

☐ Less-successful companies ■ More-successful companies

Target is to ...

A	B	C	D	E
... keep current level	... improve annually	... reach next competitor's level	... reach world-class level	... exceed world-class level

100% of more-successful and only 33% of less-successful companies have targeted to reach or exceed world-class level

Source: McKinsey knowledge management survey

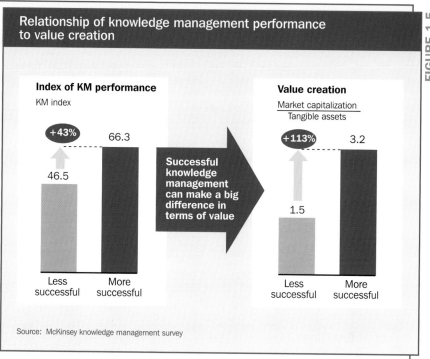

Relationship of knowledge management performance to value creation

FIGURE 1.5

Index of KM performance

KM index

+43%   66.3

46.5

Less   More
successful successful

Successful knowledge management can make a big difference in terms of value

Value creation

Market capitalization
Tangible assets

+113%   3.2

1.5

Less   More
successful successful

Source: McKinsey knowledge management survey

company's position with respect to the techniques on a knowledge scanner, we are able to assess where companies have deficiencies and conduct a gap analysis to find starting points for potential improvements (see Chapter 10). The scanner is supplemented by a diagram giving a measure of the knowledge pull that is part of generating the right cultural context for knowledge management (see Chapter 2).

The aggregated knowledge management pattern along all six characteristics plus the knowledge pull can be given as a company's knowledge index. Interestingly, we found a strong correlation between a company's knowledge index and its ratio of intangible assets over market capitalization. This result supports our initial hypotheses that successful knowledge management is a powerful lever to increase a company's success (see Figure 1.5).

In assessing how knowledge management works, it was pointless counting activities such as visits to a database. Such simple numbers would add little to our understanding because there is no indication of the substance and depth of the contribution. At one company, for example, the most active intranet page was the daily cafeteria menu. Even tracking pages more closely tied to a company's business can be misleading since, for instance, the same document may be posted in a virtual team room several times, each with minor changes, but each revision adds only marginal value to the corporate knowledge inventory.

So rather than counting clicks, we looked in more depth at the techniques that managers had put in place to help knowledge management. These went well beyond IT to include, for example, incentive systems that encourage sharing and developing knowledge and policies that allow employees some freedom from their daily work. Such measures help to push many corporate goals forward simultaneously: knowledge management, talent retention, and process efficiency to name a few. Such overlap supports our belief that the knowledge management challenge pervades an entire company and calls for a holistic approach. Randomly employing a knowledge management idea – producing a corporate yellow pages, for instance – is of little help by itself.

FRAMEWORK FOR ACTION

In the following chapters we lay out a framework for making knowledge much more manageable. We explain a number of successful and proven techniques and give meaningful insights into why knowledge is different, but not unfathomable. Understanding the characteristics of knowledge is essential for a solid grasp of the challenge and a concrete battle plan.

Chapter 2 has a detailed discussion of the overarching theme – the importance of creating the right cultural context within the company. This is about ensuring that your employees want knowledge, crave knowledge and will seek and use knowledge from all available sources. It means thinking beyond IT solutions and actively unplugging your employees from databases and getting them talking.

Chapter 3 looks at the three main tasks of knowledge management: application, distribution and cultivation. The order is important, although perhaps counterintuitive, because the tasks are arranged from application, with the most immediate potential impact, to cultivation, which has longer term possibilities. Also, faulty application can prevent advances made with the other tasks from bearing fruit. In addition, in this chapter we introduce the six characteristics of knowledge that distinguish it from other assets:

- *subjective* – the interpretation of knowledge is heavily dependent on individuals' background and the context in which it is used

- *transferable* – knowledge can be extracted from one context and profitably applied in a new one

- *embedded* – knowledge invariably resides in a static and often buried form that cannot easily be moved or reformulated

- *self-reinforcing* – knowledge does not lose value when shared, indeed its value grows when widely distributed

- *perishable* – over time, knowledge becomes outdated, especially for an individual organization, although there can be unpredictable volatility

■ *spontaneous* – knowledge can develop unpredictably in a process that cannot always be controlled.

In the following six chapters, we elaborate on each of these characteristics and outline what specific management techniques should be deployed and combined in order to work most effectively with them. By focusing on each characteristic, we recognize that the techniques may change over time – after all, few companies still rely on indentured servitude to fill their workbenches – but the characteristics will remain constant. Therefore, a deeper but practically informed understanding of knowledge will make it easier to adapt to social, technological, and cultural developments. In these chapters, we also present the results of the survey, outline best practice techniques and present relevant case studies.

In Chapter 10, we describe a method of diagnosis we have developed as a result of our analysis of the survey results, and particularly feedback meetings with the participating companies. Using the characteristics as a starting point, companies can identify how to ensure that a knowledge management program produces the desired outcome. The analysis also helps to prioritize the elements of an action plan and draw a knowledge management roadmap for the company.

Finally, in Chapter 11, we take a broader view, looking at how knowledge management might evolve. From the CEO down through the hierarchy to the line workers, every employee will have to become a self-driven chief knowledge officer. Knowledge management cannot be delegated to a separate unit, but must be an integral part of the way everyone thinks and acts. Rocket science may require a lot of knowledge, but managing that knowledge is not rocket science.

Notes

1 Georg von Krogh, Kazuo Ichijo, and Ikujiro Nonaka, "Enabling Knowledge Creation: How To Unlock the Mystery of Tacit Knowledge and Release the Power of Innovation," p. 6, Oxford University Press, New York.

2 Thomas H. Davenport and Laurence Prusak, "Working Knowledge: How Organizations Manage What They Know," p. 163, Harvard Business School Press, Boston.

3 MAKE survey by Teleos in 1998 and 1999. Teleos operates "The KNOW Network," a web-based network of leading knowledge organizations dedicated to identifying and exchanging best-practice knowledge processes. The MAKE survey is a recognized benchmark for identifying organizations that are leaders in the knowledge economy.

4 Confidentiality agreements prevent us from naming all the companies that participated in our survey, but these companies, among others, have agreed to be named as participants in this book.

chapter two

Knowledge pull required

Many companies we visited had already tried to introduce knowledge management programs, and at times these efforts were quite substantial. But despite management commitment and healthy budgets, these programs often floundered or failed. In each case something was missing. A vital ingredient of the knowledge management recipe had not just been left in the cupboard; it was not even on the shopping list. All these companies lacked the right cultural context that would create and nurture reciprocal trust, openness and cooperation.

Creating and sustaining such a corporate environment is not solely a matter of knowledge management, but there are some critical knowledge management components. To draw the greatest benefits from a knowledge management program and to match best practice, you must enthuse your employees with a desire for knowledge. If a knowledge management measure is to fall on fertile ground within an organization, every individual needs to be thirsty for knowledge. They should see knowledge management – that is, the active application, distribution and cultivation of knowledge within the company as a whole – as a fundamental part of their personal success and satisfaction.

Managers launching knowledge management programs have often begun (and ended) by focusing on pushing knowledge to the right place at the right time – a top-down strategy that leans heavily on infrastructure solutions. But channeling knowledge in such a fashion is a one-way street. Our survey showed that successful companies approach the task from the other direction as well. Instead of force-feeding their employees, they create environments that encourage them to seek knowledge for themselves and pull it out from sources both within and beyond the confines of the corporation. Developing such a knowledge pull is a key element of the right cultural context and should be included in any knowledge management strategy.

Creating this type of pull culture is not a prerequisite for initiating programs to address other aspects of knowledge management. First, no company is completely devoid of knowledge pull. Second, instigating a culture where all employees are constantly searching for relevant knowledge takes time, and treating it as a precondition that must be installed before other efforts can begin could be costly in terms of missed opportunities and abandoned knowledge. Instead, encouraging knowledge pull should be part of an overall program. But eventually, as knowledge pull gets stronger and stronger, all your efforts at knowledge management will show increasing benefits.

The profusion of push approaches is illustrated by comments we faced repeatedly throughout our study. Often, managers would tell us that they had no need for knowledge management because their IT system was just fine, thank you. Reliance on infrastructure is symptomatic of a top-down solution. However, these managers can be forgiven their attitude. As opposed to pull approaches, push schemes are generally quantifiable and can be audited, communicated reasonably clearly and launched and controlled just as managers would with any other program dealing with any other asset. But as we saw in Chapter 1, knowledge is unlike other assets. Traditional management techniques fall short of the goal unless they are recombined and imaginatively applied.

This is not to say pull is good and push is bad. It is a question of finding the right mix between the two approaches. At the more-successful companies we visited there was a balance of pull and push measures. The less-successful companies tended to focus much more heavily, sometimes exclusively, on pushing knowledge at staff.

There is naturally an overlap between the measures needed to drive such a behavioral shift and elements of other major corporate change programs, broader motivational approaches, or general modern human resource management. For example, human resource managers put much of their energy into devising personalized quantitative and qualitative target-setting systems that include financial and nonfinancial incentives. Such ideas feed into creating a knowledge pull, especially when flavored with knowledge-specific elements. What emerges should be a setting in which employees recognize the importance of sharing knowledge and feel comfortable doing so.

THE DATABASE THAT COULDN'T

The risks of leaning exclusively on a push approach are sharply illustrated by the experience of a global construction company that we are familiar with. In this case, the managers recognized a problem, saw that the solution rested in knowledge management, and did what many well-meaning, conscientious managers would.

Like all large builders, this company outsourced most of the actual physical construction work — roofs, windows, plumbing and so on — to subcontractors, allowing it to focus on its core competences of engineering, project management, and contractual matters. The subcontractor market is dominated by a large group of small players that vary substantially in their availability, quality, and price, and, since 70 to 80 percent of a project's value-added was subcontracted, identifying the right partners at the right prices was critical to the company's profitability. Also, new contractors emerged and old ones disappeared quickly, making reliable, real-time information a vital component of success.

Each of the hundreds of projects underway generated scores of subcontracts, and each of these contracts resulted in several competing bids that had to be evaluated. Obviously, the company accumulated a mountain of knowledge about the subcontractor market. This should have given it a clear advantage over its small and medium-sized competitors, but unfortunately the knowledge was held by individual project managers and in toto was not readily accessible throughout the company. Rather than taking advantage of its potential economies of scale, the firm behaved like its small competitors, putting itself at a severe disadvantage. It was selecting subcontractors as its smaller competitors did, while still paying the overhead costs associated with a large corporation. This situation almost broke the company.

Senior management decided knowledge management was the answer. Falling into a classic trap of the push approach, they decided simply to create a subcontractor database. Every project manager was given access to the server and was encouraged to fill in a fact sheet for each subcontractor. Then, whenever a project manager needed to identify and evaluate subcontractors, the information would be available instantly and the most suitable candidates could be easily selected, according to the plan. For more detailed information, each subcontractor in the database would be linked to the project manager with the most experience with that subcontractor. The project was driven by top managers because they believed that they were the only ones who could identify potential synergies between projects. The IT department only needed to set up the server and develop the template for data entry, so the project was easily executed.

It failed miserably.

Although the project addressed some of the organizational barriers to good knowledge management such as denying cross-departmental access, limited contribution rights or an uneven dissemination of data, it fell short when it came to some of the subtler, more insidious personal barriers. Project managers were reluctant to advertise their own regular subcontractors because, for example, they feared their best subcontractors would be unavailable for their own projects if others, even others in the same company, started using them. Without access to their best sources, they might have to pay more for unknown subcontractors that would take additional time to select and supervise. Profits would be hit, and suddenly the year-end bonus would be at risk. Also, filling out the necessary forms to keep the database up to date would take time away from real work. Soon, the database was stuffed with incomplete, outdated entries that project managers rarely checked.

Another fatal flaw was that project managers remained convinced that the best knowledge was exchanged over a couple of beers at the local pub. They distrusted the information that came out of the regional offices. They saw such outside knowledge as inherently inferior and not worth the trouble.

PUSH IS EASY, SO WORK ON PULL

IT-driven, top-down push approaches like this are well suited for surmounting organizational barriers to knowledge management, often simply by making the knowledge available more widely. Organizational barriers may develop organically, but sometimes they are created unintentionally as a by-product of other management decisions. One example is a database with limited access rights. This is especially common in companies rigidly split into highly autonomous divisions or departments. Without broad access to knowledge, there can be little hope of it being deployed beyond a select group of people no matter how useful that knowledge might be to the wider group. Other organizational barriers include different languages or poor formal communication channels. Addressing these can help to bring out a corporate culture of internal communication.

Push approaches help to overcome these challenges by increasing the transparency and availability of knowledge. There are many ways of doing this that go beyond IT. One is a training program that brings all your customer service staff together to learn about a new product. The knowledge becomes available and is pushed unquestioningly onto the audience. Formally changing your organizational structure is another push approach, since decisions about who should work with whom are made at the highest level and forced onto the employees. These push approaches and others can be effective in overcoming institutional barriers to optimal knowledge flow, but they fail to address a second set of barriers that are endemic to human behavior. Worse, they may even reinforce these barriers by building a consumer mentality toward knowledge. After all, why should employees worry about knowledge if they can sleep soundly knowing that knowledge is being looked after by a central department. In such a drone-like organization it can be hard to see the value in actively contributing to the process since there is no payback if their knowledge is used profitably elsewhere.

Push approaches are deeply ingrained in our society. At least as far back as the Roman Empire, successful armies have had strong, rigid hierarchies, a clear chain of command, and top officers who exercised absolute control. For almost as long, business management has copied the military style. But such an approach has its limitations. After all, modern military organizations have gone beyond simply telling soldiers to stand still and shoot. A more goal-oriented approach requires well-trained and motivated troops. The same holds true in a business context. Exclusively managing by push is quick and relatively easy, but fails to capture the full capabilities of everybody in an organization. We are convinced that the maximum potential of individuals can only be unleashed through an approach that gets to the heart of what motivates them.

We classify these as "pull" approaches. They are harder to bring into the battle because managers can act only indirectly by setting the right environment; the actual pull has to come from the employees. Pull approaches generally fall into the softer side of management. They take longer to implement and a clear cause-and-effect relationship is difficult to demonstrate. Since the strength of this pull must be closely monitored and policies adjusted accordingly, this approach is higher maintenance than push approaches. Also, managers who focus solely on such soft factors are sometimes perceived as being weak and ineffectual, compared with their tough, hard-line, bottom-line-driven colleagues.

But taking this more nuanced approach to management does not mean acting without clear targets, milestones, and end products. A management style capable of addressing these issues requires a broader range of abilities, covering both standard techniques as well as the skill and mental flexibility to deal with ambiguity. It also requires a certain degree of "letting go." This is not a field for micromanagers. As business becomes increasingly complex, micromanagement becomes less and less efficient and eventually totally impractical. Instead, you should implement self-steering mechanisms. Your role is to set the boundaries, rules, general goals, and an overall harmony, not to hover over your staff's shoulders making suggestions at every turn. In a knowledge-conducive environment, they should be encouraged to seek answers for themselves and be helped in so doing.

Just to make our point absolutely clear: we are not damning push approaches. They have an important role to play. But we are focusing on knowledge pull for two reasons. First, pull measures have the top priority because, without them, push efforts run the risk of becoming floundering white elephants – never a pretty sight. Second, there is already a natural concentration on push simply because it is much more straightforward and has an obvious cause–effect relationship. So although the rest of this chapter talks about pull, do not conclude erroneously that we advocate abandoning those costly IT systems and switching solely to pull approaches. Getting the balance right is crucial. We have already addressed the strengths of push factors, and pointed to some of the hidden traps in that approach. To understand pull measures properly we need to understand the individual barriers exemplified by our reluctant, cautious, and suspicious construction project managers.

DISMANTLE INDIVIDUAL BARRIERS

To strike at the heart of what motivates each individual employee, you have to confront the hurdles that stop them from realizing their maximum potential. These individual barriers relate to their motivation for creating and sharing knowledge. Push techniques stumble over them, whereas pull techniques aim to dismantle them. In identifying the core of these problems, you eventually end up with two major and reasonably well-understood phenomena: the twin syndromes of "not invented here" and "knowledge is power." These incorporate a variety of symptoms that need to be addressed with appropriate incentives in order to guide staff behavior.

Not invented here

The "not invented here" syndrome describes the tendency to neglect, ignore or, worse still, disparage knowledge that is not created within your own department. In the construction company example that began this chapter, one problem was that project managers believed that knowledge generated by other projects was inferior to their own. This hardly spurred them to go beyond their own knowledge about subcontractors.

This problem can arise from a genuine mistrust toward outside knowledge. After all, someone else's knowledge cannot always be readily evaluated for its quality and relevance. Accepting external knowledge also generally carries its own costs. External knowledge usually needs to be evaluated and adapted to your specific circumstances, and it is unlikely that it will fit snugly into the "knowledge gap." But such assessment and subsequent tweaking absorbs capacity that could have been developing the same knowledge internally. And, in the end the external solution just may not work, adding an element of risk and infusing the end-user with an understandable amount of skepticism. These problems are exacerbated if more time is available because if a worker feels there is enough time to plod through developing a solution – not only solving the problem, but gaining a reputation as an innovator – that worker is less likely to seek outside help. Therefore, we found that a good cure for the "not invented here" syndrome is to set ambitious targets that cannot be reached single-handedly, and generally to promote high aspirations that create enough pressure to force staff to seek quick, but effective solutions.

People are also paranoid. If employees feel that they are constantly using knowledge developed elsewhere, they begin to fear that their roles will become irrelevant or redundant. This also leads to some suspicion toward external knowledge. But again, if aspirations and targets are high enough, and you set clear goals rather than detailed methods, then what matters is achieving the goal. How it was reached is less important. Indeed, it is more likely that employees who can unearth and apply knowledge quickly and successfully will become among the most highly valued team members. Without them, the team may fail to meet the targets.

Another reason that employees may avoid external know-ledge is that it might actually be quicker for them to reinvent the wheel than to search for it in an arcane data management system. With the right computer-aided-design software, it could only be a matter of inputting a few parameters in order to design a new wheel. As a result, it might be quicker for a construction engineer to design it, rather than search for an equivalent wheel that has already been designed by a colleague. But the engineer would be robbing Peter to pay Paul. By optimizing his own work, the engineer could be harming overall company performance. There are now two wheels with comparable specifications in the database, adding unnecessary cost and complexity to the system. Here, a knowledge-specific incentive might help. Success could be evaluated not simply by the use of an individual's time, but also by the proportion of recycled knowledge employed. This requires the qualitative input of superiors, but one company we interviewed asked questions of its staff such as "Whom did you contact to get input?" and "How many other opinions were involved in the course of finding the solution?" Such a perspective should help employees to start accepting external knowledge more readily.

Knowledge is power

The "knowledge is power" syndrome refers to a mindset that places the value of knowledge to the individual ahead of its value to the company. In the construction company, we saw that project managers were more concerned with their own bonuses than with overall corporate performance, which reduced their motivation to enter comprehensive and accurate knowledge into the database. Successful knowledge management programs rely on sharing, not hoarding.

At its most basic, knowledge sharing starts by taking the time to help others. In a successful company there is always time pressure, but the extra 10 minutes spent with a colleague explaining something will be repaid later, usually in spades. But just as people distrust external knowledge, they also see their own knowledge as a part of their personal competitive advantage. This knowledge may be tips on potential customers, ideas on employing new technology or even something as simple as knowing where to find the right information. All these things help to make a worker valuable to the employer. The syndrome has many faces. For instance, workers with this mindset are too busy to return phone calls asking for help, offer only generic information under the guise of being helpful, or unnecessarily refer the question to somebody else, rather than handling it themselves. Such mechanisms can also be used to sabotage an internal rival's productivity.

The challenge is that many of the reasons for hoarding knowledge make sense as long as everyone in a company acts as though they are lone hunters. The Greek tycoon Aristotle Onassis said years ago, "The secret to success is to know something nobody else knows." But if your team becomes a group of pack hunters, downing larger and larger prey through organization and cooperation, such hoarding becomes counterproductive. This is one of the critical changes that should be targeted by any knowledge management program, and one that should have positive repercussions beyond purely the exchange of knowledge.

The most powerful weapon against the "knowledge is power" and "not invented here" syndromes is a culture of cooperation. Numerous studies have identified preconditions for cooperation, which is the core of every social system. Whether one is looking at a colony of ants, a flock of birds, a human family or a group of employees, the basic principle of cooperation is that the reward for each partner is higher when everyone is cooperating than when everyone is working alone. Managers must be aware, however, that the highest reward inevitably goes to the individual that accepts others' cooperation without reciprocating. The hoarding individual gets the advantage of all the corporate knowledge, in addition to his own unshared knowledge. Game theory describes this situation as the prisoners' dilemma (see box opposite).

The corporate prisoners' dilemma

In a classic exercise in game theory, two prisoners, isolated from each other, have the option of implicating the other or staying silent (see Figure 2.1). If both stay silent, cooperating with each other, they each receive a minimum sentence, and if both implicate the other, each gets a longer sentence. But if one implicates while the other stays silent, the squealer is set free and the other gets the maximum sentence. On the surface, a prisoner's best strategy is to squeal because the average sentence is shorter no matter what the other prisoner does.

The same mechanism holds true for two workers in the same company, although instead of trying to avoid the longest sentence, the workers are trying to capture the highest reward (see Figure 2.2). Using the isolated example of two workers, if both cooperate they each reap significant gains in efficiency, productivity and, most likely, income, while if neither cooperates they could still function, but their gains would be more modest. But if one worker hoards knowledge while the other shares, the hoarder will probably harvest windfall gains while the other worker is left to feel the fool. Again, the best strategy seems to be to hoard knowledge, because in isolation the average likely gain from this strategy appears higher than any other. This calculation generally holds when the situation is expanded to include one worker facing collectively the rest of the staff.

But just as in classic game theory, the business situation changes with repetition, and an individual's only long-term successful strategy is a tit-for-tat approach. In the office or on the shop floor, workers begin by sharing some information and gauging the reaction. If they receive cooperation in return, they will continue

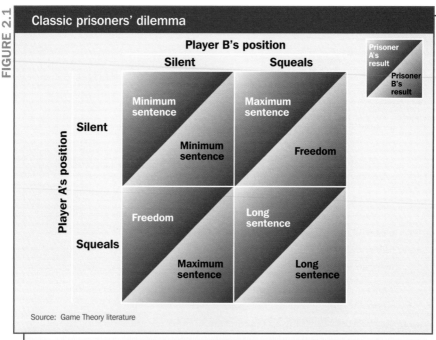

FIGURE 2.1

Classic prisoners' dilemma

Player B's position

Source: Game Theory literature

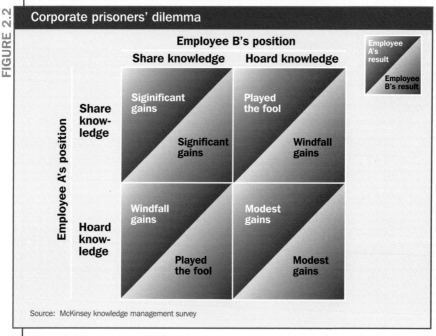

FIGURE 2.2

Corporate prisoners' dilemma

Employee B's position

Source: McKinsey knowledge management survey

sharing information at the next occasion. But if they are not recip-
rocated for their sharing, they will likely retreat rather than be
played the fool.

Of course, in the real business environment the game does not
switch sides so conveniently, but in the longer term a common
strategy will probably emerge: either everyone hoards or everyone
shares because the fool's corner will be avoided at all costs. The
situation can be modeled mathematically, and the break-even point
is a function of the likelihood of the next opportunity for cooperation or interaction and the difference in the reward between cooperating and not cooperating. This has some interesting implications
for the knowledge management of growing organizations since as
an organization gets bigger, the probability of any two employees
interacting gets smaller. All else being equal, as the chance of
interaction decreases the risk of being played the fool – that is,
giving knowledge and getting none in return – rises. Without any
intervention by management, a growing organization will find
itself sooner or later with all its employees bunkered in their knowledge shells, hoarding their expertise.

ALIGNING INDIVIDUAL MOTIVATION WITH CORPORATE GOALS

Workers base their decisions on optimizing their own return,
not the company's return, and all decisions on cooperation or
hoarding are made in order to maximize an individual's own
benefit. It is management's task to bring individual goals in line
with overall company goals. There are four primary levers for

achieving this in relation to overcoming individual barriers to knowledge management:

- Setting high, world-class targets to encourage the acceptance of external knowledge

- Mitigating the prisoner's dilemma by increasing the likelihood of repeated interaction

- Increasing the gains from cooperation with special incentives

- Fostering personal engagement and responsibility for own ideas.

High targets with knowledge management components

We have shown that setting high targets should encourage employees to look for solutions beyond their own immediate setting. The key is to bring them to their own limits by setting plausible targets that are a little higher than they can reach in isolation. Instead they must cooperate with their colleagues and pool their efforts. They should be put in a position where they begin tackling a problem by systematically scanning the company's existing knowledge to avoid duplication and, as their efforts develop, adding to this knowledge base. As employees recognize the need to access existing information, they also become more willing to provide their own knowledge to the company. This is not altruistic, they simply recognize that such contributions will help them later. If they do not contribute, they cannot expect others to do so. Consequently everybody maintains a similar level of contribution.

The more-successful companies in our survey have created an environment that fosters employees' aspirations for world-class development, innovation, and efficiency. When it came to product development and innovation, for example, almost all of them set ambitious goals. But only 33 percent of the less-successful companies had targeted world-class standards for product development efficiency and 40 percent for product innovation.

Targets can also change employees' reaction to knowledge management, although only if they are highly personalized. This means ensuring that individuals actually have some control over whether the target is reached, and that the system is transparent. Specific targets will naturally vary between departments. In a product development department, for example, the knowledge management target could be linked to the level of cooperation in competence centers in order to consolidate knowledge around a particular component. In a marketing department, it could relate to building customer databases and the frequency of interaction with clients.

Come together to avoid hoarding

As we saw during our glance at the prisoners' dilemma, increased interaction increases the likelihood of cooperation. But obviously, there comes a point when employees would be spending too much time talking – at conferences, in committees, in their bosses' offices, over the water cooler – and not enough time working. As with so many aspects of management the trick is to get the balance right. Cooperation makes the difference between a company that functions like a top-flight sports team, and one that works more like a dispersed set of scavengers. Both could look successful in the short term, but we would put our long-term bets on the sports team (see Case Study 2.1).

Case Study 2.1

BUCKMAN LABS

Pulling knowledge
along the Mississippi

Bob Buckman, former chief executive of Buckman Laboratories, made knowledge the lodestone of his specialty chemicals business. Buckman Labs, widely acknowledged as one of the leaders in knowledge management, consistently ranks first in Teleos's survey of the most admired knowledge companies. And the success is founded on an off-the-rack infrastructure strengthened by a corporate culture that welcomes and rewards knowledge sharing. Buckman, who retired in 2000, was a master of knowledge pull.

The main ingredient is a culture of trust, asserts Buckman. "This isn't slick," adds Timothy Meek, who manages Buckman's Knowledge Transfer Department. "Broad access to information and people makes this unique."

Founded in 1945, Buckman Labs is headquartered in Memphis, Tennessee, a river port city better known as the home of Elvis, Mississippi Blues and Southern pit barbecue. The privately held company has 1,300 employees in 22 countries, and in 2000 had sales of $300 million. While serving many industry sectors, its primary focus is the water treatment, pulp and paper mills, and leather markets.

The heavy lifting to create knowledge pull began in 1989, when Buckman flattened the corporation's hierarchy and instigated a company-wide open-door policy. From a business perspective, the underlying goal was to create a leaner, more agile organization that would respond quickly to customer demands. Convinced of the truth of Metcalf's principle on networks – that a network's value increases exponentially as it is expanded – Buckman created a framework of values based on open communication.

To unleash knowledge sharing, Buckman armed his staff with IBM Think Pads and gave them free rein on the Internet. He also opened a Global

Forum to everyone in the company and created restricted-access forums for project teams and industry specialists, where experts could banter about everything from whitening paper to treating leather. For the fastest results, Buckman looked for the common denominators among the company's wide-ranging IT infrastructure. He created the famed K-Netix system with a backbone built around Lotus Notes, the Compuserve computer network's forum system and standard software to facilitate newsgroups. Rather than bells and whistles, the system focuses on allowing quick and simple downloads and easy participation by the company's scattered employees.

But IT alone is unlikely to have succeeded without a strong effort to create knowledge pull. For instance, the team leading the knowledge management operates under the moniker "Knowledge Transfer Department" to emphasize the importance of sharing. Buckman also applauded and promoted frequent contributors to the knowledge network, anointed in-house experts as "gurus" in their field and privately chided those who didn't participate in online chat groups and other forums. When its Latino staff felt shut out of the English-language forum, Buckman opened a Spanish-language version. The company is also working on setting up a system equipped with simultaneous translation software to encourage greater communication among a staff that works in 15 languages.

To encourage wide participation, seven sysops offer on- and off-line help to employees and act as traffic cops in the forums. Sysops, a word from the very early years of the Internet, is short for system operators and they were essentially the prototypes for today's Webmasters. Together, they act as traffic cops for the forums, directing unanswered questions to the right people inside or outside the company and archiving discussions that lead to solutions in a database at the Bulab Learning Center for later retrieval if necessary. (The center also provides 36,000 hours of instruction a year to employees, ranging from crash courses to doctoral programs.)

The program took time to implement, and is still evolving. One project underway is to bring suppliers more actively into the virtual teams and forums, widening the circle and expanding the network. The program also faced some internal opposition, particularly from middle managers who worried that being tapped as mentors could ultimately threaten their positions. But once they saw how much time they saved by putting their sales staff closer to the customer, they were converted.

Buckman succeeded in making communication and knowledge sharing a cornerstone of the corporation's culture. With this success came a free flow of questions, answers, and, most importantly, solutions to customer problems. Buckman's understanding of the strength of knowledge continues to yield fruit. Both sales per salesperson and percentage of sales from new products increased 50 percent in 2000. And problem response time has shrunk from weeks to days. This is not just a statistical win, but a bottom-line win as well. In 1998 Buckman won a contract from a cardboard-making company partly because it was able quickly to answer complex questions about old equipment. Within hours of posting their questions, the local Buckman sales team received 10 responses from three continents.

There are ways to encourage cooperation; one is simply to put staff closer together. People working nearer to each other are more likely to share knowledge than those further apart. Obviously daily face-to-face contact makes cooperation more likely, but the relation holds despite the scale. Workers in the same continent, same country, same city and same office are increasingly likely to cooperate as they move along this scale. Short of the impossible and the ill-advised – putting everyone in a global operation across the hall from each other – what does this mean in practice? Well, for one thing, realize that you would get more bang for your knowledge buck by holding regional networking meetings rather than global extravaganzas. Cooperation can also be triggered by other similiarities such as the same functional expertise.

Cross-functional teams, which we'll discuss in greater detail in Chapter 4, are a particularly successful way that companies can increase the likelihood of interaction. Alongside the direct and deliberate knowledge transfer in these teams, they also encourage the building of informal networks. Encouraging and facilitating such informal contacts underscores the fact that interaction between divisions is a continual process, rather than a one-off effort to handle a specific problem. This informal interaction stands in contrast to the formal interfaces that lie between departments or units. Such interfaces are, of course, unavoidable when managing an entire process, but breaking down the process into a series of smaller tasks provides the impetus and structure for cross-functional teams. The team can interact informally as it is working closely together. Cross-functional teams also increase the cost to individuals of hoarding knowledge because hoarders will quickly gain a reputation of not being team players. When teams have fulfilled their targets and need to come together, formal interfaces are necessary and should not be ignored as opportunities for enhancing cooperation. Such interfaces are likely to involve scheduled meetings, agendas, and decision points.

One European high-tech company demonstrated the impact that cross-hierarchical and cross-functional teams can have on increasing interaction and on knowledge management more broadly. The attack came at two levels. At the company-wide level, the organization transformed itself into one consisting solely of multiple links. There are virtually no functions, it is just one large project organization. Project managers advertise their projects and staff choose what to sign up to – they are then attached to one or possibly two projects at any one time. But, once a week, "professional groups," consisting of people with the same functional expertise, meet over coffee for an informal discussion and to keep up to date with their field and with insights garnered from others in their peer group. This helps them to sharpen their understanding of their field, value that they can return to their project teams. The teams remain in place for the duration of each project and the relationships that are built up increase the probability of interaction at a later date and help to erode any tendency to hoard knowledge. It serves to establish a culture in which knowledge is actively transferred. The teams are also physically put together for each project, further strengthening relationships.

There are, however, natural limits to the size of such an organization. As the company has grown very quickly over the past few years, it has made some moves to split the overall project structure into two columns in order to allow the free-form team-based system to continue to flourish.

Job rotation is another way to increase the likelihood of interaction and is a technique that is especially popular in development departments. As with cross-functional teams, it helps to improve informal employee networks. As employees become more accustomed to relying on each other, the chances of being trapped in the corporate prisoners' dilemma diminish dramatically.

Incentives to increase cooperation

Challenging targets and increased interaction are two planks of a strong knowledge pull foundation, but a third plank – incentives – is often necessary. By incentives, we mean simply financial and nonfinancial rewards given for employees who are active partners in your knowledge management program. Such incentives should be designed to bring the benefits of sharing and using knowledge closer to the perceived windfall offered by hoarding. Financial incentives, particularly variable pay and stock options, have the broadest impact, but more narrowly targeted options are also available for creating a diverse rewards system. These include bonuses given for specific achievements such as reducing complexity in product design, identifying cost-cutting potential, or process improvements.

Although money is a strong motivator, nonfinancial incentives can also put impetus behind a corporate change in knowledge culture with little or no budgetary impact. Such incentives could include giving successful knowledge sharers a prestigious platform at internal events, including them in the senior executives' inner circle by seeking their advice or offering them specialized coaching to help them to reach their individual aspirations. Public recognition for good knowledge management also designates these employees as role models and serves to identify specific internal best practice in knowledge management, which can then be followed by others.

Incentives are not created in a void. They are important techniques that can support efforts to reach individual and company-wide stretch targets. Of the companies surveyed, 73 percent of the more-successful companies had individual incentive systems in place that were linked to communication and openness in marketing/sales compared with 40 percent of the less-successful companies (see Case Study 2.2).

Incentives are of course also used to further corporate goals that go beyond knowledge management, such as employee retention and traditional production targets. But knowledge management must be part of the formula, and, in particular, care must be taken to make sure that the targets used cover a balanced range of goals, including success outside an employee's immediate unit. Targets must not unwittingly help to spread the "knowledge is power" syndrome. For example, awards for top sales-people may recognize outstanding individual performances, but they could also encourage internecine rivalry and backstabbing. A manager with knowledge in mind would add another set of incentives to counter these tendencies such as mixing departmental indicators with a strong individual target so that the best-rewarded employees are those who are successful marketing/sales managers but also strong team players. It will rarely be possible to quantify the impact that such a manager might have in a neighboring department, but enthusiasm and attitude should be recognized by senior managers.

Case Study 2.2

JOHN DEERE

Plowing through resistance to knowledge

Looking back at a transition that saw dramatic increases in production and quality at the John Deere plant in Mannheim, Germany, Richard Ruf, assembly manager at Deere's Focus Factory, says he only regrets that he didn't act more quickly. "I should have been less hesitant," he says.

Since the early 1990s, plant hierarchy has been flattened from seven levels to three, lines of communications have been opened, and resistance to knowledge "not invented here" has been overcome. At the same time, most of the departments were consolidated within the assembly building, shortening the communications paths and creating a more unified atmosphere. The knowledge management efforts helped the plant overcome profitability problems and spurred impressive gains in overall production. The percentage of error-free products off the production line rose to 72 percent in 2000 from 30 percent in 1992.

"The Focus Factory at John Deere Mannheim is profitably supplying tractors and related parts to external and internal John Deere customers around the world," Ruf says. "In fact, we are the sole supplier for rear axles that are mounted in Georgia. This is proof that German sites can provide quality products at very competitive prices if they are allowed to benefit from lessons learned around the world."

John Deere's Mannheim plant, a unit of US machinery manufacturer Deere & Co., is Germany's largest maker and exporter of tractors. About 2,200 employees work at the plant, producing more than 30,000 units a year, more than half of Germany's total tractor production. Deere & Co. has about 40,000 employees worldwide and part of Ruf's task was to overcome resentment of knowledge "not invented here" as he brought the knowledge generated on this large network to bear in Mannheim.

Clear targets – Ruf wants to raise the error-free ratio to 80 percent in 2001 – and a culture that promotes knowledge pull were essential ingredients to the plant's success. But there were also obstacles. At first middle managers felt threatened by the new focus on shared knowledge, Ruf recalls, and avoided ideas that came from elsewhere.

"Mid-level managers showed more resistance to the new structure than the plant's blue-collar workers," he says. "To encourage the acceptance of new knowledge, we have included a cooperation/openness point in each employee's yearly evaluation review, which ultimately defines their chances for advancement and a higher salary. In addition, our managers have been trained to set a positive example of accepting new ideas, especially those that were not invented here. Acceptance of the new knowledge means that each group can lower its overall production costs and thus contribute to higher year-end performance premiums."

Adding to the optimal knowledge environment, departmental managers within the global John Deere organization also know each other personally. If a unit develops a superior process or product, the knowledge is quickly spread and an "absorption" team is assembled, comprising production and development specialists. The team receives added training, such as language instruction, to help them rapidly understand the new knowledge, and spends up to a month visiting the plant that developed the new process. The next step is to bring the knowledge back to their base plant.

Whether to understand a new process or to conduct business as usual, communication is a key element. "We foster an internal exchange of knowledge at all levels, starting with daily morning meetings at line group levels where the previous day's activities are reviewed and the current jobs are discussed," Ruf says. "Every week, the group speakers meet with the module manager to discuss quality issues. And every two weeks the group speakers invite key personnel from engineering or development to exchange knowledge to raise quality and production efficiency."

Such obvious top-level support is also a vital component for creating a knowledge culture.

You may well have already experienced some of the tough decisions to be made when devising incentive schemes. One option is to set highly personalized targets for each employee. The advantage of this approach is that the employee feels that it is possible directly to influence knowledge management performance, fostering a lust for knowledge, but this could pose a threat to the overall company optimum. To some extent such employees become the masters of their own destiny. For example, if an employee is set an incentivized target of building expertise in a certain field, it is important that achieving this does not adversely affect his day-to-day duties. The counterapproach is to set team-specific goals, but these are further removed from the individual's sphere of influence, reducing the motivational effect as the single employee feels impotent in influencing any of the outcomes that count toward rewards.

At many of the less-successful companies, striking such a balance between individual and team-oriented knowledge management incentives was not given priority. Instead, bonuses were seen as almost automatic, relegated to a regular part of the pay packet and not really performance related or flexible. Yet flexibility is the first critical factor if incentives are really to have an effect. This lets you reward exceptionally strong performance and potentially penalize exceptionally poor performance.

One example we came across in the survey shows how highly sophisticated systems can be set up to generate the knowledge pull by setting high targets, including knowledge targets, and attaching the right combination of incentive to these targets. At a recognized best-practice company, a balanced scorecard system was in place with the following five categories:

- *Financial focus:* Income resulting from new business operations; income per employee; market value per employee;

return on net assets resulting from a new business operation; loss ratio compared with market average

- *Customer focus:* Number of customer accounts; days spent
  visiting customers; customer visits to the company; satisfied
  customer index; customers lost

- *Human focus:* Empowerment index; time in training; motivation index; employee turnover; employees working at
  home/total employees

- *Process focus:* Error-free applications; administrative expense/
  total revenue; cost for administrative error per management
  revenue; processing time and outpayments; contracts per
  employee

- *Renewal and development focus:* Satisfied employee index;
  competence development expense per employee; training
  expense per employee; R&D expense per administrative
  expense; marketing expense per customer.

As you can see, this system combines clear quantifiable targets
with more individualized knowledge-oriented targets revolving
around empowerment, motivation or the satisfied employee
index. These scorecards operate at the company level, the
deparmental level and for each individual employee. They
always account for the extent to which the targets can be influenced by the individual. The target fulfillment at all three levels
determines the year-end bonus.

Fostering personal engagement and responsibility
for own ideas

The fourth lever for generating a knowledge pull and the right
cultural context for knowledge management is connected to

employees' personal engagement, enthusiasm and willingness to take responsibility for their own ideas. Naturally, some of your staff will be more entrepreneurial than others, but that just means you need to work on the others. By generating a people-oriented atmosphere, supporting entrepreneurial behavior and fostering commitment, a company can mobilize potential that otherwise is left sleeping. Casting employees as role models, being open to your employees' suggestions and simply being enthusiastic are all possible ways to achieve this. We also found that actively and positively involving employees in decision-making could play an important part in making them feel more inclined toward a knowledge-oriented company. The extent to which you can actually do some of these things is highly dependent on each specific situation.

Although infusing staff with a personal commitment to corporate success is not as widely used as other techniques to generate a knowledge pull, 53 percent of the more-successful companies allowed relevant employees to participate in product innovation decision-making, compared with 20 percent of the less-successful ones. Also, 60 percent of the more-successful companies leaned toward including employees in product portfolio decisions, compared with only 27 percent of the less-successful ones.

CONSTRUCTING A NEW SCENARIO

Having examined ways to encourage employees to embrace a culture of cooperation and knowledge exchange, let us return to the construction company we introduced at the beginning of this chapter. It recognized the organizational barriers and sought to address them with an IT-driven, top-down solution.

As a result, knowledge was pushed around the company, but there was no real effort to encourage its profitable use.

What could it have done differently? A first step might have been to set transparent knowledge management targets, such as a certain proportion of suppliers drawn from the database, not from a project manager's own experience, and to link these targets to the project managers' bonuses. It could also have linked these bonuses or other incentives to successful projects outside the immediate unit or region. Another possibility would have been to rotate project managers to other offices in order to generate bonds within the company and build trust among the managers. On a more practical level, it might also have helped to test the database with a smaller group first. This would not only have helped to identify the individual barriers to its optimal use, but would also have got key project managers personally involved through conferences, and success stories from the pilot program would have helped to ignite excitement around a company-wide launch.

Might have, but did not. It is said that you can lead a horse to water, but you cannot make it drink. You can also lead employees to the refreshing water of knowledge, but you *can* make them drink. The secret that successful companies understand is that you do not make them drink by holding their heads under or by leaving them alone. Rather, you make them very thirsty and help them to recognize that the only way to keep the water supply replenished and pure is to cooperate with their colleagues and dig a deeper knowledge well.

FIGURE 2.3

Summary – Knowledge pull best-practice KM techniques

Method of application of differentiating KM techniques

Percentage of participants in each category

	0	25	50	75	100

World-class aspiration

– Development efficiency — 33 · **60** · 93

– Process efficiency — 27 · **60** · 87

– Quality standards — 33 · **54** · 87

– Product innovation — 40 · **53** · 93

Public recognition of creative ideas — 33 · **47** · 80

Financial incentives linked to product development — 27 · **46** · 73

Active involvement of employees in process improvement decisions — 20 · **40** · 60

Financial incentives linked to marketing/ sales communication — 40 · **33** · 73

Active involvement of employees in product innovation decisions — 20 · **33** · 53

Active involvement of employees in product portfolio decisions — 27 · **33** · 60

Financial incentives for cooperation, information flow in production — 40 · **20** · 60

● Less-successful companies

● More-successful companies

● Gap

Source: McKinsey knowledge management survey

chapter three

Knowledge character building

A strong corporate knowledge culture will fuel a successful knowledge program. But to make such a culture meaningful and productive rather than a mess of Brownian motion requires firm-handed steerage and a clear grasp of your craft's characteristics. Just as a ship's crew can become more adept sailors as the journey advances, your employees can gradually build their desire for knowledge even as other aspects of a knowledge management program are already underway. Even without a complete knowledge culture, your company should begin actively addressing the three main tasks of knowledge management: application, distribution, and cultivation.

Despite the linear exposé, managing knowledge is not a step-by-step process. Each task should be addressed simultaneously. But there is a reason we are discussing these tasks in an order that might seem counter-intuitive. After all, if you were starting from square one, you would first have to cultivate some knowledge, then distribute it, and finally apply it. But no company starts from square one. You are already sitting on knowledge that is waiting to be applied, and you have already cultivated knowledge that is waiting to be distributed. Instead of following what might seem a natural flow, we are ordering the tasks based on the speed at which they can be tackled and how quickly they could show some bottom-line impact. Application has the most direct effect on a company's performance, followed by distribution and finally cultivation. But to stress our point, this does not imply working through the tasks sequentially. Unless they are addressed together in a holistic program, your company is likely to develop costly and perhaps dangerous air pockets in its knowledge pipeline.

Although the process is not linear, companies starting a knowledge management program and looking for quick wins in order to generate enthusiasm for the project should look closely at applying knowledge that is already available. Not only will this focus on application bring more immediate and visible results, it will also quicken the gains brought by improved distribution and cultivation. Without developing the necessary skills in applying knowledge, progress in distribution and cultivation may go unnoticed and unutilized.

APPLICATION CREATES VALUE QUICKLY

Your employees already apply knowledge daily. Whether reading, calculating, thinking, driving, or operating heavy machinery, knowledge is applied automatically, even subconsciously, just by doing their jobs. From a corporate perspective, the key is to be aware of knowledge that has yet to be applied, but that could contribute to your company's success. This could be done by using knowledge to carry out a particular task more efficiently, to reduce costs, to increase output, or to boost revenues.

Application is the use of knowledge within a specific context in order to produce a desired result that will generate value for the company. Its degree of success can be seen in the success of the task fulfillment within the company context.

Without knowing how to apply knowledge, there is little point in worrying about cultivation and distribution. Still, that is the trap that snares many companies. They focus their knowledge management efforts on cultivation, tirelessly trying to invent a business solution or killer product, but doing little more than filling shelves with research results; or on distribution, building a sophisticated IT infrastructure. By failing to give at least equal emphasis to application, much of their residual knowledge is left underutilized, and an asset that is not fully utilized could easily fail to generate enough returns to justify the investment.

One example where a company failed to gain the most value by not applying its knowledge involves Xerox's famed Palo Alto Research Center (PARC) in California. PARC was extremely good at cultivating knowledge, but the company did not always take that knowledge and work with it itself. Such ground-breaking inventions as the graphical user interface that were initially developed by PARC were applied to great advantage elsewhere, in this case by Apple. Xerox decided to gain short-term value from this new technology by selling it to Apple rather than applying it itself. Given the huge success of the graphical user interface, in hindsight the decision would probably be different.

DISTRIBUTION UNLEASHES EVERYONE'S POTENTIAL

While application focuses on putting knowledge directly to work, distribution ensures that knowledge is available to the right people, in the right place, at the right time. Knowledge should be made selectively accessible for use across your whole organization. This needs to be approached with caution: being selective does not mean establishing an all-powerful authority that judges which employees are allowed what knowledge. At the other extreme, it is important to avoid information overload, and knowledge pull is a significant factor for this. If employees desire certain knowledge for their target fulfilment, there should be no lengthy administrative procedures for gaining access to it. The right pull, even as a knowledge culture is being developed, assures that only relevant knowledge is sought, and therefore there is no need to deny access. The self-organizing and self-balancing mechanisms fostered by the right cultural context will avoid information overflow. This is the difference between pushing all the corporate information at all staff, and making it available for them to access. Good knowledge distribution also ensures that knowledge flows through the correct channels, gets to the right people, and has the maximum impact irrespective of location. Of course, basic rules of confidentiality must also be applied.

Of the three tasks, distribution is the most dependent on a solid infrastructure populated by databases, virtual team rooms and other channels. But successful companies – even those with sophisticated IT systems allowing the smooth and broad exchange of data – know that the challenge goes beyond building information networks. As we saw in the last chapter, pushing IT systems into a company can only go so far. Truly effective distribution of knowledge relies on personal networks and personal interaction with internal and external partners.

In the 1970s a leading computer manufacturer started to link all its hardware and software technicians worldwide using an on-line system. The goal was to generate expert answers to any technical question within 24 hours. The system provided easy communication facilities with search-and-retrieval capabilities covering all the questions posted and became a huge asset for the company's technical community. With a strong IT found-ation, success resulted from frequent interaction and active use of the system. Building on this success, and as part of a drive to improve technical and customer service, the system was selec-tively opened to key customers, creating an effective knowledge distribution system that offered benefits to all participants and helped to raise customer satisfaction and loyalty.

CULTIVATION GENERATES LONG-TERM OPTIONS

Despite the temptation, cultivation should not be reduced to a mad rush to invent prototypes. Developing a eureka product or service is indeed the golden fleece of knowledge management, but it is only one of many treasures that can be captured through cultivation. And many of these other gems – new busi-ness solutions, processes, procedures, and more modest product evolution – are within easier reach. In many ways, being a knowledge cultivator is like being an aggressive venture capitalist. You accept and expect that some of your investments will fail, but are secure knowing that enough will be successful to produce net gains.

Cultivation is a necessary exercise to ensure that your company's innovation pipeline and knowledge storehouse remain full. Like all enterprises, your company is losing know-ledge constantly. It walks out the door as employees change jobs. It becomes outdated because of market forces. It is lost in human forgetfulness or in an overgrown database jungle.

Myriad perils await your company's knowledge. All told, your knowledge holdings fluctuate significantly and unpredictably.

Although there is an inherent randomness in working with knowledge, managers must strive to keep control of the cultivation process. They must identify as early as possible where critical losses in knowledge might occur, and focus cultivation efforts to fill those gaps. They must also recognize when a surfeit of knowledge accumulates in a particular area, for instance repetitive marketing studies, and redirect efforts down more promising avenues. One of Europe's largest companies provides a good example here. Nokia evolved from a conglomerate with products ranging from paper to chemicals and rubber to a true telecommunications company. The groundwork for this change was laid by the efforts within its research center in Espoo, which began cultivating knowledge about radio transmission and ended up as an innovator for mobile communications and audiovisual signal processing. This was good timing for Nokia as no other company had yet come to grips with the new technology.

The challenge of cultivation is most pressing in industries in which knowledge generally loses value more rapidly, for instance because of short product life cycles or the threat of copycat competition undercutting the market. High-tech and pharmaceutical companies are clear examples of industries that put significant emphasis on knowledge creation, as evidenced by their large R&D budgets. As product life cycles shortened, there was a tendency among the more-successful companies to focus more on knowledge management techniques that cut the time necessary to accomplish the three tasks we have described.

Of the three tasks, cultivation has the longest time lag between implementation and payoff, giving it many of the attributes of a strategic investment rather than an operational fix. All industries have the need for cultivation; some simply begin withering from a knowledge drought more quickly.

KNOWLEDGE SHOWS CHARACTER

Managing knowledge means working toward the tasks of applying, distributing and cultivating knowledge effectively. To understand the critical techniques for successful knowledge management, it is necessary to look at what distinguishes knowledge from other assets. By being aware of these characteristics and what they mean in a corporate environment, it becomes much easier to find the appropriate techniques for managing knowledge.

Six characteristics distinguish knowledge from more traditional assets, and understanding the nature of these differences separates the clued-in manager from the clueless. We benefit from and struggle with knowledge daily because of these characteristics – often subconsciously. But a more explicit understanding is needed in a corporate context.

Subjectivity

Picture a group of people watching a news item about flooding in the UK. Personal backgrounds, interests, points of view, and personality will affect what they take away from the report. The insurance executive, while sympathetic, will focus on the damage claims that will deluge his company and wonder whether premiums might be affected. The farmer upstream from the flooded areas will consider what precautions he should take in case the problem spreads. The family with washed-out relatives may concentrate on how they can help. And the hydrologist would become intrigued by the fluid dynamics – or possibly, dynamic fluids – of the crisis. They all look at the news subjectively.

Businesses have long lived with fact-based assets. You can put a figure on your cash, count your workers, and measure your land, and everyone will sign off on the same numbers. But knowledge can mean different things to different people. Managers, for example, might agree that communication across hierarchies needs improving. But one country manager follows this decision by building informal networks, while another country manager starts to implement increased line reporting. In this case, these different understandings of a piece of knowledge – the corporate communications goals – might lead to mistakes, confusion, and, probably, failure.

Transferability

Knowledge can be transferred to different contexts. Sports, for example, have been developed by transferring knowledge from one activity to a new environment. Surfers who wanted a new buzz made the leap from the waves to the slopes, and the sport of snowboarding was born. The technology and the culture of surfing was adapted to the snow. Ultimately, the knowledge of surfing was transplanted to a new context so successfully that snowboarding is now an Olympic event.

This illustration leaps easily to a business context. In one example, an airline improved its handling of stopovers by studying how motor racing teams orchestrate pit stops and applying the knowledge to the cargo loading and preparations processes of its aircraft.

Embeddedness

Just because knowledge exists does not always mean it is handy. One of the problems with knowledge is that it is often embedded. It may be buried deep within someone's mind or lying undisturbed and hidden in libraries, databases, or filing cabinets. Imagine learning a carpenter's skill by reading a book on woodwork. There is more to designing and crafting a chair than simply taking a few pieces of wood, a saw and a few pages of instruction. Trial and error is one approach and, over time, you would probably end up with something that you could sit on without risking your dignity. But you would have gone through a lot of wood, a couple of saw blades and a few Band-Aids to get there. Extracting embedded knowledge is the cornerstone of apprenticeship programs, where pupils learn not from a book, but from a master.

For a business, if knowledge is embedded it is laying fallow or, worse, it may be stepping out of the door. When employees leave a company their embedded knowledge leaves with them. Before this happens, a program must be in place to encourage or force employees to spend the necessary time to distribute their knowledge to others, either in person or in documenta-tion. This holds true both for the knowledge embedded in their mind, but also for the knowledge stored in their filing cabinets – real or electronic.

Self-reinforcement

Within an organization, knowledge often increases in value when it is shared. This stands in direct contrast to other tradi-tional assets. If you know of a great Web site for checking the progress of your favorite sports team, you may share it with your friends. This does not reduce the value of the Web site to you, and may even increase its value because you can now discuss the same news with your friends. In addition, by contributing to the site – in chat rooms or discussion boards, for instance – the value of the site to all users is increased.

This is easily seen in a corporate environment. For example, if a company finds a better way to fit a new safety device – airbags or radar distance checkers, for instance – into a car, it could potentially spread this knowledge to other product lines within the company and the knowledge would gain in value if this converted into higher sales or margins. Of course, if the knowledge leaked outside the organization, its value to the company could diminish.

Perishability

As we noted when discussing knowledge cultivation earlier, the value of knowledge can change instantaneously and unpredictably. Generally, over time its value tends to diminish. If you know which newsstand is the first to get newspaper deliveries, you have a better chance of getting a head start on the competition in seeking a new home. But if everyone finds out, then you may turn up one morning to find yourself at the back of the line. The value of that knowledge to you has plummeted as your competitors in the housing market have caught up. Alternatively, that particular newsagent might close down, an external factor causing your knowledge to be worthless. Or, technology might lead to the demise of your knowledge if the local paper begins to publish its property ads online ahead of the print edition. All these problems can contribute to perishability.

The unpredictability of the value of any particular piece of knowledge makes knowledge as a whole hard to manage. A company might search for a highly promising production machine for years. The patent is in sight, but developers feel that more changes are necessary and redesign follows redesign. Your company gains a lot of knowledge and anticipates success. But, if a competitor manages to patent a similar product before you, your knowledge decreases in value as soon as the patent form is stamped.

Spontaneity

Knowledge cannot be generated on demand, but develops spontaneously. Everyone has had the experience of searching desperately for the solution to a problem. But just sitting down and concentrating on it carries no guarantee of finding it. If an important birthday is looming and you are trying to find the ideal present, walking around the shops may not be inspiring, but the perfect idea may come to you out of the blue hours later when you are doing something completely unrelated.

Traditional resources are predictable. You know how to get them. But getting knowledge does not work the same way. Sitting in front of a computer and doing routine work will not ensure that the new killer idea appears by the end of the week. But that killer idea may be the one that keeps the company afloat as revenues from the core product drop off. Brain-storming sessions or simply moments away from the grind can be effective ways of sparking a new idea, but in the end managers are usually faced with the Gordian knot of trying to create creativity.

TYING IT ALL TOGETHER

Having laid out the six characteristics, let us return to the three management tasks of application, distribution and cultivation. The characteristics should be kept in mind when managing all three tasks. However, some characteristics are more relevant to a specific task than to others.

It is easy to see this when considering subjectivity: having a common understanding of something is particularly important when applying knowledge. If people are pulling in different directions, then clearly the knowledge will be worth far less. Embeddedness and self-reinforcement are more closely linked to the distribution of knowledge, since you should remember that, although some knowledge is hard to distribute because it is embedded, it will increase the value once you find a solution. Exploiting the spontaneity of knowledge is confined to managing the cultivation of knowledge.

On the other hand, transferability and perishability cannot be as neatly allocated. Transferability intuitively is most closely linked to distribution, but it must also be considered when applying existing knowledge in a new context. It also falls under cultivation as knowledge transfer can help to trigger the creation of new knowledge. Perishability must also be managed in all three tasks. Speed is necessary in both distributing and applying knowledge to ensure that the maximum value is obtained from the knowledge before that value falls. And, of course, perishability must be managed in cultivation otherwise you run the risk that new knowledge will already be outdated by the time it is applied.

In the following chapters, we explain each characteristic in more detail and equip you with a set of techniques to help to manage them. Although many of the best-practice knowledge management techniques are well known, a recurring theme of our book is that they must be realigned in order to manage knowledge most effectively. Doing so will contribute significantly to your company's performance. Over time, naturally, some of these techniques may change with technological and social evolution, but the challenges inherent to each characteristic will remain constant.

chapter four

Subjectivity: reading from the same page

In addressing knowledge management problems, the inherent subjectivity of knowledge can be like sand in the gearbox. On first inspection, everything looks fine, but still the machinery is not working quite right. If the machine must be used anyway, the results will be spotty at best, but most people will choose to abandon the machine altogether. Likewise, grains of subjectivity can spoil an otherwise well-designed initiative. Efforts to move in a common direction can be scuttled by misunderstandings, for instance, or readily available solutions may be ignored because employees do not see how they can be applied.

As we visited companies, managers often complained that much of their company's knowledge was lying fallow because employees simply did not realize or understand that it could help them to solve problems. As we showed in Chapter 2, some of this can be attributed to distrust of external knowledge and can be countered by building the appropriate cultural context. But another facet of the problem is that employees may not understand how to use the available knowledge or how it fits into their own situations. What may seem to be clear instructions and documentation can become muddled and the knowledge left unused because knowledge is subjective. Differences in expertise, education and status, as well as varied professional and personal experiences, all contribute to the difficulty of finding a common language or a common starting point. Subjectivity is a component of every knowledge management problem, but we have found that the less-successful companies tend not to understand it or ignore it altogether. The more-successful companies have found ways to clean the sand out of their gearboxes.

A US high-tech company decided to build up its production sites worldwide in order to produce identical products with the same quality globally. A team of developers designed a production process, tested it at a central lab, and prepared for a company-wide launch to the different sites. But despite all this planning, product quality in one of its overseas plants differed to that in the US. The first attempts to diagnose the problem also failed, because, even discounting actual language barriers, workers in plants outside the US were unable to describe clearly what went wrong to the team of US-based development engineers.

The underlying problem was that production employees described their situation from a personal, subjective point of view. At the same time, the US engineers could not explain to their foreign colleagues where specific pitfalls could occur in the production line. Although they all shared the same professional background, the way of considering and understanding certain problems was influenced by each worker's subjectivity. In re-analyzing the problem, managers saw that simply defining standards was not enough to build successful production lines throughout the world. They saw that their program must stretch far beyond simply duplicating the process in manuals, an approach that merely laid down dictates without any attempt to generate a common context or understanding.

To counter this problem, the company now ensures a common understanding across its different sites by intensive cooperation and having staff from the development center spend time at the production sites and vice versa. The very early involvement of employees from all the production facilities in a new process development helps to build a shared context and supports the specific understanding at every production site. This shift to a common understanding allowed the company to accelerate production globally, with the same quality levels. This is a decisive competitive advantage in a business where product life cycles are less than 18 months.

This example illustrates how companies must grapple with one of knowledge's core characteristics: subjectivity. An understanding of subjectivity means recognizing that there is no single, common approach to any one piece of knowledge. There are always different interpretations, various viewpoints, and multiple context-based variations.

Overcoming subjective interpretations of the same knowledge becomes even more important as companies get larger and spread globally. Such companies rely on economies of scale, but subjectivity problems can spoil the potential gains. Unless these issues are addressed, each plant or branch will essentially be operating independently, relying on their differing understandings of instructions and information emanating from the head office. This makes it virtually impossible for them to tap into the company's knowledge base or for the company as a whole to capitalize fully on the strength of its size.

Global retailers, particularly in the food service industry, must obviously grapple with subjectivity if they are to offer uniform quality at each of their outlets. McDonald's Corp.'s well-documented Hamburger University, based in Illinois and with satellite campuses in 10 countries, is a prime example of instilling a common foundation for managers at its franchises worldwide.

BUILD COMMON EXPERIENCES

Subjectivity is not always about differing cultural and social backgrounds. Remember the meeting last week that started with confusion over what exactly was concluded at the previous meeting? Subjectivity rears its ugly head again. Or how about that time you asked a colleague for some quick help and got a stack of useless documentation dumped on your desk? These small day-to-day incidents indicate different perceptions of the organizational or business environment.

But where do you start? Problems presented by the subjectivity of knowledge occur most frequently at the different interfaces within a company. Different perceptions or viewpoints are often a result of different departmental affiliations, professional backgrounds, or hierarchical positions. For instance, managers exist in a different environment than line workers – some would suggest a different world. This is a necessary fact of business life since both groups have a different vantage point for viewing the company, but few companies have taken that next step of opening a window between these two worlds.

One automotive company took that next step. It sent board members to the production line to assemble car modules, giving senior managers first-hand experience of the working conditions faced by line workers. The executives struggled with the rigorous timing required on the assembly line and discovered how hard it was to handle all the tools within the limited space of the car body. During the executive shift, the line missed its quality targets but scored a bull's-eye for knowledge management. Such efforts are reasonably risk and cost free and can help to shrink the gap between the common understanding of top management and frontline workers. It also sends an important message throughout the company: management is genuinely committed to listening to workers and understanding the company's processes, conditions, and day-to-day problems.

The mélange of individual experiences that exists within every company with more than one employee must be integrated and aligned in order to reach the overall company goals. Only the implementation of a set of techniques that foster the generation of a common understanding within a company will help it successfully reach the goal of efficient knowledge application. Some of these techniques, as above, may be a little more unusual, but the core point is that you concentrate on getting a shared context. There are a set of systematic techniques that we discuss below, but you should not be afraid of being imaginative. Getting board members to work on a production line sends a very strong signal to the rest of the staff that there is corporate commitment to gaining a shared understanding.

GENERATE AN OPEN KNOWLEDGE FLOW ACROSS HIERARCHIES

While effective communication is necessary to reach almost every corporate goal, effectively communicating across hierarchies can be very tricky. As we mentioned earlier, staff can feel that managers have no grasp of their day-to-day problems and managers can feel that staff have no grasp for the big picture. Both groups are interpreting knowledge differently. Added to the mix, subjective views at all levels of the corporate ladder on the real impact of status can make two-way communication difficult. Sending communications down the line is usually easier, but the modern corporate general must also listen to the foot soldiers.

A European capital goods manufacturer was facing efficiency problems. To try to correct the problem, senior managers decided to begin using a new software package that offered more detailed product data management. But ineffective cross-hierarchical communication meant that employees who had to use the new software did not understand the ultimate goal of the switch. Indeed, they were still struggling with the old soft-ware because they had not been properly trained in how to use it. But this confusion was never conveyed directly to senior managers. Throughout the different hierarchical levels the real problem – the lack of appropriate training for handling the old software – was misinterpreted as not having the right software.

Managers and staff ended up very frustrated by the immense process delays, but could not find an effective solution. Top-down and bottom-up communications were impaired. Without effective knowledge flow between the two groups, combined with a true common understanding and shared company context, it was tremendously difficult to overcome this problem.

In a second example, an automotive supplier stumbled as it tried to debut a new navigation system. Senior managers wanted to enter the market aggressively and backed their decision with a huge budget. The new system was emphasized in meetings with product development, procurement, and marketing/sales staff. But despite this, managers failed to come to a common under-standing with their middle managers or more junior employees. Senior managers felt the strategic shift was self-evident in launching a product, whereas frontline marketing and sales staff missed their cues and were not aware of the new emphasis. They treated the new navigator as another addition to their portfolio and continued to focus on their core products. Top managers had neglected to carry the strategic shift to the hearts and minds of all employees and as a result lost much of the momentum associated with a product launch. The company missed an opportunity to become a market leader by making the wrong assumptions about what was commonly understood.

Effective top-down and bottom-up communication is a simple but essential first step to overcoming subjectivity in order that existing knowledge can be used profitably. As a knowledge strategy, cross-hierarchical communication goes beyond just talk, but is an active effort to build a common understanding and perception across the entire organization. Underlying values and the overall company-specific context must become clear to everybody. Particularly when handling decisions, strategic planning, and daily problems, for instance at the production line or customer service desk, a top-to-bottom understanding of corporate goals that is not distorted by subjectivity is vital. These topics are invariably infected with subjective notions that must be combated head on. This may seem obvious, but our survey showed that the less-successful companies did not follow even this simple rule of cross-hierarchical action. Installing an appropriate corporate communication culture holds many of the keys to a common understanding of direction and implementation. And the loop must travel full circle. After a message is delivered, it must be clear that it was understood and feedback must arrive promptly in order to identify and tackle any misinterpretation as quickly as possible.

BREAK THE STATUS BARRIER

Status symbols can undermine efforts to open lines of communication across hierarchies. Luxurious offices, several layers of assistants, executive dining rooms and other trappings of success only reinforce any subjective notion that as managers move up the corporate ladder they become less and less approachable. An overemphasis on status symbols and an overvaluation of titles or positions widens the gap between people, making it harder to generate a shared understanding. Corporations are inherently hierarchical, and avoiding a sharp differentiation between different levels is not always easy even for the best intentioned. Status, after all, is ingrained in traditional habits and established procedures that are part of a long-established rewards system. But some of the more successful companies have found steps, whether simple or revolutionary, that can lower the barriers associated with position.

One global automotive company, for example, decided that its staff should simply break bread together. For years, the company ran three separate dining rooms at its headquarters – one each for top managers, middle managers, and the rank and file – that were referred to disparagingly by staff as the gold, silver, and plastic spoons. The three different canteens sharpened the divide between managers and employees. Viewpoints shared during informal lunchtime chats were all from colleagues at the same level. Executive dining rooms have a long tradition, but managers at the car company decided that the price for better tableware was too high. Among its measures to improve cross-hierarchical communication, it abandoned the different "spoons." Now, board members share tables with line workers and the conversation flows more freely allowing, among other things, a common picture of the company to be held by all staff. A huge potential exchange of knowledge and direct communication has opened up using a simple, almost symbolic, act.

At Oticon, a Danish hearing aid manufacturer, the shift was far more radical. The chief executive's "residence" – an absurdly huge office with rich wooden furniture, thick carpeting and a gold wall clock – best illustrated the old culture, basking in traditional corporate conservatism. Status meant a bigger office for you and a better parking spot for your car. Communication barriers between hierarchies were almost insurmountable, helping to trigger a crisis that brought in a new CEO and a new attitude. In a positively Bolshevik maneuver, all the fancy furniture was auctioned internally and the status symbols that had served to preserve the status quo were quickly dismantled. The company replaced single offices with an open-plan environment in which no one had a reserved desk. Even the CEO changes his desk if, for instance, a neighboring development team needs more space for its expanding team. The company's modus operandi became more dynamic and flexible as the open environment fostered direct informal communications across hierarchies and laid the foundation for a common vision (see Case Study 4.1).

Abolishing status symbols and an open-door or no-door policy are recognized management tools for creating a common corporate culture. But realizing how status symbols and plush offices can sabotage efforts to reach a cross-hierarchal understanding puts you in a better position to calculate the trade-offs being made. Knowledge application, distribution, and cultivation are more difficult if problems associated with subjectivity are exacerbated by such symbols of power.

Case Study 4.1

OTICON

Today's knowledge special: spaghetti

Danish hearing aid manufacturer Oticon had to deal with an unexpected bout of subjectivity when representatives from the International Organization of Standardization visited as part of the company's bid for ISO 9001 certification, an international hallmark of quality management. "You should have seen how perplexed the ISO evaluation team was when they first looked around and found none of their traditional organizational structures or physical arrangements," says Henrik Holck, human resource director and head of Oticon's Competence Center. "They really didn't know what they were looking at. But our 'spaghetti' organization tends to make that impression on first-time visitors to Oticon. And, we were certified."

Oticon's radical redesign of corporate structure has gone a long way toward eliminating psychological barriers to communication by tearing down the physical barriers. Links between employees from the chairman on down are so amorphous that an organizational chart would resemble a plate of spaghetti. At Oticon, team membership is constantly shifting and the enhanced cross-functional and cross-hierarchical communication that results have been key factors in overcoming subjectivity.

The Danish group is one of six major players in the global hearing aid industry with a total market share of 15 to 20 percent. Altogether, it has 23 foreign sales subsidiaries, along with about 100 independent distributors that handle its products. Behind that success is an organizational model that helps to smooth the application, distribution, and cultivation of knowledge by reducing the drag of subjectivity as much as possible.

Designing, developing, and manufacturing modern hearing aids involves expertise from about 15 different fields, covering a gamut that includes mechanical engineering, acoustical engineering, programming, marketing, chemistry, and assembly. When he took control of the company in 1990, Lars Kolind fought to create an organizational model that reaped as much value as possible from this plethora of talent and knowledge. "There's never been a breakthrough that has occurred by writing a memo," was Kolind's guiding idea. "Breakthroughs occur when two or more people get together, get inspired, have fun, think the unthinkable." By the time he retired in 1998, Kolind had pieced together a structure that ensures informality, short decision paths and an easy exchange of information within and among projects.

"We approach our work on a project basis," Holck explains. "Each project team, which can have up to 70 members, has all of the required expertise needed successfully to complete its project. Teams also have access to our pilot manufacturing plant and testing facilities located within the building so they can quickly check if their ideas are practical. All teams work in open areas and no one, not even the CEO, has their own office."

Once a project is completed, members split up and join other project teams. The dynamics of the work flow encourage networking, and the flow of knowledge through the open-area offices is almost visible as experts shuttle between teams. "There is continuous fluctuation within the building as staffers pack up their personal 'Rolling Maries' (portable filing cabinets) and join new groups," notes Holck.

> The projects themselves are grouped into three areas – advanced product, high volume, and technology products – and each of these areas is coordinated by two leaders who are responsible for overall performance. At Oticon, staff rotate routinely between projects within the three areas, expanding and disseminating their knowledge. The result is enthusiastic, well-informed employees clad in jeans and sweaters as they sit at microscopes fitting microchips into tiny housings, discussing circuit architecture with acoustic engineers, or passing the time with the chairman, who happens today to be sitting at the next desk.

GET THE EXPERTS TOGETHER

Hierarchies are not the only culprits in ineffective communication and thus a subjective interpretation of knowledge. Separate functions are also suspect. Employees are often too focused on their specialized, individual tasks and may not see or understand the broader context of their roles. They may not take the perspectives of neighboring disciplines into account because these perspectives are not known, are not understood or are not trusted (the "not invented here" syndrome).

One US investment goods manufacturer was suffering from quality setbacks that were eventually traced back to a production module designed solely by development engineers. Although the developers knew and followed standard manufacturing and assembly practice, they created the processes without help from production, assembly, or procurement experts. The products that came off the line were expensive and of poor quality, and each department cast the others as scapegoats. A cross-functional team was assembled to solve the problem and quickly saw it was rooted in a lack of understanding of the requirements of each team. In redesigning the process, development engineers, working more closely with their colleagues in procurement, real-ized that huge savings could be captured by using standardized parts more frequently. Another benefit of the multiskilled team was that production engineers were able to help the team to reduce quality failures and speed up production.

To expand on the Oticon example, the company dismantled hierarchical barriers partly by adopting an open-office environ-ment and the change also brought improved cross-functional communications, which in turn helped to meet customer demands. For instance, its highly advanced products were too bulky and not popular, but poor communications meant that the marketing team was not able to convince developers that their high-tech solution was not customer friendly. The marketing team also did not understand that the necessary design changes that would please its customers could be made relatively easily. By overcoming this subjective understanding between departments, the company is now able to produce more marketable products.

Employees participating in cross-functional teams can learn about other perspectives and dimensions of a multiteam task and overcome some of the problems linked to their subjective, narrowly focused understanding of the task. The relative roles become clearer, and existing knowledge can be applied more effectively. A key to making cross-functional teams work is ensuring that all the different roles and functions required to achieve the goal are directly integrated into the core team. Experts from different disciplines working together to ensure that the best solutions from the varying perspectives are brought to the table. If trade-offs must be made, they are made explicitly. Also, people with different professional backgrounds tend to have different capacities and procedures for problem-solving, as well as differing perceptions of corporate goals, marketplaces, how the company works generally, and their individual roles.

Bringing all these together in a cross-functional team, employees learn from each other and create a common starting point. This not only pushes the effective application of knowledge, but may also generate new knowledge and improve distribution. Each individual's idea of what exactly must be accomplished is set within the team's overall framework, making it easier for the team to move forward as a unit. Individual subjectivity can be overcome and targets will be met more easily. Taking a knowledge management perspective allows a company to increase the benefits it can garner from cross-functional teams, but just calling a team "cross-functional" does not make it a knowledge management-oriented team. Without explicit instructions, teams with representatives from several functions might languish amid perfunctory reports from each branch with little effort exerted to reach a common understanding. Another benefit from an explicit knowledge management perspective is that team members should be encouraged to take a long-term view of their team relationships and the lessons they learn from other functions. After the problem at hand has been solved and they return to their daily work, this should result in a more nuanced approach to their job in which they bear in mind how their work fits into the bigger picture, bringing benefits to the whole company.

As with communicating from top to bottom and back, there is much room for improvement in cross-functional communication. Many companies have started to integrate selected functions into one team, but only a few have set up full cross-functional groups with members from the relevant units needed for task fulfillment, or that take part in the overall process. For example, in the product development process this would include the developers, testing experts, procurement staff, production and service employees. The survey results show that collaboration between product development and testing teams are established at all the more-successful companies, as well as the early integration of the procurement department. But only 60 percent of the less-successful companies integrate testing teams, and only 27 percent integrate procurement.

SYNCHRONIZE HIGH-LEVEL GOALS

Whether working in teams or individually, each employee must be conscious of the company's primary corporate goals. Synchronizing this understanding results in guiding creative energy in the right direction and, most particularly, bringing divergent tasks into harmony. Along with a common understanding, each department learns to adhere to the same rules, avoiding any conflicts of interest. As your business gets more and more complex and interconnected, settling such problems can become a life-saving activity. The power of knowledge will rapidly erode if the synchronization of forces is missing. Each team or employee will focus on individual targets, neglecting the overarching company viewpoint as they pursue their own goals. Recognizing both individual and team performances, as well as how teams act in the company-wide context, is an important component to achieving synchronization. Otherwise, you run the risk of having inefficiencies that might lead one team to successful fulfillment of its goals at another team's expense.

During a visit to an international conglomerate, a production manager told us that he recognized the company needed better interdepartmental collaboration, but ultimately his department's performance was measured by output and efficiency. As a result, his primary goal was to keep capacity utilization high, which was easier to do with large, uniform orders or batches. The sales department, however, was evaluated on delivery time targets and customer satisfaction. These goals are easier to reach with small batches and flexible machine utilization – exactly the opposite of the production team's ideal. As long as senior managers recognized only the departmental target, the conflicting expectations produced tension, frustration and inefficiencies in both departments. Of course both parties understood that they should not optimize their functional targets at the expense of the overall company outcome, but if senior managers do not actively acknowledge the need to balance individual and corporate goals, department managers are almost forced to act selfishly. But the top priority must always be to improve the company's overall performance and cost position, and a clear signal of this priority must be made by the top managers. With this understanding, the two departments will move toward a compromise position that benefits both and, more importantly, the company in general.

This highlights the high impact that the synchronization of goals, overall rules, and shared values can have. Agreeing on a framework for action is not always easy, and it may not be enough simply to do it once because when employees fall back into their daily work they may lose the focus on these synchronized values. Employees usually have only a vague understanding of the interdependencies of goals among neighboring functions, but however flimsy that understanding may be, it is often abandoned completely – consciously or otherwise – when it comes to fulfilling one's own target. What is needed is a long-lasting commitment to the shared values and rules within the company. One technique that has proved very successful here, as simple as it may sound, is having workers sign a binding document that lays down the overarching goals and values of a project or solution.

At an international telecoms equipment company, the development program combined a standard gate process with a signed commitment. A gate process is a common product development tool in which strict milestones are set and must be reached before the project passes through a "gate" and into the next phase. At this company, members of the development team must sign a commitment at "Gate 4," agreeing to the specifications of the project. At this point, the design parameters are frozen. No further changes are admissible since each member has literally signed off on the design, attesting that they understand and agree to the specifications. By investing the effort to create synchronized goals and a common understanding early in the process, the teams accelerate the final phases of development, and knowledge application is much more efficient.

TURNING TRADITIONAL TECHNIQUES TO GREATER ADVANTAGE

Successful companies have already realized that the relatively straightforward techniques we have discussed here can help to leverage the knowledge within the organization tremendously. Providing a common understanding is a very important starting point for successful knowledge application. If your company is constantly confronting misunderstandings or internal struggles, this is a clear warning that discord is rife within the organization. The foundations that you have built to support shared understanding may be crumbling, leaving you with employees scrabbling around in the rubble, more concerned with their own section of masonry than the whole corporate edifice.

The best-practice techniques for reaching that joint mindset are not, as is often assumed, sophisticated IT systems or technology-based network platforms, but derive from the organization itself. Cross-hierarchical and cross-functional integration and goal synchronization may not be startling concepts, but using these techniques while focusing on knowledge shows the great potential of these tools and raises the prospect for further value creation by exploiting the existing knowledge base through successful application.

FIGURE 4.1

Summary – Subjectivity best-practice KM techniques

Method of application of differentiating KM techniques	Percentage of participants in each category		

Technique	Less-successful	Gap	More-successful
Cross-functional collaboration between product development and procurement	33	67	100
Cross-functional collaboration between product development and process development	20	53	73
Face-to-face communication in order generation and fulfillment	53	47	100
Open-door policy for troubleshooting in order generation and fulfillment	13	47	60
Agreement on common values and rules among product development and related functions	20	47	67
Cross-functional collaboration between product development and test teams	60	40	100
Cross-functional collaboration between product development and service	47	33	80
Cross-functional collaboration between product development and production	47	33	80
Cross-functional collaboration between product development and marketing/sales	47	33	80
Agreement on general values and rules among order generation and fulfillment and related functions	20	33	53
Face-to-face communication in product development	67	20	87

Less-successful companies
More-successful companies
Gap

Source: McKinsey knowledge management survey

chapter five

Transferability: knowledge on the move

We have just seen how communication is a key component of overcoming subjectivity. Communicating knowledge is only possible because knowledge can readily be transferred. This characteristic of knowledge allows companies to open new business fields or find new sources for value generation by detaching knowledge from its original context and applying it to a different one. This happens every day in business: an employee finds a successful way of performing a certain task, and, if the results are positive, the employee tries to replicate the success with other pending tasks. From small tasks to huge, business-changing tasks, this is how the transferability of knowledge is primarily exploited.

Few companies have successfully managed to maximize the opportunities presented by the ability to transfer knowledge. However, taking advantage of this characteristic is relatively straightforward, and knowledge moved to new contexts can lead directly to additional value creation. Still, managing transferability demands lateral thinking and a general openness to innovative ideas.

An unusual example comes from a large telecommunications company. Its service department was inefficient, and generally the organization was slow at troubleshooting, but because of constant time pressure managers found it difficult to address these problems directly. Even finding the right contact person when specific problems occurred was problematic because various departments contained the relevant information. But responding to a tragedy changed that. An earthquake in the late 1990s demanded a huge commitment from many of the company's employees to reinstall the telecommunication infra-structure throughout the damaged region. Spontaneously, employees started working together to coordinate their activi-ties. Some took the role of interface managers, providing the expertise that was needed immediately at the frontline. An internal operator center was also set up to support and expe-dite the work. In these distressing conditions, an improved structure emerged.

Afterwards managers, recognizing the benefits of this new self-organized method of working, carefully analyzed the processes and connections between different employees and functions. They investigated how this sudden change in work flow and accelerated processes actually worked in practice, trying to understand the interdependencies and relations that made the emergency team so successful. What emerged was a set of key success factors for process improvement. They then took this knowledge out of the emergency context in which it had been so successfully deployed, and transferred it to the everyday work context. They established operator centers for "quick info" within organizational units, and they gave teams more freedom, but also more responsibility for target fulfill-ment. These changes accelerated many processes and eroded the erstwhile indolence. This dramatic example shows how the relatively straightforward transfer of knowledge helped a company to improve its performance significantly.

BENCHMARKING KNOWLEDGE UNDER YOUR NOSE

Transferring knowledge to a new context, as we saw above, does not have to mean opening up entirely new business fields. Simply discovering knowledge that can be applied in a new company-specific context can realize value, for instance by helping to reduce costs through greater efficiency. All that is needed are sufficiently similar processes or products so that comparison and transfer make sense. One set of tools that can be used for exploiting transferability are the various bench-marking techniques. These can be extended from a simple comparison of different processes or products to extracting the knowledge about the benchmark solution and transferring it to similar applications.

Internal benchmarking is most commonly used to compare competitive performance among departments or units or to discover who has the most efficient solution to a common problem. Unfortunately, the end result is usually a mountain of data covering a small part of a process. For example, a car manufacturer wants to assess the amount of glue used to attach the lens for a car headlight to its casing. The glue's temperature, the squeeze time, the squeeze pressure, the drying time and the overall throughput time, among others, are measured and compared across the different production lines. Traditionally, such an initiative ends with one benchmark result that sets the target for all units.

But the devil is in the details, and the particularities of each assembly line are different. Simply adjusting the temperature of the glue or the squeeze pressure will invariably fail to produce the desired results. This is where the second step toward knowledge-oriented benchmarking is necessary. Measuring is not enough. You must ask "why" repeatedly to get to the heart of your processes, to get to the knowledge that lies behind each process step. Returning to the car headlight example, you might observe that longer drying time will produce a stronger bond between the separate parts, but adversely affect the material of the casing at one plant because the local supplier uses slightly different materials. Just setting a benchmark for drying time would not help to optimize all production lines, but understanding the mechanisms and relations behind each individual process step and between the steps will help to come up with a more reliable and efficient solution. Transferring the knowledge from the benchmark example to other units is possible only if the underlying connections and interdependencies of the benchmark can be analyzed.

Successful knowledge benchmarking depends on a clear understanding of the interdependencies and relations within the original context. But the time taken to get to the knowledge is well spent if it allows the rapid and effective transfer of knowledge and, in turn, implementation of best practice. Few companies apply benchmarking with this clear focus on the transferability of knowledge, but those that do can feel the difference.

Internal benchmarking can span a company's entire operations as well as one small division. One global high-tech company tried to solve a problem one division was experiencing with the quality of a component used throughout its product range. The company dispatched a global benchmarking team and, after detailed analysis and evaluation of the different internal practices, the team found which business unit had the best solution to the problem. It was then a relatively simple task to detach the knowledge from its original context and apply it to the troubled unit. This use of the transferability of knowledge meant that the original unit's products improved in quality which led, in the end, to a better market position. The underlying technique was internal benchmarking, but the scope was broadened in order to generate value through knowledge transfer.

EXPLORING THE WORLD

Why restrict yourself to the boundaries of your corporate knowledge? Peering over the walls into the wide world may bring valuable insights that were not even on your company's radar. There are, again, existing management techniques available to support such a search. But focus them on knowledge, and you can generate even more value (see Case Study 5.1).

Case Study 5.1

AISIN AW

Dispatching the Seven Samurai

Aichi prefecture in central Japan is a great place for Aisin AW to build its bread and butter product: automatic transmissions. About 20 kilometers from Toyota City, the headquarters of its largest customer, Aisin rests amid

---

a sprawl of small businesses and rice paddies. There is plenty of space to work, and few distractions.

Too few distractions, really. In 1986, then president Minoru Toyoda lamented that staking the company's future on just transmissions was too risky. Shuzo Moroto, then vice president for general management and later chairman, took up the challenge and pushed for the company to enter the car electronics sector. For his plan to succeed, Aisin would quickly have to acquire knowledge in this new field, so Moroto dispatched a team that later became known as the Seven Samurai to gather knowledge that could be transferred to a new product line.

Koji Sumiya, now a managing director, was picked to lead the team. "Moroto gave me great freedom in this project, and told me to choose whoever I thought was really needed for the job," Sumiya recalls. "He advised me to pick the best staff I could, the kind whose supervisors might complain that they had been selected and thus removed from their regular work position."

Moroto sent his samurai, mostly mechanical engineers with little electronics experience, to live and work in Akihabara, Tokyo's electronic gadget Mecca. Bathed in neon lights like the cover of a pulp fiction novel, Akihabara is awash with shops selling electronics components, computers, and consumer gadgets. There, the team would glean some of the thinking that went into the best products, and work out what their own product should be like – transferring knowledge from the consumer electronics sector.

"There were two reasons for going to Akihabara," explains Sumiya. "One was that we could buy all sorts of products, and take them apart to use the components. The other was that we could play with products to see which ones were easiest to use. Our motto was: 'Think with your hands.' That meant, was the prototype easy or difficult to use?"

The team eventually focused on about 10 ideas and developed numerous plans and prototypes during the first year of brainstorming. Among these were a road surface sensor for four-wheel-drive vehicles that adjusted power distribution to the wheels based on whether the road was icy, snow covered, or wet. But this was too expensive. Another was a car periscope that consisted of a camera propped two meters above the car. Images were projected onto a screen inside. But after test drives through downtown Tokyo, the project was shelved as impractical.

The winning idea, however, was a car navigation system, which, as a prototype, comprised a modified motherboard from a desktop computer installed in a car's trunk and a small color television monitor on the dashboard. Other companies were developing car navigation systems at the time, but Aisin's was different. Thinking with their hands and transferring the knowledge about consumer electronics that they had been gathering during their haunts in Akihabara, the team came up with several unique features: audible directions, rather than text displayed on a monitor; directions that relied on landmarks, such as banks and stores, rather than addresses; and destinations that could be registered using their telephone numbers.

Toyota initially rejected the system, saying the voice instructions were a nuisance, and recording and updating databases for landmarks and phone numbers would be too much trouble. But Aisin was undaunted and persuaded a Kyoto car rental firm to offer the system as a premium feature on some of its cars. One customer was Toyota's chief Celsior engineer Ichiro Suzuki, who liked the system so much that by 1992 the navigation system was optional equipment in new Celsiors.

"Now these three [features] are all standard items on car navigation devices," says Sumiya. "Our concept for car navigation systems has become standard." And by the end of 1999, the systems made up 5 percent of Aisin AW's total annual sales of 376.3 billion yen.

For example, a European automotive parts supplier was very strongly focused on its own innovative power and development expertise. Over the years, this stance helped it to emerge as the technological leader in its industry. But its competitors' products, although missing the cutting edge technical innovations, were more reliable, durable, and cheaper. For a long time the company just accepted this situation, doing little more than starting a few efficiency initiatives. But as competition grew, just having state-of-the-art technology was not enough to remain top dog.

The initial response was to devise an internal benchmarking program to identify where there was room for improvement. But the breakthrough came when one ambitious engineer set up a benchmarking circuit in which competitors' products were analyzed and evaluated by employees from different functions within the company. The rival products were simply passed from one expert to the other through the company and each wrote a brief summary of their observations. In R&D, for example, experts tried to reverse engineer the product's underlying technology and examined technological compatibilities. Line managers assessed how easy it would be to make, what components were used, and the process technology behind it. Others specialists did likewise, and all their comments were compiled on an intranet site open to all members of the circuit. The knowledge gained from benchmarking competitors' products was transferred to the supplier's own internal products and processes, and efficiency rose significantly. The circuit didn't copy the rival's product, but in reconstructing the knowledge behind these products it was able to garner insights that could be transferred to its own operations.

A more extravagant approach is to go not just beyond your company, but beyond your entire industry. Such a transfer of knowledge between two totally different contexts can generate very high benefits for the company. One example from outside our survey that we found interesting involves a US airline. When the airline began looking for ways to reduce stopover times and raise efficiency, it did not want just to match its competitors. Instead, it wanted to set itself apart from the rest of the industry. It looked for a benchmarking partner outside its own business, and ended up at an Indy car race track. Logistics engineers from the airline watched how an Indy crew organized its pit stops – a veritable mechanical ballet where every part and person is choreographed at high speed and under tight space constraints. The airline took this highly specialized knowledge from the Indy pits to the tarmac and applied it to loading and unloading its aircraft. As a result, it reduced downtime, while increasing quality and customer satisfaction dramatically.

Other examples abound. An international hotel group improved its guest check-in process by using knowledge gained in the patient admittance process at a hospital emergency room. And a cement manufacturer turned to a pizza delivery company to help it improve its own on-time delivery performance.

All these companies have benefited from the knowledge they were able to extract from an external benchmarking program and transfer to their own products and processes. The value they have gained hints at the huge potential that is out there. But when looking at our survey results, while the gap between more-successful and less-successful companies was apparent, even the more-successful companies have vast room for improvement in this area. For example, product-oriented benchmarking is used by only 40 percent of the more-successful companies, but this is still ahead of the 13 percent of the less-successful companies that use this technique.

PARTNER FOR KNOWLEDGE

Benchmarking is not the only way to find knowledge outside the company. Working closely with external research partners can also reap extraordinary rewards, whether the programs are structured or unstructured. A US chemical company simply pays the fees for employees conducting doctoral research in cooperation with a research center or university. The management assumes that those employees will automatically transfer the new research findings to a company context, whether they are working on chemical, technical, psychological, or management topics.

In a more systematic example, a European engine company participates in a variety of public research projects with different partners from research centers, universities, industrial customers, and, occasionally, competitors. Employees working on the projects not only accomplish the project's specific aims, they also gain access to the diverse knowledge brought to the project by the other participants. When they return to their daily work, they naturally transfer some of this external knowledge to their problem-solving. This systematic transfer of external knowledge is a key success factor for this company, especially in an industry with substantial development costs.

Going further, tapping into your partners' knowledge could also lead to more formal strategic alliances. Strategic corporate alliances are as old as capitalism, but as knowledge moves to the center of every company's agenda, it is this aspect of alliances that should increasingly become the driver of cooperation. More traditional reasons for alliances – market expansion, access to new distribution channels, economies of scale or simply growth – are becoming far less important than before.

Sixty-seven percent of the more-successful companies in our survey set up strategic alliances in order to gain access to partners' knowledge, while only 33 percent of the less-successful companies tried to establish such long-term partnerships. It is also interesting that external knowledge sources are used for both product and process improvements with alliances being formed by development as well as by production departments.

Efforts to link with external knowledge sources can even lead as far as mergers and acquisitions (M&A). After assessing your own core competencies and those of a potential partner, you may decide to accelerate the integration of its knowledge by taking over the entire company. Although such an integration should help to ease the transfer of knowledge, managers must also bear in mind that post-merger management is very tricky. If buying knowledge is one of the primary goals of an M&A initiative, extra care must be taken to make sure that that knowledge doesn't walk out the door following the merger. Post-merger management is a voluminous topic, but among the ideas for preserving knowledge in an acquisition target is to assure relevant employees of their value to the company, create a dynamic, creative environment full of knowledge pull, and make sure that the knowledge synergies are exploited.

By cooperating with external partners, companies gain access to another pool of knowledge that might provide new insights for their own current processes and products. The transferability of knowledge allows it to be detached from the partner's context and transferred to your own applications. Of course, there are many pitfalls to be avoided in setting up alliances with other companies, and these multiply substantially if you actually go ahead and acquire the partner. When aiming to transfer knowledge between companies it is very important to reach a certain degree of trust and accountability between the partners. This is not just to ease the flow of knowledge, but, as we saw when considering subjectivity, the transferred knowledge must be understood in this new context in order to be applied. If the partners do not trust each other, they may not be fully open with their ideas and insights. And without such transparency, the transferred knowledge could be as useless as missing luggage.

KNOW YOUR CUSTOMER

Our discussion so far has focused primarily on how transferring knowledge can improve a company's performance broadly. But transferring knowledge to new products can also trigger such significant victories as direct market success and improved customer satisfaction. This could be understood as classical market research but again, taking a knowledge perspective adds another very important ingredient to this discipline. Techniques that provide insights into customers' requirements, subconscious demands, and hidden wishes also uncover new market potential by showing where existing knowledge could be transferred.

One Japanese company launched a new generation of consumer electronics goods worldwide, but paid little attention to cultural differences of taste. It knew that it had the most modern and innovative product in its segment and was convinced that this was the killer sales pitch. But while the product was a star on the Japanese market, sales in Europe, the US, and other parts of Asia were very disappointing. Following a huge market research program, the company discovered that it had failed to recognize the nuances of the different markets.

The design was too futuristic for the US market; the color choices did not work well in Europe; and, in other parts of Asia, the product name had negative connotations.

For the next generation of this product, marketing staff and developers were told to observe their markets and pass along all the relevant knowledge. Developers attended product clinics to hear from customers which features were most popular and which most disliked and the product's main selling points. Managers worldwide visited stores to meet customers and observe their buying behavior. This knowledge about customer requirements and needs was then used to identify the areas where knowledge transfer would be most successful. If customers wanted better remote controls, for example, then that department would have to focus on getting new knowledge. Changes were incorporated into the product's next generation, and it was very successful not only in Japan but also on the international market.

Discovering emerging customer needs might indicate areas for knowledge transfer that would have been otherwise overlooked and it might guide you away from efforts to transfer knowledge in areas that are not relevant to consumer trends. But it is important to implement the best-practice techniques that go beyond merely asking which products customers would like. You should aim to collect information about your customers' latent wishes, as well as trying to tap into new customer pools. This requires redefining the role of marketing/sales in the product development process. Marketing and sales knowledge about customers, markets, and changes in the competitive landscape should be directly integrated into product development so that engineers can translate these emerging customer requirements into product specifications.

Market research must be a core activity of every company, whether a start-up software developer or an incumbent auto manufacturer. But seen from the vantage point of knowledge management, this traditional tool gains importance by identifying the areas in which transferability has the greatest potential for creating value. You might get lucky by randomly seeking internal or external knowledge worth applying to your corporate context, but by using market research and customer preferences as guides you can focus on transferring knowledge in ways most likely to lead to market success. This is underlined by the knowledge management techniques that focus on customers' current and potential requirements.

When looking at our survey results, customer orientation and market focus proved to be most important. Of our more-successful companies, 87 percent dedicated employees from different units to analyze customer behavior. Outside the sales or service units, the same strong commitment to customer orientation was observed in 47 percent of the less-successful companies. The same pattern holds true for involving marketing/sales staff in product development to bring together all the knowledge about the customer in order to generate a better product. Only 20 percent of the less-successful companies actively do this, compared with 67 percent of the more-successful companies.

DISCOVER THE LAND OF NEW OPPORTUNITIES

One of the most appealing aspects of transferability is its potential to open completely new lines of business. This goes well beyond improving process efficiency or adding another bell or whistle to a microwave oven. In the knowledge-based economy, the opportunity to sell your own knowledge, opening a new market to your company, can bring the highest rewards. Even in businesses characterized by decreasing returns, increased competition, and shrinking market volume, transferring knowledge to a new context can reinject dynamism into the balance sheet. The opportunities are as large as your creativity, willingness, entrepreneurial power, and knowledge base.

At one European investment goods company, managers launched a new service unit based on the expertise and know-ledge gained in the company's core competence of constructing plants. The company took its expertise in spatial planning, ventilation, and electricity, water and sewerage ducts, among others, and applied it in the maintenance and facility management business. By using its knowledge twice, it built a new column of constant revenue. In a cyclical industry like construction, this is particularly useful. Today, this unit accounts for almost half of all revenues.

A second and more dramatic way of transferring knowledge to new business lines embraces the entire company. One European investment goods company went through a remark-able transition from a metals producer to a highly profitable knowledge-intensive enterprise. Based on the knowledge it already had from its unique manufacturing processes, it opened a new business line focused on advising other metals companies on process management and supplying the tools necessary to replicate its own processes. To power this new revenue stream, the company took advantage of the transfer-ability of knowledge to bring this expertise into a new context. The selling argument was simple – the company was recognized as an innovative plant operator – and potential customers were very enthusiastic about possible business relationships. By taking the plunge and veering away from the standard industry model in which knowledge was a closely guarded internal resource, the company opened a growth avenue that would not have been possible had it remained a traditional manufacturer.

Such an extravagant deployment of the transfer of knowledge is rare. But it is one example of what can be done by a visionary management team that truly understands the possibilities brought about by the ready transferability of knowledge across contexts.

The transferability of knowledge to different and extraordinary contexts can unlock huge value caches to the owner of a great knowledge base. As our survey results suggest and the case studies illustrate, the opportunities offered by the transferability of knowledge are not yet wholeheartedly exploited. Most managers still seem bound to their traditional ways of doing business and overlook that promise of bringing knowledge into entirely new contexts. Too often, managers in traditional businesses cling to their traditional value propositions, even as growth prospects are shrinking perceptibly. By recognizing the horizons opened by the ability to transfer knowledge, some managers will break free of this static view and run with the best in the new knowledge era.

FIGURE 5.1

Summary – Transferability best-practice KM techniques

Method of application of differentiating KM techniques

Percentage of participants in each category

0   25   50   75   100

Marketing/sales staff actively involved at early stage of product development
20 — **47** — 67

Internal and external benchmarking related to production know-how
20 — **40** — 60

Intensive market observation by dedicated employees from all units/departments
47 — **40** — 87

Strategic alliances with external experts in order generation and fulfillment
33 — **26** — 67

Internal and external benchmarking concerning process improvements
20 — **27** — 47

Internal and external benchmarking of competitors' products and processes
13 — **27** — 40

Strategic alliances with external experts in product development
33 — **27** — 60

- Less-successful companies
- More-successful companies
- Gap

Source: McKinsey knowledge management survey

chapter six

Embeddedness: mining a rich vein

Everyone recognizes that knowledge is not readily quantifiable. It has no line on a balance sheet, and we even lack the vocabulary to describe a quantity of knowledge, reverting to nuggets, chunks, pieces, and, more generically still, amounts. Mining your company's knowledge is necessary, but it is difficult to know how rich the seam is because a core characteristic of knowledge is that it is embedded, hidden from view. Companies must come to terms with this if they are to have a successful knowledge management program.

Knowledge is generated in the minds of people. Unlike manufacturing a washing machine, a car, or an oil rig, neither the process nor the result of knowledge creation can be fully observed or counted after it is over. Moreover, immediately after being generated, the knowledge is saved in the mind of the individual. Even after several transformations, whether that is writing it down on paper, shoving it into a database, or telling your colleagues over a beer, knowledge is not instantly transferable. To some extent, it is always embedded.

Think for a moment: can a developer really write down all the experiences that go into designing a car door mechanism and his impression of competitors' doors? Do sales people really have the time, let alone the ability, to jot down all their observations from asking 250 customers what they would like to see in a new product? And how realistic is it to expect senior managers to write down all their insights concerning building and implementing a successful business strategy in order to smooth the way for their upcoming underlings?

Obviously, these things are neither possible nor practical. Some, maybe most, of the knowledge will always remain in people's minds. It can never be fully extracted, and yet it is often these deeply buried ideas that hold the greatest potential. Managers must actively seek ways to extract this knowledge as much as possible. The same problems arise with knowledge stored in endless shelves or databases. Lying there in books or bytes, the knowledge has little value. It must be extracted, brought into the daylight, and made easily accessible to other employees (see Case Study 6.1).

Case Study 6.1

OUTOKUMPU

Extracting high grade ore

Metal is about as old economy as one can find. Entire epochs of prehistory have been defined by the dominant metals of the time. But Finnish metals and technology group Outokumpu shows that established industries can benefit just as much from proper knowledge management as their high-tech brethren.

Based just outside Helsinki, Outokumpu is "a company in the metals business with technology as a strong value-adding element," chief executive

Jyrki Juusela says. "Adding value to metal is not only our brand slogan, it is our strategy."

That value is added by a long-held understanding of the importance of knowledge as a key factor to success. As far back as 1949, well before knowledge management was a corporate buzz phrase, Outokumpu recognized the value of the knowledge it had built up by creating a process to squeeze as much value as possible from the ore available for smelting.

"We simply had to innovate on our own in order to process economically our deposits of low-grade ore in order to survive," notes Markku R. Toivanen, senior vice president for New Business Ventures. "In 1949 we developed our flash smelting process at Harjavalta, Finland. Soon, we were receiving inquiries from other companies about our new revolutionary technology. Today, the flash smelting process we developed over 50 years ago is used to manufacture nearly half of the world's primary copper."

By using its knowledge to expand beyond the boundaries of a typical metals group, Outokumpu profits by helping other mining companies to design, construct, operate, and finance a mine or smelter on a turn-key basis. If that is not enough, if even can take care of the marketing.

Transferring the knowledge developed as a metals processor into a new business context was a very fruitful exercise in finding greater value from internal knowledge. And the metals and technology group has continued to refine its abilities to extract its embedded knowledge and smelt that ore into valuable alloys. As part of its knowledge management program, the group began a concentrated effort in 1997 to mine more of its embedded knowledge and make that knowledge available to more employees.

Helping customers with product development requires combining their product specific requirements with the deep metallurgical experience that Outokumpu has gained and documented over years of research. In 1997 Outokumpu began a group-wide knowledge audit to collect and effectively harness its rich lode of embedded mining and metallurgical know-how. The audit was inspired by a belief that the company had extensive knowledge that was not being used optimally.

Working with a small association of other Finnish companies that were also seeking ways to improve their abilities to share knowledge, Outokumpu completed its audit by the end of 2000. One result is databases of ideas and information that are available throughout the group over the company's intranet.

"The knowledge covers production processes, products, Outokumpu key personnel and competitors," explains Raimo Rantanen, senior vice president of Corporate Research and Development. "The single most important learning point of the audit was that the flow of information can be built more straightforwardly. During the audit project, key persons of all businesses and functions were listed and the flow of information ... was enhanced."

Outokumpu also relies on a solid IT infrastructure to make it easier to find and extract embedded knowledge. With about 12,000 workers in 17 plants in 11 countries – not counting scores of subsidiaries – finding the right person to answer specific questions is sometimes difficult. The group's intranet system, however, is tailored to help employees to find the right expert easily. The managers say that the appropriate foundations for sharing knowledge are essential to enhance communication, cooperation, and knowledge exchange in such a far-reaching company.

For any individual employee, the fact that their own knowledge is embedded is not a big problem – at least not from a personal perspective. They know how to do their job and whether the knowledge is extracted and made available to anyone else is probably not of prime concern. This is not a question of hoarding knowledge, just that there is no immediate reason to take the time to dispense this embedded knowledge. But extrapolate this situation to your whole company, and you can see the problem.

If a nugget (or piece or so on) of knowledge is important for one person's success, there is a strong likelihood that someone else in the company could find it useful, too. For example, if a car suspension developer has found a new solution for a luxury car, it makes sense that the corresponding developer working on the company's mid-size car should get the chance to benefit from this. Otherwise the company is in danger of reinventing the wheel – perhaps literally – and, as we saw in Chapter 2, that adds unnecessary cost and complexity into the proceedings.

Our hard-working suspension developer may also have generated insights that might be useful for other employees, such as the steering-mechanism development team, although their value might not be immediately obvious. And generally, when it comes to product development, a vast array of knowledge is of great benefit to the marketing and sales department who can then focus their efforts on the new, or unique elements of the product. Wherever the knowledge ends up being applied, it is certainly valuable beyond the confines of the suspension developer's mind. We saw this clearly in Chapter 5, but there we were concerned with showing why you should look to transfer knowledge, here we are concerned with how you overcome embeddedness in order to do that. For example, if the suspension developer is offered a lucrative position by one of your competitors, then unless his knowledge has been extracted before he leaves, there will be limited opportunity for transfer.

Most of your customers' knowledge, which can help you to identify the most profitable avenues for knowledge transfer, is also embedded. These are the people that you are working to please, so finding out how to get at their thoughts is critical. The same situation arises when looking at suppliers, manufacturers of production technology, and other business partners. They all have knowledge that is not easy to get, and unless you get it, that knowledge cannot benefit your business processes.

IT CAN HELP

The commonly accepted way of tackling embeddedness – and certainly the focus of much of the knowledge management literature to date – is the design and use of IT systems. Companies seem to want to find more and more sophisticated solutions for documenting their knowledge. This is, however, just one part of the solution – and also part of the problem because it restricts your focus in such a way that may lead you to neglect other equally important measures for extracting knowledge. After all, as we showed above, it is never possible to make all the knowledge explicit or store it sensibly in a database, especially if the contextual background needed to overcome subjectivity is lacking.

Adding to the fog, we are witnessing a strange phenomenon. Existing IT tools are being renamed by fashion-victim managers. Databases are marketed as "knowledge bases." Document management systems turn out to be knowledge management systems, and so are enterprise resource planning systems. But rather than hoping that a new name will solve your problems, it would be better to identify the specific IT tools or features that are really important for knowledge management or to set out where the value for knowledge management is in using these tools.

The surveyed companies also often focused on IT systems. Although many of them recognized the challenge of extracting embedded knowledge, they seemed to concentrate more on distributing knowledge via IT channels. This is relatively simple, and easy to manage, but misses an important element. Using an IT system carries no guarantee that embedded knowledge actually becomes more accessible or that enough of the knowledge is transported to the right place to be useful. Powerful and sophisticated search engines are needed, and some management of the system to ensure that knowledge is being presented in the most appropriate fashion and is being used.

Some companies handle the embeddedness of knowledge very well. Along with a superior IT infrastructure, they also manage the knowledge that resides in their staff. Software companies, for example, constantly face the challenge of making their programs as user friendly as possible. But the problem and the solutions go beyond the high-tech sector.

A US investment goods manufacturer combated the challenge of transferring embedded knowledge by routinely assigning process designers to the shop floor for a year to oversee the modules they had created. This helped to bring the embedded knowledge of the process designers into the open to where it could best be applied on the assembly line, and was much more helpful than simply transferring that knowledge onto paper where it would probably never be read. The program also opened lines of communication between assembly line employees and designers. This gave the designers better insight into the problems faced in production, unleashed new ideas for more efficient processes, and established continued personal contacts between the two groups. Within five years, this program, in combination with other measures, had cut costs by 15 percent and reduced throughput time by 80 percent.

BUT CHOOSE CAREFULLY

Knowledge has different guises. Some can be fairly straightforward, such as tying the names of staff to a particular expertise, but it can also be more complex, such as the best way to conclude a sales pitch or intricate design instructions for a new games console. Both present certain problems when it comes to recording the knowledge. Our best-practice companies did not try to store all the content in their IT systems. Instead, they paid particular attention to saving knowledge about knowledge, as well as on documenting basic structures of knowledge that have long-term value and are fairly stable. There are also questions concerning methods of storage. Should it just be put into a table, turned into a series of overhead charts, typed up? Or should it be an audiovisual extravaganza? You need to think about who will be using the knowledge and what format they would find most helpful. For example, will the knowledge be disseminated broadly to teams or to individuals? Is it likely to be needed on the move or by people stuck at their desks? Do not neglect such seemingly obvious tasks as discussing individuals' requirements early on in order to save time, effort, and expense.

An international financial services company, for example, has a Web-based directory where all employees are listed by name and special expertise. But the expertise is not explained in detail. There are just short explanations about the relevant knowledge – a yellow pages where you can search for the right person. Most of our successful companies had some similar form of yellow pages. The best balance seems to be to have only names and departmental structures and expertise written down, and leave out the context rich knowledge that is best extracted through personal contact. If there is knowledge that is relatively stable over time and not context rich, it probably needs no further extraction, and if it is not recyclable then there is little point in storing it at all. Many documents exist in so-called knowledge libraries that are never used, either because nobody knows where they are or the content is of limited value.

PERSONAL CONTACT IS KEY

Traditionally, the apprenticeship model has been used to extract embedded knowledge. Even in the animal world, this is how offspring learn from their parents: bear cubs learn how to fish by watching, remembering, and trying. It is perhaps the most natural way of passing knowledge from one individual to another, and is still common in societies where literacy is not widespread. Watching someone do a specific activity, and then trying it under guidance allows knowledge to be transferred from a teacher to the apprentice and embeddedness is overcome. Of course, it is the feedback and repetition that drives the success of an apprenticeship program. In a business context, apprenticeships are not always feasible, although the popularity of mentoring in organizations is finding favor again. It is the element of personal contact that is vital to understand, and you should look for ways of fostering this as another way of extracting embedded knowledge.

The more-successful companies concentrate heavily on providing dedicated rooms for collaboration, aiding the flow and personal exchange of knowledge. Less-successful companies do not put as much emphasis on bringing people together personally. People may drop by for a chat, but such sporadic visits do not bring the same benefits as working together.

Collaboration can extend beyond the departmental divide and even spread over the company walls. When exchanging knowledge with development partners, for example, it is very valuable to let the parties spend some time together. This does not mean coming together for one face-to-face, kick-off meeting and then never meeting again as you pursue your tasks in isolation. The extent and frequency of contact will naturally vary, but could culminate in full co-location, where your in-house developer works with the external developer in the same building or the same room for most of the development time. This form of cross-functional teams goes a step beyond those we discussed in Chapter 2, seeking to extract knowledge that is embedded somewhere outside the company, as well as transferring internally embedded knowledge.

A Japanese car manufacturer did just this when developing one of its cars. It brought suppliers into the development process by letting them work closely together with its own staff. This reduced the number of formal interfaces, and helped to extract the embedded knowledge from all partners. Working together removes the necessity of documenting all this knowledge. This degree of co-location is supported in the best-practice companies by regular meetings for those people who are not working physically together. Most of the more-successful companies conduct such meetings on a regular basis whereas the less-successful companies call meetings just to solve the most urgent problems. They also are less likely to have recognized the value of incorporating suppliers, partners, tool manufacturers and others in the process. But these people are both sources and recipients of valuable knowledge.

The advantage of such tools is that they allow a direct, informal access to the embedded knowledge. People do not have to write memos, type laboriously into databases, or dictate long letters. The transfer process is neither disturbed nor corrupted by any intermediate. Instead, there is a direct flow of all relevant knowledge where all the necessary context can be delivered immediately and with minimal risk of transmission failure.

Another tool the more-successful companies are using is job rotation. We saw some examples of this in Chapter 4, dealing with how it can help to overcome subjectivity. Being moved to a different job does not necessarily make the knowledge explicit before being applied, but still lets it be applied in other environments. And rather than an individual being seen as an expert-in-residence to answer queries, the person is brought to the task so that the knowledge can be applied immediately. It is possible to marry this with some form of apprenticeship program so that when the person is rotated to another position, the knowledge is not lost for that task. Equally, for the job that has been left behind in the first place, it is important that some of the tools we have already referred to are implemented — such as writing down important guidelines or instructions or providing for some sort of handover period.

There are other advantages to job rotation. All too often, a developer is not overly concerned with problems that can arise at the production stage. But if the developer moves to the production department once the product design is finished, these concerns become part of the daily routine. If such a rotation is commonplace then the developer is more likely to make sure that the design is easy to manufacture, and his embedded development knowledge will be put into action in the production environment. It may be that he has some insights that might help to optimize production that would otherwise never have been extracted.

Perhaps the greatest long-term benefit of job rotation is that your employees get smarter and accumulate more knowledge. Every time they take on a new job, they can both share their embedded knowledge and add to it. They are jumping on a new learning curve by doing new things. Staying in the same job only leads to an incremental transfer of knowledge, but thrown into a new situation with new challenges allows them to combine their knowledge in one field with knowledge from another field. That creates new knowledge and adds to the company's total knowledge reservoir. So besides overcoming the embeddedness problem, this can help with managing the characteristic of spontaneity, which we will discuss in Chapter 9.

Job rotation also clearly helps when dealing with subjectivity, as physically moving to another task and context allows employees to present and discuss their knowledge. In this way, job rotation differs significantly from meetings or training where a presentation is given but most of the knowledge walks out of the door when the session is over.

Although companies are aware that much of the knowledge they have is embedded and not immediately accessible, they are less confident when it comes to determining the balance between using IT tools to extract knowledge and using other, more personally oriented tools. Assessing the right degree of extraction requires careful thought, but our survey showed clearly that the more-successful companies focus on documenting stable, basic parts of knowledge that are not especially context rich. They also provide powerful search and retrieval tools to help employees to tackle knowledge overload in databases. And they establish close working relationships, which are equally important when grappling with embeddedness. People have to work together in order to transfer important parts of knowledge, those embedded, hard-to-reach bits that make all the difference.

FIGURE 6.1

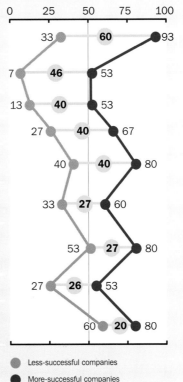

Summary – Embeddedness best-practice KM techniques

Method of application of differentiating KM techniques

Percentage of participants in each category

Method	Less-successful	More-successful
Special work spaces for suppliers in product development	33	93 (gap 60)
IT-based yellow pages and knowledge databases for product development	7	53 (gap 46)
Job rotation in product development	13	53 (gap 40)
Internal teamwork in product development	27	67 (gap 40)
Special work spaces for development partners in product development	40	80 (gap 40)
Teamwork in product development with suppliers	33	60 (gap 27)
Special work spaces for tool manufacturers, production technology specialists in product development	53	80 (gap 27)
Co-location of product development staff	27	53 (gap 26)
Teamwork in product development with tool manufacturers and production technology developers	60	80 (gap 20)

Less-successful companies
More-successful companies
Gap

Source: McKinsey knowledge management survey

chapter seven

Self-reinforcement: starting the chain reaction

Knowledge is a more ethereal concept than money or any of the other traditional corporate assets. But it is precisely because it is unquantifiable that another characteristic comes into play. We call this trait self-reinforcement to emphasize that sharing knowledge does not normally lead to a decline in its use or value. Self-reinforcement is not a trait of other assets. A machine can only be in one place at one time, and sharing €100 means that you end up with less than €100. But sharing knowledge produces different results. The original knowledge holder keeps the knowledge even after it has been shared, and the knowledge receiver gains the knowledge, which means it can be applied more widely, creating value, or, combined with the recipient's own knowledge, creating even more value.

This idea bears similarities to a typical network structure where the value of the network increases exponentially with the number of nodes added to the network. And, just like other networks, a noncompetitive knowledge network can create unforeseen opportunities for growth, profit, and success. Creating knowledge networks is vital if you are going to get the full value out of the knowledge in your company. In other words, get connected. On-line book retailer Amazon.com is well known for all the data it accumulates, but taking a deeper look at its efforts you see it is a prime example of mining self-reinforcement for as much value as possible. Amazon collects detailed user-specific information, such as books sought and books bought. Armed with this data, it tries to find usage or buying patterns that it can pass on to other potential buyers. It is hard to visit an Amazon site without being cajoled with "Other people who bought this book, also bought..." or some other tempting come-on. And each time you go to a new page, you add to the company's database and enhance the sophistication of the knowledge network. This does not just help you next time you go back to the site, but knowledge of your behavior helps the next visitor with similar interests – and of course that helps the company. A self-reinforcing process starts that increases the value of the knowledge without anything more than marginal transaction costs.

An international telecoms equipment company electronically stores ideas about improvements to its products and processes. Development, marketing, and sales staff have access to this knowledge. The company gets two advantages through exploiting self-reinforcement. First, like almost any database, the knowledge is distributed and multiplied without major additional costs, and, second, users can build on the shared knowledge and develop it further. This second-generation knowledge is fed back into the database, where others can read it and build on it, and so on. A multiplier effect kicks in, and continuous improvement cycles take place.

In another example, an international conglomerate gets all its employees to write an end-of-year report. This contains their success stories, their problems, and an outlook for the next year. Again, the knowledge is stored in an open-access database making it possible to multiply the existing knowledge base and giving staff a better idea of what has already been done in specific development fields. This knowledge can then be built on to generate new knowledge.

CONNECTING THE CRITICAL MASS

The major challenge confronting you in trying to exploit this self-reinforcing trait is to define precisely the structure of these knowledge networks. This means determining which knowledge-transfer tools should be used, who should have access to the knowledge, and who, if anyone, should manage it. One glib solution is simply to make sure that employees have as much access as is necessary for their work, without having to trail through laborious databases or spend significant chunks of time filling in forms. But what does "as much as necessary" mean in corporate reality and how should such a network be implemented?

It is almost impossible to assess the value of a knowledge network in advance. It may be clear who is receiving the knowledge, but not precisely what knowledge they are using and how much value they are generating from it. This makes it harder still to determine the most appropriate structure. Given the benefits of self-reinforcement, you might be tempted to deliver all of the knowledge to all of the people. This might seem even more sensible since it is almost impossible to estimate accurately the value that any one piece of knowledge might have for any one individual. Some companies try this global approach; their distribution systems are more akin to a giant knowledge pump than a sophisticated network of irrigation channels. But a more-is-better tactic usually leads to employees complaining about information overload or, more accurately, complaining that they cannot find the knowledge they need among the trillions of bits and bytes they can access.

And the job becomes more complex. Along with decisions about how to deploy a knowledge network internally, you must also think about which external sources – research institutes, suppliers, or customers – to include in your network and how. Among other considerations, this means securing the right mix of confidentiality and openness. Nobody wants important knowledge to reach competitors or otherwise hurt market position, but companies and institutes included in a closed network can gain from sharing one another's specialized knowledge without any adverse effect.

EXPLOITING THE NETWORK

Although it is recognized that disseminating knowledge leads to increasing returns, there are no ready-to-use solutions available for companies. It is not especially useful to link everyone with everyone, but overanalyzing the connections and distribution is also wrong. As we show in a later chapter, knowledge generation is so unpredictable that allowing only a totally formal, predictable, and controlled knowledge flow limits the opportunity for creation.

The impact of single tools is relatively well understood. As examples, intranets are a good basis for knowledge exchange, they can let you access saved knowledge, and databases are a convenient reservoir to store knowledge. However, which tools are the most important, or the most applicable in different situations, is rarely articulated. Such broadly accepted insights offer little real guidance, and companies are usually left to proceed by trial and error.

One US high-tech company has set up a program where knowledge from different departments is combined with knowledge from equipment and material suppliers during the development of the overall production process. This is done through close cooperation between the company and its suppliers, and includes financial support. Bringing all this knowledge to one table helps overcome embeddedness, as we have seen, but another effect is that during this process the participants are constantly reinforcing the value of the knowledge brought to the table. One person gives input, the next takes it and develops it further, and so on. More interestingly, the knowledge is then rolled out across the whole company, and the final result is a standardized process that all subsidiaries or production facilities must implement. Even outside this development group, the multiplier effect comes into play as existing knowledge is used again and again, each time building rather than shedding value.

BUILDING NETWORKS WITH EXTERNALS

The more-successful companies also recognized the important role that other companies can play in reinforcing existing knowledge. Treating external knowledge sources as partners – formally or informally – allows you to share and benefit from each other's high-quality knowledge. The best solutions are often found in this way, and the value of each party's knowledge is augmented, not eroded.

As we have noted, suppliers are a source of knowledge, as well as materials. But it is often only the latter that is taken from the supplier. The more-successful companies often focus on a fixed pool of partners to reinforce the available knowledge assets. They rarely choose suppliers on the basis of competitive tenders, nor do they focus completely on their own in-house development. Neither of these would allow any intensive, deep exchange of knowledge. Instead, each party would guard and use its own existing knowledge. Obviously egalitarian ideals are, in practice, impractical for the developer. The art is to work together with selected suppliers while trying to maintain a grip on the process and stay on top. This can be done with financial links, or even financial penalties, that tie your suppliers to you. Alternatively, or additionally, you can offer to work with your suppliers in process areas where you have a competence, sharing your knowledge without any threat.

Valuable knowledge is also available downstream along the supply chain where distributors, retailers and, eventually, end-users dwell. Such downstream knowledge, once acquired, can be distributed throughout your company, but will be especially potent at creating value in the areas of marketing, product development, and design.

Our more-successful companies had especially close relationships with the retailers who brought their products to market. Not all companies can justify the overhead costs of selling direct to market. Retailers are far more attuned to the demands of final customers. They are the ones more likely to hear the complaints and compliments and may be able to predict more accurately whether a new product will be a top dog or a sleeping dog. This knowledge needs to be brought into the development process. Less-successful companies fail to recognize the potential knowledge that these retailers can offer, and the interaction is often one way, away from the company. Without including retailers and other customers into the network, their knowledge is unavailable, but when they are included the knowledge is reinforced, creating value on all sides.

BUILDING IT NETWORKS

IT allows the broad distribution of knowledge in a very short time. It also allows sophisticated filtering of data so that different types of recipient have access to appropriate knowledge. The challenge is to establish who should receive what knowledge without the risk of flooding everyone with everything or closing the tap too tightly.

One solution is to do substantial work flow management, where process specialists sit down and define every single step of the flow. Such an effort would establish who needs what knowledge, helping you to map out a distribution plan. But the obstacles are almost insurmountable. How workers use transferred knowledge is not always evident, and calculating how much knowledge each worker has in order to figure out how much more each needs is a fool's errand.

The more-successful companies have chosen a different approach. They allow employees broad, cross-departmental access to available knowledge sources. But because they have also built the right cultural context, these companies can rely on employees to pull the knowledge they find most useful out of the knowledge bank, rather than having it foisted upon them. Our survey showed, for example, that, in the more-successful companies, employees from the product development department are provided with access rights to service data as well as purchasing data, as this data is often of great importance for the tasks the developers have to fulfill. A manager of a global software company neatly summed up how successful companies deal with open access to knowledge. He explained that everybody has access to every knowledge source as long as they ask for it. There must be a sense of trust and accountability within the organization, otherwise you fall back over the individual barriers that we discussed in Chapter 2. He also explained that even the more sensitive and confidential information, such as financial indicators and contract negotiations, are made available if the person requesting can provide good reasons why they need the data. This policy of trust and openness ensures a responsible handling of all knowledge sources within the company by every employee.

By contrast, the less-successful companies do not allow such access rights. For them, the tendency is to believe that data that emanates from a department is confidential and proprietary to its originators. They are only prepared to share data if someone specifically asks and if the holder of the knowledge thinks it might be of use. Essentially, they follow a strong push approach that results in a form of knowledge hoarding: those who possess the knowledge want complete control over what is sent out and to whom. But both the company and those hoarding workers fail to take advantage of the self-reinforcing nature of knowledge.

At a US investment goods manufacturer, production staff have full access to sales data. This allows them to see forecasts, as well as orders, and they can then adapt their own production plans accordingly. Benefits from such a program work in both directions. While production staff have a better gauge of demand, salespeople have access to the production department's capacity planning so that they are able to give accurate delivery dates. When an order is placed, the company can tell customers which day the product will arrive. Much of this can be attributed to the deft reinforcement of knowledge across the whole company.

Before data can be accessed, it must be entered, and generally data entry should not be limited to a small, dedicated team. People from other departments should have entry rights, as well as such external partners as suppliers. But whatever structure you set up, there must be guidelines for using the database that are strictly enforced. Databanks are not forums for free-form thinking, otherwise they rapidly disintegrate into knowledge scrap heaps. The structure should also be intuitive with keywords and sub-folder names that are commonly understood to avoid overlap or erroneous filing.

When well-crafted guidelines are followed, no knowledge is lost, no delays arise because data must be converted to different formats, and, last but not least, the danger of miscommunication is cut severely. External contributors must be held to the same strict guidelines, and both companies should ensure that their technologies are compatible. Corrupted data is of little use, and constant conversion negates other time savings.

Such seamlessness not only helps the supply chain, but also the value chain. With sophisticated product data management, the US investment goods manufacturer above was able to use the complete range of product-related data, including purchasing and financial data, all along the process from inception to post-sales support. This total knowledge management approach is a great example of what can be achieved by realizing the benefits of self-reinforcement.

Several automotive manufacturers have a similar level of integration. They build a virtual assembly line before launching a new model, which requires data from tool, machinery, and parts suppliers. Such a simulation is very data intensive and needs constant change and review. Transferring data on paper is not feasible because it is too expensive, time consuming, and error prone, so these car makers and their suppliers work to integrate fully their IT systems in order to enable a smooth flow of knowledge.

A global high-tech company provides another example of how knowledge can be shared and gain in value. During its product development process, it regularly performs virtual quality checks of the prototype under design by simulating typical malfunctions. Two 70-inch monitors allow teams to compare the results of two different types of machines or two versions of the same machine simultaneously. Staff from the development, manufacturing, safety, quality, and service departments all participate in these virtual quality checks. During the quality test workshop they discuss the current development status and go through a standardized quality checklist that is available for all development teams on the corporate intranet. There are two self-reinforcing effects that emerge from this meeting. On the one hand, participants reinforce their own knowledge by talking to each other. This joint problem-solving naturally increases the value of the knowledge that is shared within the group. Additionally, the knowledge embedded in the standardized checklist is leveraged. The checklist contains the aggregated experiences of former teams that also had to go through the virtual quality check procedure. Each time a team has to go through the quality check, it downloads the checklist, controls every item and adds those that arise during the meeting which are deemed useful. By permanently updating the checklist, which is mandatory for every team, self-reinforcement is fostered.

TRAINING WITH INTERNAL AND EXTERNAL EXPERTS

So far, we have only discussed knowledge reinforcement as a part of regular work. But successful companies have also recognized that there is scope to go beyond this. To restrict your company to day-to-day work is to ignore much of the self-reinforcing potential. Training, that old workhorse of knowledge dissemination, should not be neglected in a knowledge management program (see Case Study 7.1).

Case Study 7.1

SAP

Making knowledge click and easy

Like all high-tech companies, German platform software and solutions group SAP watches its markets change almost every day. Product life cycles have compressed dramatically since the company was founded 28 years ago, and customer tastes and demands have become more fluid as they themselves are forced to react to a more dynamic global economy. To remain not only competitive, but also a leader in its industry, SAP must take full advantage of its resident knowledge.

Among its other knowledge management efforts, the software developer opened SAP University in 1999. Using three separate approaches, the university leverages the self-reinforcing nature of knowledge by distributing knowledge quickly, broadly, and efficiently. The world's third largest independent software supplier, SAP employs almost 22,000 people in more than 50 countries. From SAP's headquarters in Walldorf, about 55 miles south of Frankfurt, the in-house university offers live on-line seminars, recorded lessons that can be downloaded in English or German from the SAP eLearning Library, and face-to-face courses.

As a measure of its success, staffers regularly contact SAP University with suggestions for course topics, occasionally offering to teach a subject. Andreas Lotz, SAP University director for eLearning, explains, "Once an expert has contacted us, and there is a need, we will arrange the sessions, set up the necessary logistics, ... and advertise the session. We will also ensure the information is catalogued and becomes available via the eLearning Library. Frequently a learner in one session will be inspired to teach one. So we say that we're all learners and teachers at the same time."

One approach offered by SAP University is live virtual classroom sessions. Employees can log onto an intranet site to check the scheduled sessions. If they are interested in participating in one of the courses, they must register to ensure a slot. Once the session starts, staffers at any of SAP's global offices can participate, watching streaming video broadcast from Walldorf, Palo Alto, or almost anywhere else and submitting questions and comments as part of the live on-line discussion. The sessions are conducted by in-house experts, as well as visiting external specialists.

If time differences or other logistics problems preclude live attendance, a second approach ensures that the knowledge offered by these courses is still available. The live sessions are recorded and made available through the SAP eLearning Library. Staffers can download the courses at their convenience from any office. Not only does this give students more flexibility in getting the knowledge, but it also saves the instructors from having to repeat the courses at different locations around the world.

Traditional classroom-based courses are also available as a third approach offered by SAP University. Because of the time and expense involved in classroom instruction, staffers need permission from their supervisors to attend one of the face-to-face courses, which can be held in Walldorf or any other SAP location. Although there are acknowledged advantages to personal meetings, such as improved networking and increased transfer of knowledge, the additional hurdle encourages staff to try the nontraditional approaches to training.

By getting the most out of its IT infrastructure, SAP has created an efficient and convenient way to distribute knowledge throughout its global network. Lotz credits the program for helping to accelerate the rollout of new products, giving broad access to expert knowledge, and providing a repository of up-to-date internal learning. Among the additional benefits SAP has garnered since opening its university are reduced transportation costs and less productivity lost to travel.

"One big difference between SAP's information backbone and learning programs we've seen at other corporations is that at SAP each division, or even each person, can build a Web site and present a skill set," Lotz explains. This open approach has snowballed at SAP, and top managers are also using the curriculum to promote key strategic product areas such as customer relationship and supply chain management.

Training by in-house experts can multiply internal best practices, while external trainers can provide insights and perspectives that may be completely new for the staff. Both help to reinforce employees' embedded knowledge. Less-successful companies tend to focus almost exclusively on on-the-job training, while the more-successful companies recognize the potential of training as a separate and distinct part of employees' work life. Training allows staff to gain knowledge and to reflect on their achievements and on the company's position.

In the traditional approach to training, the instructor and employees meet face to face, often with a classic lecture hall atmosphere. But, as seen in the Case Study, a more innovative approach takes advantage of modern IT tools. For example, lessons can be Web-based or available on CDs. Both approaches have advantages and disadvantages.

One US software company had a particularly innovative approach to spreading knowledge via internal training. It used the many different features of its intranet. On one hand it set up Web-based training sessions, but this was not a stand-alone solution where each employee was left to struggle alone with the learning program. Instead the company also organized on-line training sessions. The times of each training session offered are posted on the intranet and each employee can decide whether they are interested in participating. At the appointed time all the participants and the trainer log on to the chat room. Here they can pose questions to the teacher, the answers to which are seen by all participants and are recorded for dissemination at a later date to other interested parties. If someone has a particular problem within the learning program, the trainer can monitor the steps the trainee is taking and give direct advice. Again, this can be watched by the others. The students also can learn from each other and give each other tips, a clear self-reinforcing opportunity.

But it is not just the on-line session that serves to reinforce the value of the knowledge. It is the availability of all the material, of the recorded session, the list of FAQs (frequently asked questions) and the opportunity to e-mail questions to the trainer after the session. The most important problems and solutions are analyzed and made available for the other students. In addition to the learning material, many presentations, speeches, and even traditional classroom training sessions are recorded and put on-line. There are video clips from a moderation training as well as the latest CEO speech from a supplier meeting.

There are two strong benefits from this IT-dependent solution. First, the knowledge is documented and put on the intranet so that it can be accessed by everybody with almost no distribution costs. Second, people have more independence in their method of receiving training. One employee told us that if he is engaged in relatively routine work, he often starts a video clip from a training session and watches it in a small window of his monitor. This self-reinforcement of the corporate knowledge base is extremely valuable.

The traditional approach allows for intense interaction among the participants, while IT approaches, short of video conferencing or live on-line chats, are rarely able to reach such depths. The traditional approach also eases the transfer of embedded knowledge. The technologically driven approach enables workers to learn on their own schedule and at their own pace. It can also bring a uniform, core package of knowledge to a wider audience more efficiently, including students who might not otherwise have been identified. Successful companies usually use both methods, but the traditional method is fading in importance.

The individual obstacles described in Chapter 2 — the "not invented here" and "knowledge is power" syndromes — have their counterparts in entire corporate attitudes toward knowledge. Many of the less-successful companies we visited shied away from gathering external knowledge and tried to keep tight control over internal knowledge by making it difficult for divisions or units to share. These companies are missing out with their need-to-know policy. But while there are recognized risks of knowledge leaking into the wrong hands outside a company and prudent precautions must be in place, the more-successful companies take a mixed approach toward knowledge distribution. Through self-reinforcement, they take as much value as possible from the knowledge at hand. These companies use structured techniques such as formal training, as well as providing workers with the freedom to visit and add to a wide range of databases. Once reinforcement takes hold, a chain reaction of value creation through knowledge sharing begins that can propel your company toward the next horizon.

FIGURE 7.1

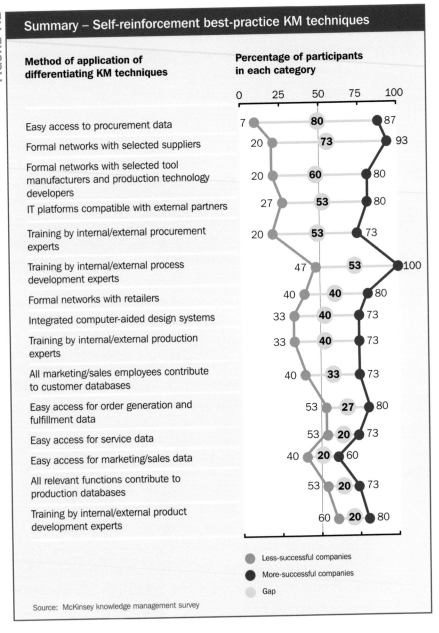

Summary – Self-reinforcement best-practice KM techniques

Method of application of differentiating KM techniques

Percentage of participants in each category

| | 0 | 25 | 50 | 75 | 100 |

Easy access to procurement data — 7 · 80 · 87

Formal networks with selected suppliers — 20 · 73 · 93

Formal networks with selected tool manufacturers and production technology developers — 20 · 60 · 80

IT platforms compatible with external partners — 27 · 53 · 80

Training by internal/external procurement experts — 20 · 53 · 73

Training by internal/external process development experts — 47 · 53 · 100

Formal networks with retailers — 40 · 40 · 80

Integrated computer-aided design systems — 33 · 40 · 73

Training by internal/external production experts — 33 · 40 · 73

All marketing/sales employees contribute to customer databases — 40 · 33 · 73

Easy access for order generation and fulfillment data — 53 · 27 · 80

Easy access for service data — 53 · 20 · 73

Easy access for marketing/sales data — 40 · 20 · 60

All relevant functions contribute to production databases — 53 · 20 · 73

Training by internal/external product development experts — 60 · 20 · 80

● Less-successful companies
● More-successful companies
● Gap

Source: McKinsey knowledge management survey

chapter eight

Perishability: capturing value quickly

The value of knowledge tends to decline over time. This trend can be interrupted by sudden and unpredictable bursts of value, but these spikes are rarely sustainable. While a company can garner windfall rewards from such sudden updrafts, measures in this area must concentrate on coping with the perishing value of your corporate knowledge base.

A recent example of how knowledge can perish centers on the music industry and was spurred by a shift in technology. For much of the 20th Century, vinyl records – whether LPs or 45s – dominated music stores, surviving the challenge by eight-track tapes and coexisting with cassette tapes. But vinyl, and the knowledge needed to create vinyl albums and their players, took a punishing blow following the introduction of digital technology. The changeover did not happen overnight, but today relatively few consumer electronics companies still offer LP players in their product portfolio. Although most manufacturers managed to survive the shift in technology, some did not. European LP player manufacturer Dual was one such victim. Its knowledge of how to make vinyl record players was perishing as it came under severe pressure from the efficient, and cheaper, mass-production techniques coming out of Asia. It could not compete in the price war that followed and was already struggling as CD technology started to swamp the market. Despite Dual having that technology, its Asian competitors were able to continue to churn out lower priced units and Dual was not able to make that jump. In 1982 it declared insolvency. That summer it was merged into the Thomson group. Interestingly, despite several changes of ownership since then, the brand name remains – an enduring reminder of the value of intangible assets.

FACING THE THREE VALUE DESTROYERS

There are three particular issues that make it hard for companies to cope with perishability. First, competitive advantages are often built on proprietary knowledge that is of high value precisely because no one else has access to it. Second, as we have just seen, broad shifts in technology can replace old knowledge in an industry. Third, external factors can attack the value of your knowledge. All of these can be mitigated by the same thing: speed.

Competitors are closer than you think

If your company has developed a particular expertise or has a competitive advantage built on a technology that you own the rights to, you probably see this as a major competitive advantage over your rivals. But the chances are that they are not so far behind. As soon as they catch up the value of your knowledge drops and much of your competitive advantage vanishes. Patents can slow this process, but they are time consuming and often the knowledge included is too complex to ensure effective protection. Competitors can steal a march simply by adapting some knowledge from the patent and going on to develop a better solution. Of course, if your expertise is exclusive and you are fast enough with the patent approval process then it can be a revenue source through licensing. But you should not lean back and feel comfortable just because you have a patent. Your competitors may find alternatives or complete substitutions for your protected technology.

To some managers, this might suggest that companies should make even greater efforts to protect their development department and its existing expertise. But erecting barriers and completely blocking any external party from your knowledge development efforts prevent you from taking advantage of the self-reinforcing effect of knowledge that we described in the previous chapter. Effective knowledge management requires taking both characteristics into account and combining techniques that let you benefit from self-reinforcement, without jeopardizing the company's knowledge base in the process.

The sheer pace of technological innovation over the past few decades makes it hard to predict when your competitors will catch you. What was valuable knowledge and a differentiating factor for your company yesterday, might be completely worthless today. The increased use of common product standards also presents a greater risk of knowledge losing value faster for all the companies in a specific market. The solution is to use your organizational and individual knowledge faster. You must make as much money as possible from your new knowledge before the competition strikes back and the value of that knowledge perishes.

Technological change can short-circuit value

If a new technology emerges that substitutes for an old one, then knowledge of the previously hegemonic technology is inevitably less valuable. Of course, the succession can take some time and companies may adapt themselves to the new situation, but the perishability of the older knowledge will be a painful experience for any company that specialized and relied on that particular knowledge. We discuss in the next chapter how you can try to encourage knowledge generation in order to be better prepared for the next wave or, better still, develop it yourself.

The example of vinyl recordings cited earlier shows how technological advances can short-circuit the value of carefully created knowledge. Another illustration from the consumer electronics industry is the famous VHS/Betamax saga, where technology was one of several issues that led to the dominance of VHS video tape and players. It is hard to counter substitution, as Sony found out in its failed battle to enshrine Betamax as the industry standard. But speed to market, especially if it includes first-mover advantage, can give a company the power to set the standard, maximize profits before new technology sweeps in, and give a company the flexibility needed to respond to these shifts.

Events can wash away value

The final threat to knowledge value is the rest of the world. Political, social, or economic changes well beyond the control of individual companies can wash away the value of accumulated knowledge. Some of these changes are fairly foreseeable and companies can try to plan around them. Take the European recycling legislation that has been pushed forward over the past few years. By setting mandatory statutes for the amount of recyclable material used in, for example, cars, some materials have been completely abandoned by the automotive sector. Knowledge surrounding the manufacture of these materials is therefore of far less value than it was. But this is a long-running discussion and the directive has a transitional period, so that all players in the market – the original equipment manufacturers, the component suppliers, and the basic material suppliers – could anticipate the decline in value. But for a supplier that based one branch of its business on a now-redundant material, there could be serious problems as the knowledge of this business unit still falls relatively rapidly.

Nuclear power is a good example of an industry that has suffered from social, political, and unpredictable external problems. Over many years the value of knowledge in this highly complex sector steadily increased. It was bolstered by the oil crisis in the 1970s, which left energy consumers reeling from soaring fossil fuel prices and seeking an alternative. But after the Chernobyl accident in 1986 and amid growing worries about safety, the value of nuclear power station technology expertise plummeted. The accident rammed home the dangers of the already controversial nuclear power sector, and when the facts about fallout from the accident became clear, there was a growing wave of distrust toward the technology. This accelerated the decline in the value of the knowledge.

The degree of decline varied geographically. In Germany for example, the government has ordered that all nuclear power stations be decommissioned in the first half of this century, so the opportunity to profit from this expertise is fading faster than in other countries. In general it is the speed of exploiting the knowledge at hand that becomes the critical success factor.

In a changing environment only speed can help an organization to gain the maximum value from the existing knowledge.

But while the value of knowing how to run a nuclear power plant as an electricity generator has been undermined by these social and political developments, many companies have been able to transfer this knowledge and unlock value in other contexts. For instance, the market for radioactive waste management and nuclear plant dismantling expertise is expected to remain healthy despite the waning fortunes of nuclear power generation.

THE NEED FOR SPEED

So how can you combat these problems? There are many techniques that can help to minimize the threats. Scenario techniques, where you build different visions of what the future might look like with best, worse and most probable alternatives; risk or option analysis; depreciation accounting; or broad risk management can all help to prepare for external change, but for many of the more-successful companies, such techniques are supplemental measures rather than the core of their programs. Analysis and planning based on external forces are a defensive, reactive attitude. The best-practice companies in our survey were far more focused on acting quickly. They lean on standardized processes to accelerate development and production, make decisions quickly so as not to miss market opportunities, and adopt process experiences rapidly in order to keep ahead of the curve (see Case Study 8.1).

Case Study 8.1

INTEL

Speeding chip development

Few sectors suffer more from missed markets than the semiconductor industry. Change is so rapid that the value of knowledge can shift faster than an Internet rumor. In this environment, US chip giant Intel has watched its markets veer from primarily PC based to new applications in everything from home game systems to handheld personal assistants. All along, chip complexity and speed have increased, resulting in a significant increase in chip size. Faced with such challenges, getting the recipe right on the factory floor is a Herculean effort with little room for error, and introducing a new process opens the potential for problems. Shutting down a chip factory for even one day if the process formula is not right can cost a company millions of dollars in missed revenue.

In order to get the most out of the knowledge being generated throughout its worldwide operations before that knowledge loses value and perishes, Intel unveiled its Copy EXACTLY! program in 1988. The idea is essentially simple: by standardizing the way development and production processes for its vast range of products at factories throughout the world are transferred between sites, not only is best practice replicated precisely throughout its operations, but innovations can be disseminated quickly. As markets shift or production improvements are developed, Intel can react quickly by exploiting the Copy EXACTLY! program. For a company such as Intel, with about $30 billion in annual revenue and 73,000 workers in 43 countries, getting it right cannot happen by chance.

The program focuses on taking the time necessary to create the right technical and business processes, then distributing them quickly to segments of Intel's operations. "You can't bake a cake at 800 degrees in order to cook it in half the time," explains Intel training director Jeanette Harrison. "But with consistency, rigor, and structure you can transfer key learnings from one factory to another much more rapidly."

Under the Copy EXACTLY! program, new processing capabilities developed by large engineering teams at Intel's technical development labs in Santa Clara, California, and near Portland, Oregon, are turned into manufacturing processes and prototypes are designed. Once the prototype is ready, it is transferred to Intel's high-volume wafer fabrication facilities, such as Fab 12 in Chandler, Arizona. Proposed changes to the prototype are tested vigorously by cross-functional teams with up to 20 members that can include engineers, technicians, manufacturing supervisors, and others. Problem-prone areas are parceled out to different teams and members assigned to come up with quality solutions. When the team gives the go ahead, factories in Albuquerque, Israel and elsewhere implement the changes together, so the process at any plant is an exact copy of any other.

Leaders from the various cross-functional teams also meet regularly to compare notes. At this level, these team managers try to identify best-known methods that were developed during the work on the process prototypes, for instance how best to keep equipment from becoming contaminated. Joint management teams meet in person and in intranet forums to vet these ideas and form a consensus on which methods should be highlighted and pushed as best practice. Team members are encouraged to challenge assumptions and conclusions in an effort to polish the proposals brought to the table.

"Even though having so many teams and formalized processes is bureaucratic, it's about battling the bureaucracy," says Harrison. "By aligning teams we involve people across the enterprise and can move very rapidly." The discipline imposed by Copy EXACTLY! allows knowledge to be harnessed quickly and disseminated widely before its usefulness expires, she says.

But the work does not stop once the process is in place. After implementation, the engineering team conducts a postmortem analysis and compiles the results in "bluebooks." The autopsy usually turns up ideas for further production and productivity improvements, and the program returns full circle in an effort to harvest continual gains from knowledge.

By compressing the time needed for consensus building, Intel has shaved off nearly two-thirds of its chip turnaround time, cutting it from seven years, to slightly more than two. The Copy EXACTLY! program has also helped to generate profits from its flash memory operations, which were once just breaking even. "Shortening the learning curve is what it's all about," Harrison explains. "And Copy EXACTLY! is a forum to share and shine."

In the end, speed is the only efficient countermeasure against perishability. The more-successful companies do not rely on building up barriers to their knowledge base, which can reduce the competitive threat but do little against technological shifts or external influences. Nor do they waste resources that could be better focused on forward thinking by obsessively trying to hide their latest technological breakthroughs. Instead, they launch new products early and, before the din has died down, are already making inroads with the next generation. In contrast, their less-successful counterparts try to maintain the status quo.

In times of accelerating innovation cycles, the more-successful companies are always searching for the latest solutions, even if this means destroying their old structures to make way for renewal. This is precisely where less-successful companies fall down. They are too busy encoding their knowledge, raising barriers to hide their technological progress, and worrying about confidentiality every step of the way. Such efforts may serve to delay the decline in value of knowledge but can ulti-mately do nothing to prevent that decline. They also run the bigger risk of missing the next big wave of innovation because they are fixated on the last wave. Focusing on protecting existing knowledge hinders dynamic implementation and even-tually returns start to decrease anyway. This tends to trigger more conservation efforts, and a spiral begins that will hurt the bottom line. The proactive and aggressive strategy is the more successful one. And the techniques that help to exploit and renew knowledge constantly must be implemented rigorously.

Accelerating with standards

An international telecoms equipment company was struggling with the perishability of its knowledge, partly because it was too slow to market. To tackle this challenge, senior managers realized they needed to introduce process standards that ensured the fast conversion of its latest research into products fit for market launch. They developed a gate process, which we have already mentioned in Chapter 4, that covered both product development and order fulfillment. These efforts were more closely linked than normal because of this company's strategic orientation. Altogether, projects must pass through six gates. At each gate, and for the development phase between the gates, clear rules are written describing which expertise must be integrated at that point, which checkpoints must be passed, what general procedures should be applied, and what precisely is the target of that phase.

The decisions to be made and the team responsible for making those decisions are clearly defined, as are the consequences of missing targets. This rigid procedure may seem overly bureaucratic, but it removes obstructions from the path from beginning to end. Everything is aligned and timed for maximum efficiency, reducing friction and improving co-ordination. Everybody knows exactly where along the process the project is at any time. And since everyone on the team understands that the standards are obligatory, no time is wasted discussing timelines or procedural nuances. In a techno-logically complex industry where so many different experts are involved, this process adds value.

Many employees see process standardization as additional complexity that can strangle innovation. They are wrong. The goal of standardization is to establish a uniform process flow throughout the organization and to reduce complexity where possible in order to accelerate bringing innovations to market. Fast implementation is a necessary factor in outwitting perishability, and a project can move faster if as many obstacles as possible are removed ahead of time.

It is also important to exorcise the misconception that standardization limits creativity. Standards have to strike a fine line between efficiency and the effectiveness of knowledge cultivation. Creativity is vitally important and of tremendous value when it occurs early in a process, as we explain in the following chapter. But it can be dangerous, and costly, if practiced at every stage of a process, especially during implementation. The result can be moving targets and missed deadlines. Standards should allow for early creativity, while maintaining the level of efficiency required to ensure fast knowledge application to avoid the evaporation of the value of the knowledge.

Speeding up the conversion of knowledge into new products is not just about process standardization, but can also involve standardized design rules and instructions. A European manufacturer active in the logistics sector emphasized customized solutions as part of its value proposition, but found that development engineers tended to overdo this customization. Each new product was built from scratch, taking no account of pre-existing modules and components. The engineers were proud of their unique solutions. But since colleagues had often tackled similar problems, a lot of work was replicated, slowing the development process. Meanwhile, competitors had accelerated their innovation cycles, jeopardizing the manufacturer's continued success.

To combat the situation, managers realized that they had to define clear design rules and instructions for constructing individual customer solutions. They implemented a product data management system with strictly defined rules. Now, whenever developers start designing a new component, the system will offer existing alternatives. Developers are forced to use existing standards because the routine for introducing any modifications discourages variation. Reducing complexity by strictly following the standard design and construction rules allowed for a dramatic process acceleration.

From our survey, 60 percent of our more-successful companies have introduced mandatory process standards and design rules. They support the efficient use of these standards through training sessions on standards and rules. Although this is perhaps a relatively low proportion, only 27 percent of the less-successful companies have introduced process standards or centrally defined design rules and a mere 13 percent of them offer continuous training to introduce these central standards.

Deciding quickly

Another problem that can hold up companies is the speed of decision-making. An automotive company had introduced standardization as part of a plan to accelerate its processes. It had a well-defined process standard that was strictly implemented, but the decision-making procedure was not so clearly defined. As a result, some projects met their deadlines, but others fell way behind schedule. Analyses showed that standard processes were maintained perfectly in both the timely and the tardy projects. The difference was that in the laggard teams the project leaders had a completely different understanding of their role within the project; they tried to be involved at every step. Such hands-on involvement led to the leader taking decision-making responsibilities at all levels, which slows the process unnecessarily. It also erodes the confidence of other team members to make their own decisions, for fear of over-stepping their authority. The problem was exaggerated because the project leaders also had functional responsibilities. Often when the team went to the manager for a decision, they had to wait for a meeting to end before getting one. Competitive advantages were lost because of the delays in market entry, which could have been avoided by quicker decision-making by other team members.

A European automotive parts supplier overcame a similar problem by clearly defining the role and authority of decision-making committees, project leaders and the team members. Senior managers do not interfere with the day-to-day development activities of individual project teams. Their task is to help to set the strategic goals and values guiding the teams' work. Their interaction with the team is organized around frequent, formal steering committee meetings, where critical problems and ideas that go beyond the teams' authority are presented and the necessary decisions are made. At these junctures, senior managers must stay focused on the overall view and the orchestration of activities, making the necessary decisions quickly, and delegating most decision-making to the project leader and team members if possible. Postponements are not allowed.

At this parts supplier, project leaders are responsible for coordinating, managing, and controlling the development process, rather than interfering with detailed content decisions. The maxim is to observe and oversee, but to try to delegate decisions to the members in charge of each task, thus speeding up the whole process. The project leader's duty boils down to responsibility for early market entry before perishability reduces the return on R&D. Functional experts can make decisions independently as long as this does not jeopardize the overarching project goals, while project leaders are at hand if something threatens the overall success of the project. The limited involvement of senior management reduces the time needed in liaising between the two groups. Everybody involved understands the necessity of rapid decision-making. As a result, the company applies its knowledge very quickly, bringing benefits to the bottom line.

These two cases show that traditional, hierarchical decision structures, based on frontline employees gathering information, reporting it to their superiors and awaiting a decision, are time consuming and risk losing supplementary critical knowledge about the matters under discussion that could allow for a far more informed decision. The importance of a clear definition of decision-making authority and assigning this authority to the most appropriate level is reflected in our survey results. Assigning project-specific decisions to project members and leaving senior managers and project leaders decisions with a broader scope could be seen at more than 50 percent of the more-successful companies, while most of the less-successful companies fell short of realizing these clear delegation principles.

Policing the police

We have already set out why standardized processes are an important aspect of efficiency and speed. But these standards can only be helpful if they are strictly maintained and updated. In a twist to the age-old question, Who polices the police?, you need to ask who is keeping the standards up to standard. This implies not only keeping the relevant databases updated, but also making sure that the standards are adjusted as necessary. Without a watchdog, process manuals turn yellow with age and databases are clogged with perishing knowledge. Process standards are only efficient when aligned to the overall business situation, and maintenance of the standards is as important as implementing the process itself. Otherwise you can become a victim of the vicious cycle of outdated standards, haphazard modification of the standards, and an increase in friction and delays, which renders such standards useless.

One international high-tech company established a unit that takes process experiences from across the company and integrates them into the company-wide process standards. The unit also ensures easy access to and application of the experiences, as well as the systematic collection and forwarding of new process experiences. Knowledge that emerges in the company must be made available to other teams before its value perishes. Rather than fronting for a centralized research and development division, this unit is primarily the vanguard of operations. One of its tasks is to distinguish between knowledge with little relevance outside a specific project and knowledge that can be valuable more broadly. As part of the effort, project schedules include time to allow members to step back from their immediate concerns and summarize their experiences from the project. All employees working on development projects have access to this database, whatever their precise role or expertise. This real-time availability removes frictions and delays, which helps overcome the problem of perishability.

The survey results illustrate that systematic retention and updating of process experiences are important for both product development and order generation and fulfillment processes. Still, many of even the more-successful companies seemed to underestimate the role that this can play in order generation and fulfillment, with only 60 percent practicing this compared with 33 percent of the less-successful companies. In product development, 73 percent of the more-successful companies used this technique compared with 20 percent of the less-successful companies. In order generation and fulfill-ment, 87 percent of the more-successful and 53 percent of the less-successful companies store lessons learned, FAQs, and improvement suggestions, while in product development this drops to 67 percent and 20 percent, respectively.

ENJOY THE RIDE UP WHILE IT LASTS

There are some thrills in this roller coaster, too, sudden hikes in the value of knowledge that might have been dormant or underappreciated. For example, in the 1970s knowledge of Cobol programming was very valuable, but its value perished slowly and steadily as new programming languages emerged. By the 1990s, there was barely any value left in knowing Cobol and most experts had either retired or migrated to C++ and other computer languages. But as the turn of the century approached, knowledge of Cobol suddenly became highly valu-able again as companies sought ways to correct the infamous (and eventually impotent) Y2K bug lurking in old Cobol coding. The old experts were suddenly in high demand and could again make good money from their expertise.

Nice, but the spike was short lived. Once 2000 arrived, the value of Cobol knowledge sank quickly again. Such a bumpy ride is not comfortable for companies that want an accurate assessment of their asset value. It is easy with techniques such as depreciation accountancy or risk management to do this with other assets, but the unpredictability of knowledge makes this challenge much harder. A reversal of fortunes is impossible to predict and comes with no guarantees of long-term sustainability. The best insurance is a fast operation that can cash in on converting knowledge value to profit quickly.

FIGURE 8.1

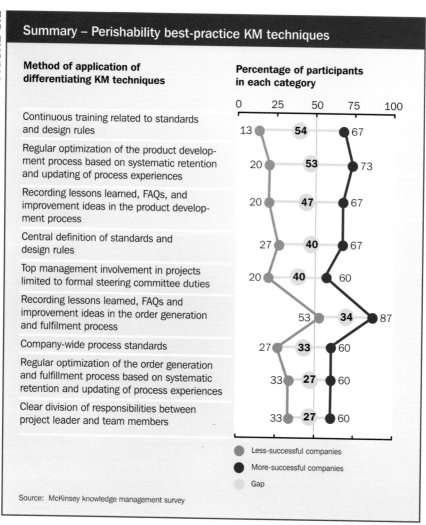

Summary – Perishability best-practice KM techniques

Method of application of differentiating KM techniques

Percentage of participants in each category

Method	Less-successful	Gap	More-successful
Continuous training related to standards and design rules	13	54	67
Regular optimization of the product development process based on systematic retention and updating of process experiences	20	53	73
Recording lessons learned, FAQs, and improvement ideas in the product development process	20	47	67
Central definition of standards and design rules	27	40	67
Top management involvement in projects limited to formal steering committee duties	20	40	60
Recording lessons learned, FAQs and improvement ideas in the order generation and fulfilment process	53	34	87
Company-wide process standards	27	33	60
Regular optimization of the order generation and fulfillment process based on systematic retention and updating of process experiences	33	27	60
Clear division of responsibilities between project leader and team members	33	27	60

- Less-successful companies
- More-successful companies
- Gap

Source: McKinsey knowledge management survey

chapter nine

Spontaneity: sparking profits

The outbreak of new knowledge cannot be scheduled or predicted accurately. Dispatching an individual or team to solve a problem or work toward a breakthrough innovation will likely result in some knowledge being formulated, but whether it is the right knowledge at the right time, the best solution, remains anyone's guess until the process is well underway. That moment when an idea finally erupts or when a consistent picture emerges from seemingly disconnected thoughts is an individual experience. Neither the timing nor the content can be forced because the appearance of new knowledge is spontaneous. But it can be anticipated and encouraged, at least in broad terms. The mistake that companies make, however, is to equate spontaneity with randomness.

Often, managers are overwhelmed by the false concept that spontaneity cannot be managed. While it is true that the spontaneity of knowledge makes its creation difficult to predict, the process can be managed in a way that increases the frequency of valuable knowledge being generated. Successful innovators such as 3M Corporation, Sony, and Nokia demonstrate that this process can be tackled efficiently. And it is not a question of filling your desks with certified creative thinkers, but of bringing the creativity of all of your employees to the forefront. The results will likely be refreshing.

At one innovative company, developers are allowed to dedicate 15 percent of their work time to pursuing individual research, which is neither coordinated with nor checked by supervisors. Resources such as laboratory instruments and materials, test equipment, and colleagues' expertise are available to help developers. They are free to do whatever they want in this time. If somebody wants to kill a project, the onus is on them to prove their point. If an idea begins to look like a viable business opportunity and is taking more than 15 percent of the developer's time, then they must present their case to senior managers. One research group even hired a communications trainer to help the more introverted developers present their ideas more successfully. The number of patents from this group rose from 25 to 100 that year. This is different from most organizations where typically the inventor must argue their case right from the outset. Traditionally, the managers at this company have fostered innovation by standing aside and letting product developers take the initiative, while developers, in turn, have worked under the aphorism: "It's better to seek forgiveness than to ask permission." This open attitude to new ideas and knowledge is a strong driver to innovation. As a result, more than 30 percent of the company's revenues consistently come from products that are less than four years old, and the company still reaches its demanding profit and growth targets.

The company has successfully created a culture that fosters the spontaneity of knowledge. It did not try to lay down a path to innovative ideas, instead it set up an organizational context that provides the wherewithal for its staff to realize their own ideas. Ideas are, after all, the seeds of knowledge and must be cultivated and allowed to mature in the organization.

HARNESSING THE BEAST

Despite the presence of success stories, many corporations still try to limit their dependence on spontaneity because the path to profitability is not well marked and the distance to the destination is uncertain. You might be able to imagine the ideal context in your company in which to encourage creativity, but developing and sustaining such an environment may be unfathomable. This is usually because there are no guidelines that can lead to thorough and successful implementation.

In this chapter, we will focus on more formal structures that encourage knowledge creation by setting the stage for spontaneity as much as possible. This is the more manageable face of spontaneous innovation. Of course, the other side to this coin is knowledge development that comes from outside formal structures, which can bring rewards that are just as enriching. Solutions, ideas, and insights can appear in the oddest places – the shower, an airport lounge, a car stuck in traffic – and can address issues big and small. It is this side of the coin that makes many managers shrug their shoulders in frustration and condemn the process as too random. But even such unpredictable bursts of inspiration are really extensions of the first phases of managed knowledge creation and can be enhanced by bringing the ideas generated into the structure as soon as possible, giving them a broad audience, and encouraging them with the right cultural setting.

The structure for tackling spontaneity can be broken down into a straightforward four-step process: search, collide, decide, and try (see Figure 9.1). To keep the illustration focused, we will describe a process that ends with generating new businesses or products. The decision was not arbitrary, but reflects the corporate reality that directed attempts to develop knowledge

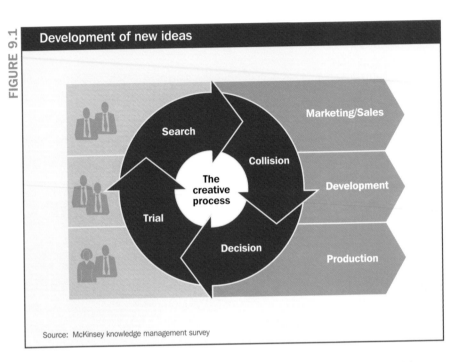

FIGURE 9.1

Development of new ideas

Source: McKinsey knowledge management survey

are most often linked to new product development. With minor variations, the approach can also be used to target process efficiencies and more modest goals.

SEARCH FOR NEW IDEAS

The search phase is an obvious starting point. The spontaneous eruption of knowledge arises from a combination of different, previously unrelated thoughts coming from various directions. At this early stage, managers should make sure that the doors are open and unobstructed, rather than worrying too much about the absolute relevance of the knowledge being absorbed by employees. There is time to assess quality (and worker performance) later. In this phase, the greater risk lies in closing the wrong doors, not in opening unnecessary doors.

Letting employees sift

Many senior managers are unaware of the significant problems that prevent their employees from gaining access to inspirational knowledge. Most might even think that they are doing their jobs as managers by controlling the information flowing into and through their companies in order to prevent their workers from wasting their time on irrelevant reading and browsing or from drowning in a flood of information. Blame the 1990s, when business leaders and their advisers were preoccupied with lean management and organizational restructuring. Efficiencies and other cost savings that keep a company's competitive edge sharp are vital for survival, naturally, but in some cases we may have thrown out the baby with the bath water.

One obstacle that often inadvertently prevents knowledge creation is limited access to sources of inspiration, both internally and externally. This is linked to the false belief that creativity is so random that it can happen in a void. Creating knowledge that is valuable to your company requires a rich diversity of inspiration. The more you can throw into the knowledge pot, the tastier the stew. All channels for accessing existing knowledge should be opened to provide a huge field of stimulation for spontaneity. Restricting employees to their own functional or product-specific knowledge is not helpful if you want them to come up with completely novel ideas.

Bias in knowledge that is already being disseminated throughout a company can also be a problem. If only a few departments are responsible for obtaining and broadcasting external information internally, then by necessity much of the content will be filtered and condensed. And, if the filtering criteria remain opaque, the value of the resulting knowledge is not immediately clear. Think, for instance, about how your customer service staff handles a call. The call center employee focuses on categorizing and reporting the problem following a standard template that must, by its very nature, ignore many of the specifics. But how many customer suggestions were ignored simply because there was nowhere to write them down? Tremendous value can be created when anomalies are not filtered out, but rather are sought after as a driver of inspiration.

As we have mentioned, many efforts to limit the inflow of knowledge can be traced to measures designed to improve overall efficiency and reduce waste. Efficient processes are also critical in knowledge management if you are to maximize the value from knowledge before it perishes. But they are also a potential threat to creativity. A balance must be struck, despite the challenges.

Weighing the value of individual efforts to open the doors to knowledge can be like judging whether a cup is half full or half empty. For example, a US software company is obsessive about customer service and support. In the short term, customer support helps to keep customers happy by answering questions and solving any problems that occur with its products, and in the longer term the company translates what it learns during these interactions into improved products. To highlight this priority, almost everybody, including senior managers, spends at least a few hours occasionally working on the customer support lines. A waste of time and resources, or an abundant source of inspiration for the entire organization? You do the math.

Along with mandatory shifts on the customer service lines, other approaches to searching for inspiration can be successful, including visiting partner or competitor sites, as well as companies from different industries, and attending conferences and trade fairs. These and many other channels should be used by the employees to get in contact with various knowledge and ideas, but the focus must be maintained. One large automotive company used to take a rather skewed approach to trade fair visits. It sent its development staff to the most important automotive fairs, but each developer had strict orders. Some, for example, were told to watch for unauthorized use of the company's logo. Such strict mandates hindered the team from finding inspiration in competitors' solutions or approaches, suppliers' innovations, or customers' reactions to prototypes. Now, the company has realized the great opportunities at these fairs and has freed its staff from their policing duties.

Ideally, managers would be able to ensure that their employees search internally and externally for knowledge that is appropriate and useful. But without adopting a stifling Big Brother approach, which in itself would be disastrous, such close oversight is impossible. Managers must accept that their staff needs a variety of information sources and that as many employees as possible should be exposed to up-to-date thinking in a variety of areas. Inspiration results from intimate knowledge of your business, which includes your competitors, technology, customers, and business partners. It is useless to try to set an arbitrary limit on how much exposure is too much or to try to determine at what point inspiration stops and distraction begins. This does not mean that there is no control. In the end, workers must provide value to the company. The trust implied by opening access to knowledge sources is accompanied by the responsibility to use these sources wisely. The control comes in evaluating individual employee performance.

Log on, tune in

In today's business world the Internet and its internal corporate cousin, the intranet, are great ways of allowing individuals to access a wide variety of information. Both channels allow employees to acquaint themselves with different areas of knowledge and, by using newsgroups and other interactive tools, to access this knowledge first hand without excessive filtering or bias.

Internet access enables people to seek inspiration from a seemingly infinite pool of information. Users can define their own search profiles, and increasingly sophisticated technology can help to pull relevant knowledge from the ever-expanding Web. Focused and moderated newsgroups allow employees access to on-line discussions. At organizations that provide their employees with a large degree of entrepreneurial autonomy, even the shop floor workers get Internet access if they ask for it. In the more enlightened companies there is an atmosphere of entrepreneurial enthusiasm and a commitment to let new ideas bubble up. Ford Motor Co. made headlines recently by promoting Internet literacy among its workforce by providing all employees with free Internet access at home, and other companies have followed suit.

Internal databases can also nurture your inspirational efforts, particularly repositories for new ideas or customer requests. In the more-successful companies, both of these are open to the entire corporation, allowing each employee first-hand access. At one international telecoms equipment company, the content of the idea database is fundamental to each development project. All ideas are evaluated, and feedback is given within two weeks of a topic being entered into the database. When it is time to create and design new products, the database is scanned for the latest iterations of relevant concepts, which are then incorporated into the product design as appropriate.

Our survey results show that generally the less-successful companies do not realize the opportunities that a modern and open IT infrastructure can bring in terms of searching and scanning external knowledge pools. Only 20 percent allow direct

Internet access for the development department, and only 33 percent for the marketing/sales department. At the more-successful companies, Internet access is almost de rigueur for these teams (67 percent and 73 percent, respectively). However only 47 percent of the more-successful companies have established an internal idea database, well ahead of the 7 percent of the less-successful companies with such a database, but still leaving plenty of room for improvement.

Don't get bogged down by structure

There are basically two organizational models for breeding new ideas, the in-house, autonomous think tank and the R&D effort that is scattered throughout the company. Although diametrically different, both approaches can be successful. Rather than becoming embroiled in a debate about which model is better, managers should concentrate on cultivating an open corporate culture. Environment can make or break either of these models. What counts is the intensity of exposure to diverse knowledge in order to increase the probability of sparking spontaneous knowledge generation.

A centralized effort has a longer history and remains the favorite for most companies. These powerful corporate R&D units are protected from the daily business and its operational pressures, but are expected to accumulate diverse knowledge and ideas from different directions in order to identify innovative opportunities. By bringing together a critical mass of knowledge, centralized development programs can produce a series of winners. Companies such as Xerox with the PARC research center and Lucent Technologies with Bell Labs have proven that this model can be highly successful, although not all companies manage the latent tensions of the system as well. Operational units often feel that these centralized think tanks are not plugged into the real world and do not share their experiences across the company. As a result, frontline managers may shun ideas emanating from central R&D and feel that they entire effort is just a cost burden.

The founders of one US high-tech company followed a path much less traveled. Coming from an organization with a large, ineffective, centralized R&D unit, they decided to abandoned this model and made each individual business unit responsible for its own R&D. Clearly there are potential drawbacks to this approach, such as fragmented R&D budgets or redundant projects, but these were overshadowed by the innovations that have resulted from the close interaction between R&D and the operational business, including customers and partners. Such an approach is becoming increasingly popular.

Centralized research is generally suited for taking large steps in innovation, often focusing on radically different product lines or businesses. They draw their strength from their independence and in-depth knowledge. On the other hand, the decentralized, cross-functional model is better at incremental or evolutionary advances, such as continuous cost reduction and expansion of current product lines. These programs generally require a close link to the business environment and access to diverse sources of knowledge.

FORCING IDEAS TO COLLIDE

The next phase in a structured program is mixing these raw ideas together like so many atoms in a particle accelerator and watching the collisions. Logically, collision follows search, but in practice the two phases are almost parallel. New, raw ideas are constantly being added into the mix, and collisions take place at all levels from within an individual mind to among hundreds of meeting participants.

This is the "Eureka!" moment that results from bringing sources of information together in new ways, forcing collisions of ideas that result in new insights. If they occur frequently enough, they can provide multiple recombinations of earlier thoughts that can then be shared in order to bring different perspectives. In an open forum, the process of conflict and debate helps to evaluate prevailing views and eventually stimulates the birth of ideas that can turn into fundamentally new knowledge. This stresses the importance of a team environment that allows individuals to let their ideas bounce together.

The search process builds up a critical set of knowledge and thoughts, but it is the collision phase that helps to shape a ground-breaking idea and produces the spontaneous spark of creativity. New combinations of thoughts and ideas are constantly occurring in your company already. For example, the cross-functional teams that help to build a common understanding of a topic, can also be seen as incubators for creative ideas. The diversity of team members should generate positive conflict, disputes, and discussions where individual preferences are defended. These discussions produce the atoms of knowledge that can then collide to create new ideas. Such collisions may occur already, but if you are to manage spontaneity more actively you must push the intensity and quality of these collisions to levels that result in knowledge explosions.

This requires using a range of creativity techniques, the most common of which is brainstorming. At its best, brainstorming is a dynamic chain reaction of ideas. Initial thoughts trigger subsequent ideas and the resulting deluge of new ideas and new knowledge can sometimes be overwhelming in its intensity and volume. Unfortunately, managers tend to dismiss brainstorming as an unsystematic and inefficient problem-solving tool. But like any tool, brainstorming will not be effective unless it is handled correctly. Like trying to drive a nail with the wrong end of a hammer, misuse leads to frustration and eventually discarding the tool altogether. Many managers told us during our interviews that they expect creative spontaneity to be a part of daily work, not the result of special brainstorming sessions. But letting staff drown in day-to-day operational struggles and repetitive routines makes it less likely that new ideas will erupt easily. Allowing and fostering additional creativity sessions and bringing individual ideas together produces the greatest results.

Managers must be ready to avoid the three traps of brainstorming sessions: a lack of openness, a lack of experience, and a lack of focus. Brainstorming is a sensitive exercise, and the chain reaction can only be perpetuated as long as participants do not have to censor their own ideas for fear of ridicule. In an atmosphere that lacks trust and openness, the exercise is seriously handicapped. Brainstorming sessions should also be part of a general task fulfillment business. It requires repetition to get people accustomed to it, and the more-successful companies practiced it frequently. And finally, these sessions should not be free-floating, unguided, and never-ending exercises that might be enjoyable, but yield few results. Best-practice companies clearly believe that brainstorming requires a well-defined target, such as finding a solution to a concrete problem, and that sticking to this target is vital lest the process become wasteful and inefficient.

While brainstorming is the most common technique for producing a critical mass of ideas, there are many others available such as association methods where people intensively discuss a certain problem until no further progress can be made. They are then shown a sequence of different pictures from totally different contexts – such as nature or sport. Refocusing the mind on different subjects and new associations can help to bring new solutions to the problem. Another effective tool for fostering the creativity of people is off-site creativity workshops. The team leaves its usual corporate environment and moves to a more inspiring setting. This can range from a conference room at another company site to a meeting room at an old castle. Either way the new setting should open the participants minds to new thoughts, independent from their daily routines. But, like brainstorming, all these techniques require trust and openness, training and repetition, and strict targets.

One automotive company uses a range of creativity techniques in a very structured process- and product-improvement program. A cross-functional and cross-hierarchical team is given four days to define, structure, and launch an improvement program. All team members are assigned full time to the program for those four days, and at the end they must present a clearly defined program ready for immediate implementation. Generally the effort begins with brainstorming, then the team structures, prioritizes, and evaluates alternative solutions. These are then cross-checked against possible future scenarios, assessing how reliable and successful the improvement measures will be. With a tight deadline, a good mix of people, and the freedom to use different methods, these teams become very dynamic and creative.

The more-successful companies frequently deployed open and targeted creativity techniques throughout their organization. Our survey showed that these techniques are important in product-oriented innovation management (80 percent of the more-successful companies) as well as in process-oriented continuous improvement programs (100 percent of the more-successful companies), while the less-successful companies underestimated the opportunities, with 53 percent using these techniques for innovation and 47 percent for continuous improvement.

SELECTING THE WINNERS

The next phase is selecting the promising ideas. If you are able to establish an environment where your staff is constantly sparking new knowledge, then it is critical to screen these ideas in order to assess their strategic value to the company. A clear selection process with well-defined and publicly shared criteria is key to extracting new ideas. This phase operates as a threshold to formal development, where the innovators must prove the impact of their ideas on the bottom line. Rejected ideas may also offer lessons, but the ideas that are approved are truly cultivated by dint of receiving all the necessary support.

After the search and collision phases have produced a series of refined thoughts, the selection process makes sure that the company's resources are dedicated to those ideas believed to have the greatest potential. Without a rigorous selection procedure, old ideas can linger like a bad smell, while new ideas die for lack of oxygen. In a case in point, a product development manager at a large automotive company told us that with every new car project, the same idea would pop up, even though it had been rejected repeatedly by various management committees. The company was suffering from the absence of a rigorous and transparent idea selection procedure. Neither the selection criteria nor the selection committee were well defined, and engineers did not understand why managers had rejected the concept. As a result, the engineers kept tweaking the idea and resubmitting it, rather than opening their minds to new ideas and new concepts. The car maker needed a much more transparent selection process so that the whole company could understand what was deemed useful, what was not, and why. Of course, hand in hand with such transparency is rigor, which guarantees a fair, open, and motivational process, even for engineers whose ideas are rejected.

Idea contests have proved to be a very effective technique to inject entrepreneurial behavior into a laissez-faire organization. The contests are extremely valuable as a huge number of ideas are produced, and out of them will be that small handful of really promising ideas that make the difference for the company (see Case Study 9.1).

Case Study 9.1

FUJI XEROX

Lights! Camera! Knowledge!

When Fuji Xerox started searching for a way to spark excitement, creativity, and even iconoclastic thinking throughout the firm, it found no better prototype than Hollywood. Top managers wanted to break away from traditional thinking and practice for boosting business, which essentially meant rounding up the sales force for a megameeting and launching a focused campaign to drive growth. This traditional method had worked nicely. For instance, the 1998 campaign concentrated on understanding the customer's needs and helped to increase the company's share of the digital copier and color printer markets. But customer satisfaction began to fall in all areas.

"All these [earlier efforts] were sales oriented, which meant that the whole of Fuji Xerox wasn't involved," says Taro Sengoku, a leader in the company's Knowledge Dynamics Initiative (KDI). "We were getting weak at really satisfying customers. So we thought, what kind of thing excites people?"

Their answer: the movies. In 1999, Fuji Xerox, a joint venture between Xerox Corp. and Fuji Photo Film Co.[1] with annual sales of about $8.5 billion, launched a project called Virtual Hollywood. The goal was to unleash spontaneous thinking in order to bring the imaging company's product closer to customer needs. Under the program, directors (employees) had to generate enthusiasm for their ideas and pull together a creative team of script writers, cinematographers and screen stars (colleagues from different functions) around the story. The team then presents scripts (improvement ideas) to a group of investors (general managers). The best are implemented in the hope of generating a box-office hit.

Although gimmicky, the project promoted out-of-the-box thinking and in the first year generated submissions from 200 teams addressing process improvement as well as product development. For example, one idea that came from the intellectual property department was to develop a printer that can be installed in convenience stores and used to print documents downloaded from WAP-enabled mobile telephones. Although some senior managers were initially against the project, fearing that it would distract their staff from their main work, the program generally has been embraced. Sengoku says about 20 percent of Fuji Xerox's employees are involved in Virtual Hollywood projects.

Along with helping to encourage spontaneous thinking, Virtual Hollywood has scored other wins for Fuji Xerox's knowledge management program. For instance, the firm has seen greater cross-functional and cross-hierarchal networking as a result of gatherings linked to the project.

KDI itself is a temple to spontaneity. The seven workers assigned to KDI have set up shop in a campus-style oasis of creativity in the middle of buttoned-down Tokyo and think up ways to make Fuji Xerox more imaginative. They dress casually and operate from a former underused fitness center, amid plants, easy chairs, and leftover exercise machines. A skull and crossbones flag and even their business cards add to their iconoclastic trappings. Kazue Kikawada, head of the institute, has a card identifying him as "senior freelance bandit," while Sengoku works under the title "knowledge torchbearer."

Kikawada says the KDI program, with its emphasis on free thinking and empowering workers with their own knowledge, also had to overcome some cultural barriers. "Japanese manufacturers are vertical organizations, and this way of working was thought to be impossible," he says. "But we are now getting lots of inquiries about this from outside."

---

1 In early 2001, Xerox agreed to sell half of its stake in Fuji Xerox to Fuji Photo Film. Following the transaction, Fuji Photo Film owns 75 percent of Fuji Xerox.

BUILDING BUSINESSES

Without implementation, the strongest idea is as useless as a fork in a soup kitchen. The final phase of our structure is building new businesses. Here, the most promising new knowledge is carefully tested and applied. Testing the assumptions behind the concept, developing prototypes and, if all is successful, a plan for launching the idea onto the market are all necessary to generate real value for the company. By this point, the embryonic idea will have matured into a rich, textured concept. This is the home stretch.

Experimentation necessarily takes time and resources, but it also allows individuals to take their idea and make it live. It is critical that the workers who originated the idea are also given responsible roles in the testing and implementation process. This is probably the single largest incentive for workers to offer their best ideas to their company. These ideas are their brainchildren, and each employee should be treated as an entrepreneur driving a business or product idea to market. In some cases, the originating employee may be assigned full time to the final development of their idea, but more often it should be handled as a supplement to normal operations.

Experimentation should be seen here in a broader perspective. It is not only about working in a laboratory or building up prototypes; it is also about trial and error processes that make ideas work. Experimentation is not the dedicated business of a limited group of people, but a task that all employees should take on alongside their operational duties. This process instills a sense of ownership in the employees, resulting in the company-wide realization of spontaneous ideas. Employees can benefit from the positive tension between their day-to-day work and their conceptual experiments. This positive tension combined with clearly defined time frames and consensus on the end products leads to a very effective and efficient way of generating the right ideas and solutions and implementing them rather than just building castles in the air.

The more-successful companies clearly understand the potential of individual experimentation. One international telecoms equipment company set up an in-house venture capital fund that focuses entirely on promoting internal ideas. This fund was open to the entire company, and employees were taught how to apply and structure a proposal for funding. The program featured clear evaluation processes and selection criteria, which were communicated throughout the company, and was managed by a new recruit with venture capital experience. If an idea is backed by the fund, the employee can receive a significant cash investment to develop a prototype, as well as phantom shares in the new enterprise. Partly by giving employees a sense of ownership to their ideas, the company pulls these ideas onto the table. Also, if the idea leads to a spin-off company, these phantom shares become a real stake in the new business. About 400 employees have participated in program, and a few flagship ideas have made it all the way to an initial public offering, giving the parent company an enormous payback, both in terms of ideas and capital.

These examples underline the importance that the more-successful companies attach to being proactive with concepts such as idea contests, as well as to less blatant approaches such as allowing employees freedom to research. They promote the realization of spontaneous ideas throughout their organization. This span covers product marketing, product development, and the continuous improvement of processes.

Creativity and spontaneity can be guided and encouraged by astute managers who don't throw up their arms in despair at the challenge. Only by taking an active role in bringing the creative power of all your employees up to peak levels can you ensure that your company is maximizing the innovative possibilities of the knowledge it controls. You may not be able to predict when an idea will pop up, but you can turn the heat up and be ready to capture the most promising kernels.

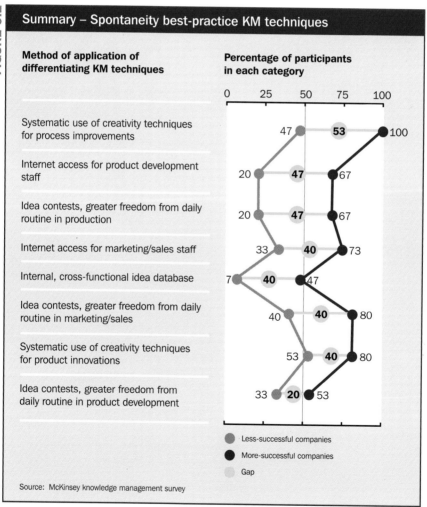

FIGURE 9.2

Summary – Spontaneity best-practice KM techniques

Method of application of differentiating KM techniques

Percentage of participants in each category

Systematic use of creativity techniques for process improvements	47 — 53 — 100
Internet access for product development staff	20 — 47 — 67
Idea contests, greater freedom from daily routine in production	20 — 47 — 67
Internet access for marketing/sales staff	33 — 40 — 73
Internal, cross-functional idea database	7 — 40 — 47
Idea contests, greater freedom from daily routine in marketing/sales	40 — 40 — 80
Systematic use of creativity techniques for product innovations	53 — 40 — 80
Idea contests, greater freedom from daily routine in product development	33 — 20 — 53

Less-successful companies
More-successful companies
Gap

Source: McKinsey knowledge management survey

chapter ten

Kicking off a knowledge management program

Design to cost, design to ease of manufacture, overhead value analyses ... we could go on. The list of tools for improving operations and the profitability of a business is long. And for each one, a proven approach is readily available. Most use three or four distinct steps to solve the problem: there is typically diagnosis followed by program design, then implementation is started in a pilot before the concept is rolled out broadly. Some of these elements are well suited to improving a company's knowledge management, but the broad approach differs significantly. Good knowledge management should certainly help to improve operations, but a fully fledged knowledge management program is more comparable to the development and implementation of company strategy than to a classic operational improvement program. A knowledge management program should be conducted with parallel, rather than linear, phases. This means implementing some measures very early in the diagnosis to capture the low hanging fruit. It also means continuing to do analyses of various aspects during the major period of implementation.

To get a knowledge management program up and running or to improve a lethargic program, we suggest three focal points that will lay a solid foundation for your efforts:

■ Define precise, business-oriented targets that your knowledge management program must support

■ Visualize your current knowledge management situation by conducting a broad assessment of corporate practices

■ Concentrate on a pragmatic approach that can bring early wins with limited investment.

BE PRECISE ABOUT THE OBJECTIVES

Do not do knowledge management for the sake of doing knowledge management. Your aim should be to improve your company's performance in very targeted areas. Of course it is worthwhile to improve the flow of knowledge between units, but linking it to a business target is much better. At the core of each knowledge management effort should be a metric directly linked to performance, such as the rate of innovation, a customer satisfaction index, or quality control improvements. The techniques to be implemented should be selected in order to support the improvement of this metric with good knowledge management.

To refine the objectives it is helpful to compare yourself to the world's best both in terms of business performance and knowledge management performance. Based on our interviews with chief executives, the top priority for a knowledge management program was improving quality of products and services over the medium to long term. The second highest objective was attracting new customers, followed closely by near-term operational improvements. Achieving customer service goals and expanding product portfolio were also cited as targets, but less frequently.

The more-successful companies recognized that pure knowledge objectives also play a role. But it is not only defining the right goals that is important, who does the defining is also critical. The survey strongly suggests that the goals must be defined at the top. At most of the more-successful companies, senior managers set the knowledge management objectives. While the details should still be worked out in individual units, without senior-level support and involvement employees will not recognize the importance of the issue. But, on the other hand, everyone affected should be included in defining the goals at the micro level as they know their own work best. Additionally, such early involvement will draw them into the project from the outset, and participation usually leads to motivation.

One of your first exercises should be to develop a solid vision of what you want knowledge management to do for your company. Often managers make the mistake of starting a knowledge management program with only the vague goal of, well, improving how they manage knowledge. The vision must go beyond that to pinpoint corporate objectives that can be reached through the program. Whether maximizing cross-selling possibilities between two newly acquired units, improving key account management across products, or some other well-defined goal, if you do not set a clear target, your knowledge management efforts will likely end in disappointment.

In initiating a program, the central tasks of knowledge management – application, distribution and cultivation – are useful in identifying where to find the quick wins. As we explained in Chapter 3, applying knowledge that is already available in your company will lead to the fastest impact on financial and operational performance. Particularly if your self-diagnosis showed a significant gap in handling subjectivity and transferability, there may be plenty of low hanging fruit ripe for the picking.

ASSESS THE STATUS OF YOUR COMPANY

The initial assessment of your company's knowledge management must focus on getting a broad understanding, rather than a highly detailed deep drill. At this stage, you need to find out where your biggest challenges lie. Almost certainly you will find potential for improvement at a variety of levels: the business unit, a geographical department, entire divisions, and, naturally, company wide.

At first blush, the greatest potential for improved knowledge management may seem to await across the highest organizational level, where economies of scale could underpin your efforts. But we are convinced that almost every change or improvement activity should be started from the bottom, within a small unit, preferably headed by a manager with a proven track record of driving change. A key factor to success is to have a direct link to the people at the frontline of the knowledge management program. Discussions in the corporate headquarters will have limited impact and may well be perceived lower down the company as an academic exercise with no relevance to day-to-day work.

Quick scan

To bring together this broad overview of your company's current knowledge status, look at your efforts in terms of knowledge pull and the six characteristics we have described. To help you with this preliminary scan, we have compiled a short list of questions. Although this list is considerably abbreviated from those that formed the basis for our questionnaires and interviews, it provides a convenient starting point for your knowledge assessment.

	Not used at all	Seldom used	Occasionally used	Often used	Always used
1. Knowledge Pull					
■ Setting targets to achieve or surpass world-class level					
■ Combining these targets with individual incentives					
■ Active involvement of employees in product portfolio and product innovation decisions					
2. Subjectivity					
■ Frequent, informal bottom-up and top-down communication					
■ Setting up cross-functional teams					
■ Common goals and values within different functions/departments					
3. Transferability					
■ Application of benchmarking techniques					
■ Using external knowledge sources via strategic alliances					
■ Commitment of all employees to track customer and market requirements					
4. Embeddedness					
■ Co-location, especially with external partners					
■ Job rotation and teamwork in development					
■ Joint teams or personal meetings with external partners					
■ Employee knowledge profiles available on the intranet					
5. Self-reinforcement					
■ Regular training with internal and external experts					
■ Network building with external partners					
■ Open access to knowledge infrastructure					
6. Perishability					
■ Company-wide process standards					
■ Systematic retention and updating of process experiences					
■ Regular process optimization based on experiences					
■ Decisions are made at the lowest appropriate levels					
7. Spontaneity					
■ Internet access for all employees					
■ Open idea databases to store product ideas					
■ Application of creativity techniques and idea contests					
■ Degrees of freedom for all employees away from daily work pressure					

Answers range from "not used at all" to "always used." So, if you are sure that a certain set of techniques is being implemented and used throughout your company you should answer "always used." After going through the quick scan, you get a view, albeit a subjective one, of your current knowledge management performance. The techniques included in this list are among the ones that our survey identified as being used significantly more widely by the more-successful companies to attack business problems compared with the practices at the less-successful companies. Areas where you are furthest from the "always used" column obviously have the greatest potential for improvement hikes.

But it is easy to imagine a technique that is heavily used, but not successful. After a first run through the questions, it would be helpful to take a closer look, particularly at techniques that are marked in the right-hand column, and ask yourself whether you are achieving demonstrable successes through these programs. If you are not, rethinking the program with an understanding of the characteristic influenced by that technique could help to uncover the flaws.

From your answers, you can roughly identify where your company is lagging in knowledge management. You may also find areas in which you apply best practice, but the point of the analysis is to reveal your shortcomings.

Plotting the results

Analysis is futile without a strategy to communicate the results comprehensibly. This requires some form of aggregation, since simply listing the answers to a few pages of questions is not particularly enlightening. To make the message clearer, we developed a tool, the "knowledge scanner," that can visually depict your knowledge management performance at a highly aggregated level (see Figure 10.1). Each of the six axes represents one of the six characteristics of knowledge, and the more a company uses best-practice knowledge management techniques the higher its performance rating. Plotting your performance is an efficient way to communicate your findings and demonstrate the necessity for action in your company.

The scanner's outer circle relates to 100 percent correspondence with the best practices that we identified, whereas in the center there is no correspondence with this pattern. Of course, no company surveyed completely matched the best-practice pattern, and no company was completely devoid of knowledge management. However, the more-successful companies managed every characteristic comparatively well, even though they still had areas that could be improved.

FIGURE 10.1

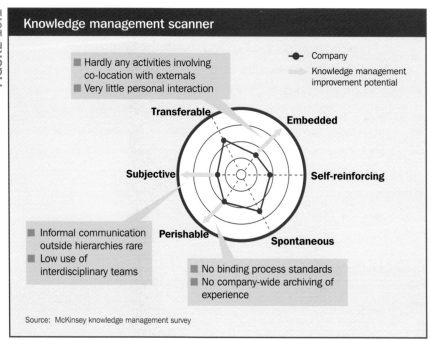

The best knowledge management company in our survey, for example, matched total correspondence to best practice when it came to managing spontaneity and generating knowledge pull. In embeddedness and subjectivity, it was very close to the 100 percent pattern. But in other areas, especially the management of perishability, it was much further away from best practice. The scanner is a proven tool to communicate these gaps, and even the top performers can identify areas for further improvement.

The scanner can show you in which areas you are falling short, but be wary of using it as checklist of techniques. Not all techniques will be as suitable for your particular business as others, and some may not justify the investment of resources. For example, smaller companies may have little need for an expensive idea database if employees routinely gather to brainstorm informally. The scanner merely suggests where you should be focusing your efforts. To understand your shortcomings in detail, you need to examine your answers to each question individually and compare them to the corporate targets you hope to achieve through knowledge management.

The analysis can also be used to compare different divisions of a single company. Knowledge management should be uniformly good across the company, but our survey revealed that in large companies one division can have a great handle on the challenge, while another is left struggling. If this is thrown into relief by the scanner, you can take appropriate action to bring the divisions into line by encouraging knowledge transfer across the boundaries and other efforts.

CONCENTRATE ON GETTING RESULTS

In knowledge management, as everywhere, success breeds success. When deciding where to start and whom to involve first, look for people who already show enthusiasm – and start small. This reduces risk, speeds up the process, and is more practical. If you have a plant or office where some informal, unstructured knowledge management is already going on, start there. Clearly someone at least has the right idea and an appetite for knowledge. Starting with a smaller area is also less daunting and – for those of you still skeptical – less expensive. But eventually the whole company needs to be addressed. This is the only way that you can tap the full potential of knowledge management. However, to have a fruitful company-wide program, it is important to have early successes that are well publicized internally.

Be courageous enough to take risks and confident enough to realize when a program is not reaching its targets. Also, do not sweat the details, at least not initially. A solid outline for a program should be enough to get it going, and good management will fill in and adjust the details as the program progresses. These mid-course adjustments will also help to steer the project more directly toward its targets. And finally, keep these targets focused on a small number of specific and measurable business objectives. By prioritizing, you increase the chances for early successes before expanding the effort into new challenges.

Once you have identified the unit or team that is primed to embark on a knowledge management effort, the program must be implemented aggressively. Focus on that unit rather than spreading resources thinly and strike forcefully. Workers involved in the initial effort must pull out all the stops. Do not have people working on the knowledge management program just 5 percent of their time; get them involved at least four days a week. In working with diverse companies in many different situations, we have seen dramatic results from pulling eager employees away from day-to-day business in order to ignite a change from business as usual. Even at the risk of adding uncertainty or insecurity to their situations, throwing them into the deep end of the pool is a strong trigger for new thinking.

Also, do not staff the team just with junior employees. Your employees will only really believe that a program is deemed important if the best people are attached to it. Knowledge management should rank in the top five items on your corporate priority list, and this should be reflected in the team composition: high-level managers lead the effort (sponsored by the CEO); well-respected team leaders serve as opinion leaders; and the team should be augmented by young high-potentials from the company's talent nursery.

Another component of an aggressive plan is ambitious time frames. Just as we demonstrated when explaining knowledge pull, stretch targets are a great technique to use here. Put the team under pressure; pressure turns carbon into diamonds. The worst thing that can happen to a knowledge management program is for it to turn into a never-ending procession of fuzzy objectives. A crystal clear, demanding target coupled with exposure and other incentives will create a high-performance team and make your knowledge management effort successful. And, as we said at the beginning of this chapter, the engagement plan should recognize that all aspects of the program should be carried out in parallel rather than step by step.

Once the program is in full swing, positive results should ensure that the effort gains a momentum of its own. But this will not be the time to sit back and relax. Remember the danger of organizational and individual barriers, and remember the perils of both information overload and knowledge perishing before your eyes. You must instill in your company a sense of caring for knowledge so that it becomes part of everyday life, rather than something that ebbs and flows as the mood suits.

chapter eleven

Coming to terms with the knowledge economy

Knowledge management has been a fashionable topic in business circles for more than a decade, but our survey showed that many companies can talk the talk, but few can walk the walk. This is probably because the theme has been surrounded by a general mystique that makes many dyed-in-the-wool business leaders uncomfortable. It is time to throw out the jargon. Soon, it will be useless to distinguish knowledge workers from non-knowledge workers or knowledge companies from non-knowledge companies.

Without doubt, we stand on the threshold of a new economic era. Whether it is called the new economy or even, as we prefer, the future economy, the emerging scarce resource in the corporate milieu is knowledge. As we have seen, knowledge is quite different from land, labor, and capital in many ways. But managers who find the determination and means to manage this asset will harvest breathtaking returns. Henning Kagermann, chief executive of German software developer SAP, once said that knowledge can bring returns of 700 to 800 percent a year. Kagermann might be overstating his case, but we are certain that knowledge, correctly invested, can bring returns well beyond the interest that can be gained on pure capital.

Understandably, many executives face this new era with exaggerated trepidation. But our survey has shown that this reluctance is unwarranted. Once you start to look at knowledge as another asset that must be exploited for optimal results, its mystery begins to fade. Knowledge may be different from traditional assets but, as we have seen, it has recognizable characteristics. Traditional management techniques can be applied to overcome some of the troublesome characteristics of knowledge, such as perishability and embeddedness, and to take full advantage of the opportunities presented by others. By facing these characteristics head on, managers can maximize the gains available from the knowledge they own and the knowledge they create.

IF WE ALL AGREE, WHAT IS THE PROBLEM?

The shift to a new asset structure that values knowledge above other factors and cements the role of intangibles in a company's net worth seems so apparent that there is rarely a debate among corporate managers over the emerging importance of knowledge building and knowledge utilization. The importance of knowledge in the high-tech sector is clearly obvious. But our survey also showed that a wide gamut of industries can capture rewards from effective knowledge management, including better performance and increased innovation.

But if everyone embraces the idea of knowledge management, why have only a few top managers shown a deeper understanding of how to put theory into practice? The outstanding question is not whether knowledge management is important or even how important it is in relation to other strategic measures. The real question is how can a company systematically exploit all dimensions of knowledge and fully utilize them to improve revenues, profit, and growth.

From a leadership perspective, knowledge management has been viewed more like a craft and less like a science. Because of the very nature of knowledge, it is difficult for managers to predict what measures can really improve performance, and how to encourage and guide knowledge flows within an organization. As we have seen, simply divining a definition of the field that is acceptable to academics and practitioners alike is nearly impossible. Scholars worry too much about how many knowledge angels can fit on the head of a pin, and practitioners too often brush the field aside as the soft underbelly of management that either works or does not. Top executives, trained in hard facts and schooled in strategies that can be decided largely by comparing costs of input to revenue potentials and other likely benefits, are often at a loss when trying to account for knowledge. These managers are accustomed to making decisions under uncertainty, but many may avoid the added layer of uncertainty brought by actively attempting to manage knowledge. They embark with the general notion that knowledge management is important, then spend lavishly on the journey without a clear idea of their likely destination or even a good estimate of how long the trip might take.

Knowledge is much more difficult to handle than information because it is about relationships rather than data. In a single generation, the amount of data available to any one of us has exploded to such an extent that we now talk about information overload. As a small example, remember that Christmas card you threw away that played "Jingle Bells" over and over again? The amount of data stored on that one chip that ended in a landfill outside Tokyo would have made corporate computer banks from the 1950s green with envy. Along with stored information, we have also become far better at retrieving information. A few minutes of surfing on the Internet and you will find the musical score for "Jingle Bells" and hundreds of other holiday classics. Without leaving their offices, most senior executives can get their hands on complete corporate financial histories and volumes of other information.

But try to find comprehensible instructions on the Internet on how to play a guitar in order to pluck out "Jingle Bells" like Eric Clapton. Or search your intranet for the experience necessary to interpret those sales figures in a way that will drive the chart higher. It is not as easy. The more data we accumulate, the harder it is to manage the knowledge needed to understand the interrelationships and use that data effectively ... and the more important it is to do it right.

There is an obvious temptation to approach knowledge management armed solely with time-tested management criteria. But those managers who try to apply long-held ideas of efficiency and, to some extent, the normal methods of exploiting market potential will miss the main point of managing knowledge. Instead of pulling in a bountiful harvest, they will find their silos bare and stomachs empty.

CHARTING THE NEW GROUND

If knowledge is an asset that resists being crammed onto a ledger pad and is nearly impossible to extrapolate in a way that can be used to predict future value, how can an executive possibly manage it? The data and analysis from our survey has given us a useful basis for understanding the challenge and deciding where additional efforts may bring the most immediate good.

The six characteristics – subjectivity, transferability, embeddedness, self-reinforcement, perishability, and spontaneity – define the challenge in a way that allows managers to get their bearings in this unfamiliar landscape. By using the best-practice techniques we have identified benchmarks for comparison. Companies can scan their practices with what we have called the knowledge scanner to create an image of their knowledge management efforts. The scanner produces a visual of a changing object – the corporate knowledge effort – and helps to identify where growth has been retarded and where the organism is thriving.

While evaluating your company's knowledge management efforts, it is wise to remember that ultimately, knowledge management is a quest for a corporate holy grail. The effort carries its own rewards, but it will obviously never be possible for anyone in the company to know everything all the time. Hitting 100 percent in any one of these dimensions alone is impossible, but just as King Arthur's knights gained personal enlightenment while seeking their Holy Grail, companies striving for knowledge management perfection will discover manifold benefits along the way.

As with many business solutions, a workable solution that promises 80 percent of the potential impact is better than striving for 100 percent and failing. Targeting perfection in knowledge management ends up burning more and more resources, particularly on data processing, for each step taken toward what might be a purely hypothetical goal. Does everyone in the company have to know everything all the time? Obviously not. A production worker at a stereo factory does not have to know every detail of a unit's design, but that worker and his company may benefit, for instance, if he has an understanding of the basic principles of design to cost. A service technician need not know the minutiae of corporate strategy, but that technician must be up to speed if, for example, that strategy focuses on improved service and offering more value to the customer over a product's life cycle.

Knowledge management is using and developing a company's understanding of relationships in order to bring direct benefits, either in cost savings, process efficiencies, utilization of market potentials or even developing that eureka innovation that leaves rivals in the dust. For some, this definition may be too broad, but we believe that such a wide net is necessary to develop a practitioner's guide. It brings a broad spectrum of activities into the realm of knowledge management, from incentives to operational processes to talent retention.

There is another reason to avoid a narrower definition of knowledge management. If you ignore the techniques that focus, for example, on incentives or product development, you are quickly left with only information technology, and knowledge management becomes synonymous with data management. Such a narrow definition is tempting. You can touch a computer, and there are thousands of software developers and other service providers waiting in the wings to help to deploy databases, teleconferencing, and other technology solutions. Reducing knowledge management to this level is very dangerous because it leaves untapped potential available to competitors, and can be very costly.

That was a trap that many of the less-successful companies in our survey had fallen into. They falsely saw knowledge management as infrastructure, such as databases, virtual team rooms, or e-mail addresses. They thought that, with the right infrastructure, they would be able to move data and real knowledge around smoothly and their task would be all but finished. Of course computers are necessary, solid infrastructure is necessary, and e-mail is necessary. But it is not sufficient for successful knowledge management. Managers cannot neglect the softer, opaque, more difficult side of knowledge management. It is on this terrain that the greatest potential for improvements rests.

WHERE TO START

Eventually every company, even those considered best practice, should make a thorough knowledge management assessment. Such an internal study should result in a detailed battle plan for using specific management techniques to address gaps in a company's knowledge management efforts. But there are also ways to identify quickly where the potential for immediate improvement lies. And, as we have shown, there is likely to be a lot of potential.

Mirror, mirror ... reflecting corporate structure

First look in the mirror, the CEO and each top manager sets the example for the rest of the company. If you have not explicitly made knowledge management your priority, no one else will. You must be an active and visible participant in all facets of knowledge management.

Second, look around your company. There are some easy tests to figure out whether you have the necessary infrastructure, but are not using that infrastructure effectively. Look at your databases, for instance. Are they dusty storage bins for documents that are rarely opened or are they fresh and dynamic, filled with information that has been recently updated? Also, check your intranet and extranet Web sites. The content should be replaced regularly, and visitor statistics should show frequent activity. Quiz a couple of people in the corridor. Everyone in the company – including the senior managers – should have access to the IT system and know how to use it. Employees must also have the time and encouragement to participate in discussion forums and join other online activities. You should exemplify this by jumping into some of the discussions yourself.

... reflecting corporate strategy

Examine your strategy and see whether knowledge management is a thread that is woven throughout the corporate tapestry. A quick test is a rather simple question: has your company had a knowledge breakthrough recently, for instance an improved process, better market understanding, or a new product or service? If you have to think about it, then the answer is no.

Incentive systems must encourage teamwork. They should foster group goals as well as excellent individual performances, and there should be significant disincentives in place to discourage knowledge hoarding and any aversion to knowledge "not invented here." Organizational structures that foster backstabbing or other destructive measures in order to secure an attractive assignment or promotion work against the goal of creating a knowledge culture. In outstanding organizations, everybody who is good, as measured against standards that include knowledge management, gets promoted and rewarded, and if hierarchies do not allow for enough titled positions to denote increased responsibility, there are other methods, such as the creation of expert career tracks or interim positions that signify imminent advancement.

... reflecting operations

At the operational level, there are also signals that can show whether knowledge management is well integrated into your company's practices and that suggest how well you are doing in cultivating and distributing knowledge. For example, there should be processes in place that quickly document experiences in a way that others can easily learn from. This might suggest a clever IT solution, but that is only part of it. Documenting knowledge often takes additional time, and senior managers must allocate that time to their employees. Even as a high-pressure project is nearing completion and the pace becomes deadening, time must be set aside to document the knowledge gained. Otherwise, important lessons could be lost as team members scatter to the four winds.

Also, make sure that knowledge management is a formal part of the agenda at regular meetings, whether of top executives or in broader groups. Time should be reserved to discuss progress made within the company, or simply to exchange anecdotes about how knowledge has been shared and used to improve the company's overall performance. The idea is to get into the habit of talking about knowledge management, not as a special project, but rather as an integral part of day-to-day operations.

It is very difficult, if not impossible, to quantify spending on knowledge management beyond spending on infrastructure. This is particularly true for the opportunity cost of managing knowledge effectively. But you should have a sense of which investments and expenses are promoting knowledge management in a very clear and defined way. And there should be clear, if indirect, milestones and targets to make sure that the outlays are contributing to your corporate success. Even at the risk of doing some fuzzy math, your company should have developed some metrics to gauge how well the tasks of knowledge management are being accomplished. The trick is to avoid confusing information accumulation with real knowledge management.

The metrics used can be overarching corporate goals, such as faster product development and improved order generation and fulfillment, which we used as two of the standards for comparing companies in our survey. Such targets offer a clear connection between knowledge management and corporate performance, but the risk is that they are also influenced by many other factors. The metrics can also be tied to individual projects, for instance brief questionnaires can be distributed after meetings to gauge whether knowledge management targets, such as a common understanding of goals or improved personal networking, were achieved.

CONDUCTING THE ORCHESTRA

In the past management has often taken a strong top-down approach. This was easy enough when the resources being managed were traditional assets such as land, labor or capital. The additional resource of knowledge makes the corporate world much richer and broader, adds new complexities to management's agenda, and gives way to creative, new solutions.

In traditional factory systems, top executives had the clearest ideas of how their plants and their processes should operate and what their customers wanted. And then they issued orders to the troops. Compared with today's environment, the pace of change was slow and the level of complexity needed was reasonably low. In its time, this model was successful. A closed circle of managers, many with close contacts to customers, suppliers, and employees, could create and distill the necessary volume of ideas to keep the business running and thriving. Change and innovation were not as important when making a quality product. It was sufficient to capture a significant portion of local, regional or even national demand. Even today, there are some areas in which such a traditional programmed business model still works. Many mass-market franchises, including fast-food chains and car service chains, are successful precisely because they keep the complexity low, follow standard operating procedures developed by the head office, and stick to a proven game plan. As we mentioned in Chapter 4, a major advantage of such a management style is the eradication of subjectivity. No one is marching to the beat of a different drummer.

But with knowledge as a scarce resource, things are changing. Given substantially more complexity in business, increased technological possibilities, and a better trained and educated work force, top managers at established companies are increasingly switching their focus to the most important architectural decisions and pushing many other decision points lower in the corporate organization.

Start-ups obviously face a different situation. Here the knowledge is still concentrated around the founders, decisions tend to follow the programmed model, but at a much faster pace. But even successful start-ups, particularly the larger ones, will quickly mature into organizations that will require active management of knowledge and a game plan to master it.

In both situations, executives must exploit knowledge as much as possible. Every significant idea from throughout the organization must be brought into the open, evaluated and, if found to be worthy, carefully implemented. Senior managers at established companies oversee hundreds and thousands of employees – engineers, line workers, clerical staff, marketers, salespeople – each one a potential idea generator. At most companies, this potential remains largely untapped. And as we have argued, even a modest increase in harvesting this knowledge can result in significant gains. But it can only work if everyone in the company is initiated into the knowledge culture. The challenge is not slight. It calls for a massive effort in spreading the culture, gathering and filtering the results, assuring the program functions as quickly as possible, and implementing the best of the ideas rigorously.

The CEO cannot take personal charge of implementing and tracking the scores of knowledge management techniques that we have identified as best practice. However, he can use the simple scanner to gain some insight into where he stands and where he wants to go. He has to create and foster an environment in which there is a lot of cooperation, but also friendly competition and corporate Darwinism, an environment in which incentives lean heavily on group success, but also acknowledge individual achievements. At one Japanese car maker, for example, the performance of production line workers is rated based on six categories of achievement: individual performance, team performance, assembly line performance, plant performance, car line performance, and corporate performance as a whole. In this environment, everyone shares the success financially and, much more important in terms of interesting work and a dynamic workplace, top performing employees are clearly singled out for their contributions to the knowledge base and overall success.

By successfully creating such a culture, the CEO will not need to monitor the minutiae. Senior managers will be encouraged to seek and implement techniques in their divisions in order to foster good knowledge management. And every division, from human resources to plant operations, stands to gain from improved knowledge flow. This knowledge management Mecca, a positive self-enforcing spiral, is easy to imagine, but it takes effort to implement. Companies that find themselves trapped in a downward spiral in which knowledge is leaving, being lost, or simply not being offered, may be able to reverse the trend by focusing their efforts on a small segment of the company and pushing hard for immediate results. But this would only be a first step. Once the techniques begin to show an impact, they should be aggressively replicated throughout the company as quickly as is practical.

ALL CKOs, PLEASE RAISE YOUR HANDS

Whose job is it to explore this new landscape? The best companies have seen the fallacy of a narrow definition and have charged not one but all of their employees with being self-standing chief knowledge officers (CKOs). Starting with the chief executive, then going to the middle managers, and finally the frontline employees, everyone in a company must recognize the value of knowledge, and everyone must participate in the knowledge management program.

Company leaders must take the lead

Jack Welch at General Electric (GE) is one of several well-known CEOs who have infused their companies with a thirst for knowledge that cannot be quenched. Starting with his well-known call for GE divisions to be number one or two in their segments, Mr. Welch has forced GE to rethink its knowledge.

The chief executive must, in some ways, operate as the CKO. It is the CEO that sets the tone for a corporation, and if the boss takes knowledge seriously, the rest of the company will follow. One long-serving CEO we know was chided by his daughter a few Christmases ago for not being able to read new e-mails. To meet the challenge, the executive put himself under the tutelage of one of his company's IT whizkids and learned to e-mail and surf the Internet. He then dared his executive board to meet the same challenge, rather than relying only on secretaries to communicate over the corporate system. Soon, board members were e-mailing employees throughout the company, opening a new channel of cross-hierarchical communication and bringing the company to a new level of knowledge sharing.

Acting as a CKO, the chief executive must install and implement rules that enable the application, distribution, and cultivation of knowledge. And by setting the example, the chief executive makes it difficult for anyone in the company to shirk their part of the knowledge management initiative. The leader of a global giant like GE may have more options and a wider choice of levers available that reflect the diversity and complexity of the organization – and these should be used according to the specific circumstances – but smaller businesses can also reap significant benefits from a focus that includes knowledge.

Middle managers must sign on

If the CEO sets the tone and establishes the rules, it is the middle managers who must take the ball to the field and lead the efforts. To get a clearer picture of how a middle manager's role should be influenced by effective knowledge management, let us take a hypothetical project manager for a car company charged with getting a new sports car to market. Along the way, the manager is forced to confront the six characteristics of knowledge, and only by active knowledge management can the project reach optimal success.

■ *Subjectivity* rears its head immediately just by considering what factors define a sports car. Body style, performance, driving characteristics, and many other options are all part of the mix. The project manager must make sure that everyone on the team has the same image of a sports car and the same priorities. The image could be defined by a target customer segment or – far more risky but potentially more rewarding – by the project manager's own vision, but this must be held in common by the entire team.

- *Transferability* comes into play from many sides. Lessons learned from the success of a vintage sports car made by the same company, clues suggesting what is hot in other industries reliant on flashy design such as consumer electronics or sports equipment, and knowledge about what can be copied from current models can all be applied to the design project.

- The project manager's team obviously cannot include everyone in the company with experience relevant to debuting a sports car. To bring much of this *embedded* knowledge to the surface where it can contribute to the new project, the manager can, for example, bring old hands within and outside the company together to float ideas and discuss aspects of the project. Team members could also garner more ideas by spending time meeting potential customers at sales outlets or going to places such as car museums or gallery openings where target customers are likely to gather.

- To take advantage of *self-reinforcement*, the manager must create a sense of ownership in a small group, but also be willing to share knowledge developed during the sports car project outside the project team, and be willing to consider ideas and feedback that comes from outside the core project team. The value of knowledge to a company increases when it is shared, and although it is good to have a few surprises on hand when the car is unveiled, ultimately the manager must keep in mind that the team is part of a larger organization and ask for help.

- Although *perishability* is as inevitable as reruns of M*A*S*H, the project manager must be ready to respond if, for example, consumer tastes shift suddenly or a rival's latest model steals some of the thunder from our manager's own project. Both these situations, and others, can cause some of the knowledge used in the car design to lose value quickly. Also, before the project ends, the manager must budget time to document the knowledge accumulated during the project so that it does not perish and others can benefit from his experience.

- *Spontaneity* can be hard to fit in under time and cost pressure, but the project manager must find a place for it. Whether giving team members competitors' cars to drive over the weekend, bringing the team and their families together for a kickoff party, or putting a slot-car racetrack in the common team room, there must be occasional opportunities to step away from the direct pressure of the project, stare at a blank canvas, and allow creativity.

Our project manager – a proxy for all middle managers – faced a challenge that traditionally focused on such considerations as time, quality, and costs, and found understanding knowledge management was a vital component for helping to bring the project to a fruitful conclusion. The successful project leader has indeed become another knowledge manager.

Creating knowledge workers

Soon, every worker will become a knowledge worker. The rote processes that typify the popular myth of a factory worker's daily job are increasingly being taken over by machines. Fewer and fewer industries in the developed, high-wage countries will need low-skilled labor. Automation and the increased competition brought by globalization both play a part in changing the employee dynamic.

To cite one example, blue-collar workers in the German machine tool industry have already been transformed into knowledge workers. The change is apparent just by looking at the shop floor, where workers have exchanged the traditional blue coveralls for t-shirts and jeans. Human precision is being replaced by computerized precision, and knowledge about the machines they use is far more important than craftsman skills. Many line workers have taken programming courses as they strive to learn how to handle their production equipment better. The change is evident, for example, at German printing press manufacturer Heidelberger Druck, where some assembly workers can manage a near-seven-hour assembly process, essentially building a complete module, because they know all the parts and steps along the way. This is a far cry from the repetitive 10-second tasks of yesterday's factories.

These are knowledge workers. They bring more to their workplace, offer more value to their company, and gain more satisfaction from their jobs. These workers can, for instance, help to identify the bottlenecks in an assembly process and contribute to product development. The shift in the employee landscape is inevitable, but companies can accelerate the shift by offering additional training, explicitly rewarding all workers who move in this direction and understanding the entire know-ledge chain. They can adjust job descriptions to broaden the scope of individual positions and increase individual responsi-bility, giving their employees a chance to grasp the bigger picture. And they can include employees from all functions and all hierarchies in planning and development activities, both as a reward for becoming knowledge workers and in an effort to utilize their knowledge as effectively as possible.

In the end, working with knowledge is much more creative, gives a higher sense of doing value-added work and, simply put, is much more fun. Every employee can share in the benefits of shifting to a knowledge-based workplace, which can help in employee retention.

THE KNOWLEDGE ERA

After eras dominated by land, labor, and capital, a fourth era, the era of knowledge, is dawning. Just as the world is starting to understand that there is no such thing as a new or old economy, but rather just one economy being transformed, it has become clear to us that it will soon be worthless to try to distinguish a knowledge worker from any other kind of worker or a knowledge company from any other kind of company. Just as no company will probably survive without taking advantage of the opportunities offered by the Internet, soon no worker will survive without actively using knowledge as a tool of their trade, whatever trade that is, and no company will succeed without tapping into the great potential of their employees' knowledge.

For the new knowledge workers this will mean a lifelong emphasis on education and training, as well as a focus on marketing their individual capabilities. In increasing numbers, they will demand opportunities from their employers to use and replenish their own knowledge base. And workers – especially the top talent – will weigh heavily the freedom for creativity and the overall work environment when selecting a job. This book has been devoted to what this change means for these evolving knowledge companies. The transformation is in full progress, and we are entering this fourth era with tremendous speed and force. The learning curve is steep, but the potential seems almost unlimited.

Knowledge management may be difficult for hardened business professionals to approach. But successful and ambitious executives must wrestle with it in order to conquer the new world. And they will find that proven management techniques are adequate for the task, as long as they are applied with an understanding of the different characteristics of knowledge.

Ignoring the challenge now may lead to fewer headaches in the short run, but it will also lead to a great disappointment tomorrow when you are left behind in the old paradigm. There is tremendous wealth out there to be created and parts of the necessary infrastructure, the Internet and global networks, are already in place.

The knowledge era is not the product of a few smart business professors or even a cadre of management consultants. It is the product of our times and our advancements. Others can speculate over what could replace knowledge after this fourth economic era has run its course, but for us – for businessmen and businesswomen – the true work is in carving a path into this new era and exploiting the possibilities of knowledge to their fullest extent. That will easily keep our hands and minds busy well into the 21st Century.

And that would not be a bad thing. Allow us for a moment, just briefly, to dream. Society usually bears the indelible imprint of its industry, and what if this were true for our ideal industry in this fledgling knowledge era? Society would echo efforts to confront the six intrinsic characteristics of knowledge. We would be united in values (subjectivity), open and transparent (transferability), generous and sharing (embeddedness), free of limitations and borders (self-reinforcement), true to the lessons of the past (perishability), and creative, innovative, and dynamic (spontaneous). And finally, the benefits captured, which would go well beyond economics, would place societies that embrace this new knowledge era as role models for the rest of the world (knowledge pull). But now it is Monday morning, and time to wake up and go to work.

about the authors

Jürgen Kluge joined McKinsey in Düsseldorf in 1984 and was named office manager for Germany in January 1999. Kluge is particularly active in the automotive, machinery, electro/electronics, and office equipment sectors. He has been the global leader of the Firm's Automotive & Assembly sector practice and co-leader of its technology management center. Before joining McKinsey, Kluge studied physics in Cologne and Essen. He holds a PhD in experimental physics (laser).

Books he has co-authored include *Simplicity Wins*, *Shrink to Grow*, and *Durchstarten zur Spitze* (Shooting for the Stars).

Wolfram Stein works in the Munich office of McKinsey for clients in the automotive, transportation and high-tech industries. He joined the Firm in 1998 following 11 years with IBM and in 1999 was elected principal in the global Business Technology Office. Along with knowledge management, his client work includes business-related technology deployment, e-commerce, and m-commerce.

Thomas Licht joined McKinsey in 1994 after studies in biology and geography at universities in Würzburg, Albany N.Y., Trinidad and Israel. An associate principal for the Firm, his work focuses on the automotive and assembly, transport and construction industries. He specializes in post-merger integration, large-scale project businesses, and organization. Since 2000, he led the team responsible for McKinsey's global knowledge management survey.

THE CO-AUTHORS

Alexandra Bendler joined the Institute of Production Engineering and Machine Tools in Darmstadt in 1998 as a research associate after earning her Master's degree in industrial engineering from Darmstadt University of Technology. Along with her research in knowledge management, her work has centered on corporate strategy and international production planning. She is a doctoral candidate preparing her thesis on knowledge management in international marketing and sales activities.

Jens Elzenheimer studied industrial engineering at the Darmstadt University of Technology. After earning his Master's degree, he developed training programs for standard business software. In January 2000 he joined the Institute of Production Engineering and Machine Tools as a research associate. In addition to knowledge management, his work focuses on the management of global production networks and the effects and implications of mergers and acquisitions on production strategy.

Susanne Hauschild joined McKinsey in 1998 and has worked in the energy, transportation, and assembly industries, focusing on operational improvement and organization. She has a Bachelor's degree in international business from Northeastern University, Boston, and a Master's degree in business administration from International Partnership of Business Schools, University Reutlingen, Germany. Susanne is preparing her doctoral thesis on knowledge management.

Uwe Heckert joined McKinsey in 1997 and is working within the Firm's Business Technology Office in Frankfurt, focusing on IT-based solutions and IT organization and management. He holds a Master's degree in business administration from University Göttingen and has also studied at State University of New York. He is completing his doctoral thesis on IT in knowledge management.

Jan Krönig joined McKinsey in 1997 and is focusing on the consumer goods and telecommunication industries. He holds Master's degrees in business administration from the University of St. Gallen and the University of Miami. Jan finished his doctoral thesis in 2001 on the role of incentive systems in knowledge management at the University of St. Gallen.

André Stoffels joined McKinsey in 1996 and focuses on innovation and IT management. He holds Master's degrees in electrical engineering from Rheinisch-Westfälische Technische Hochschule in Aachen, Germany, and Ecole Centrale in Paris. He studied at Ecole des Hautes Etudes Commerciales School of Management, France, and was a visiting scholar at the University of California, Berkeley. André is completing his doctoral thesis on knowledge management in product development organizations at Darmstadt University of Technology.

contents

starters & nibbles

slow-cooked spicy herbed prawns

2kg uncooked medium king prawns

4 cloves garlic, crushed

2 fresh long red chillies, chopped coarsely

¾ cup (180ml) olive oil

½ cup (125ml) lemon juice

1 teaspoon sweet paprika

½ cup loosely packed fresh flat-leaf parsley leaves

½ cup loosely packed fresh coriander leaves

¼ cup coarsely chopped fresh chives

preparation time 20 minutes ■ cooking time 30 minutes (plus refrigeration time) ■ serves 8

1 Preheat oven to slow.

2 Shell and devein prawns, leaving tails intact.

3 Combine garlic, chilli, oil, juice and paprika in shallow 3-litre (12-cup) baking dish, add prawns; toss prawns gently to coat in mixture. Cook, covered, in slow oven about 30 minutes or until prawns are just cooked through; stirring once halfway through cooking time. Cover; refrigerate 2 hours.

4 Serve prawns tossed with herbs.

Festive

next

Please note that the cup and spoon measurements
used in this book are metric. A conversion chart
appears on page 128.

First published in Great Britain in 2008 by ACP Magazines Ltd.
This edition published in 2008 exclusively for Next Retail Limited.

next.co.uk
nextflowers.co.uk

ISBN 978-1-903777-35-0

Printed and bound in China

smoked salmon &
dilled sour cream crepe cakes

½ cup (75g) plain flour

2 eggs

2 teaspoons vegetable oil

1 cup (250ml) milk

2 tablespoons drained capers,
rinsed, chopped coarsely

2 tablespoons finely chopped
fresh dill

1 tablespoon grated lemon rind

2 teaspoons lemon juice

1 clove garlic, crushed

1 cup (240g) sour cream

500g sliced smoked salmon

preparation time 30 minutes (plus standing time) ▦ cooking time 30 minutes
(plus refrigeration time) ▦ makes 16

1 Line base and side of deep 20cm-round cake tin with cling film.

2 Place flour in medium bowl. Make well in centre; gradually whisk in combined
eggs, oil and milk. Strain into large jug; stand 30 minutes.

3 Heat oiled 19cm frying pan; pour ½ cup of the batter into pan, tilting pan to
coat base. Cook over low heat, loosening around edge with spatula until browned
lightly. Turn; brown other side. Remove from pan; repeat with remaining batter to
make a total of five crepes.

4 Combine capers, dill, rind, juice, garlic and sour cream in small bowl. Place
a crepe in prepared tin; spread with ½ cup of sour cream mixture, cover with a
quarter of the fish. Continue layering with remaining crepes, sour cream mixture
and fish, finishing with a crepe. Cover; refrigerate overnight.

5 Gently turn cake onto chopping board; discard cling film. Using sharp knife,
carefully trim cake into a square; discard trimmings. Cut into 4cm squares; top
squares with sour cream and dill, if desired.

pan-fried asparagus with parmesan

preparation time 5 minutes
cooking time 5 minutes

1 tablespoon olive oil

400g asparagus, trimmed

½ cup (40g) flaked parmesan cheese

½ teaspoon cracked black pepper

1 Heat oil in large frying pan; cook asparagus, in batches, until just tender. Serve asparagus sprinkled with cheese and cracked pepper.

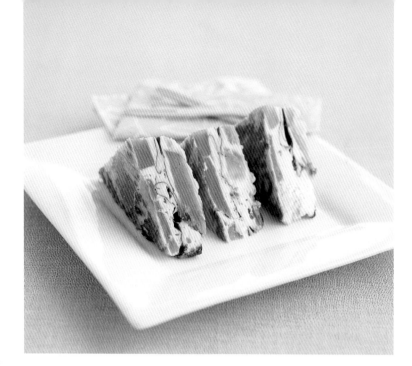

butternut squash & spinach frittata

preparation time 20 minutes (Plus refrigeration time) ▓ cooking time 45 minutes

900g butternut squash, sliced thinly

2 cloves garlic, crushed

1 tablespoon olive oil

6 eggs

½ cup (125ml) cream

40g baby spinach leaves

¼ cup (20g) coarsely grated parmesan cheese

1 Preheat oven to moderately hot.

2 Place squash, in single layer, on baking trays; brush with combined garlic and oil. Roast, uncovered, in moderately hot oven until tender.

3 Meanwhile, oil deep 20cm-square cake tin; line with baking parchment.

4 Whisk eggs with cream in medium jug. Layer half of the squash in prepared tin; pour half of the egg mixture over squash. Top with spinach and remaining squash then pour in remaining egg mixture; sprinkle with cheese.

5 Bake, uncovered, in moderately hot oven about 25 minutes or until firm. Stand 5 minutes before cutting into triangles.

roasted vegetable
& goat's cheese terrine

2 large red peppers (700g)

2 large aubergines (1kg), sliced thinly
lengthways

2 medium green courgettes (240g),
sliced thinly lengthways

150g soft goat's cheese

¼ cup (60ml) cream

1 tablespoon lemon juice

½ cup loosely packed fresh basil leaves

100g mixed salad leaves

basil oil

½ cup (125ml) extra virgin olive oil

½ cup loosely packed fresh basil leaves

10g baby spinach leaves

1 tablespoon finely grated lemon rind

preparation time 30 minutes ■ **cooking time 25 minutes (plus refrigeration time)** ■ **serves 8**

1 Line 1.5-litre (6-cup) terrine dish with cling film.

2 Quarter peppers; discard seeds and membranes. Roast under grill or in very hot oven, skin-side up, until skin blisters and blackens. Cover pepper pieces in plastic or paper 5 minutes; peel away skin.

3 Cook aubergines and courgettes in lightly oiled large frying pan, in batches, until browned both sides.

4 Combine cheese, cream and lemon juice in small bowl.

5 Line base and sides of prepared dish with two-thirds of the aubergine, draping aubergine over all sides of dish. Place half of the pepper over base of dish; spread cheese mixture over pepper then top with basil, courgettes, remaining pepper and remaining aubergine. Fold overhanging aubergine at short sides over terrine then fold remaining aubergine over long sides to completely enclose terrine. Cover; refrigerate 30 minutes.

6 Meanwhile, make basil oil.

7 Cut terrine into eight slices. Serve on salad leaves, drizzle with basil oil.

■ **basil oil** Blend or process ingredients until smooth. Strain through small muslin-lined strainer into small jug.

main courses

slow-roasted turkey with sausagemeat stuffing & port gravy

4kg turkey

¼ cup (60ml) chicken stock

½ cup (125ml) port

2 tablespoons brown sugar

2 tablespoons vegetable oil

2 tablespoons plain flour

sausagemeat stuffing

2 tablespoons vegetable oil

2 medium brown onions (300g), sliced

500g sausagemeat

4 cups (280g) stale breadcrumbs

2 tablespoons chopped fresh sage

½ cup (60g) chopped walnuts

preparation time 30 minutes ▪ cooking time 6 hours ▪ serves 8

1 Preheat oven to low. Discard neck and giblets from turkey. Rinse turkey under cold water; pat dry inside and out, tuck wings under body. Spoon stuffing loosely into cavity. Tie legs together with kitchen string.

2 Place turkey into oiled baking tin; pour stock and half of the port into dish. Cover baking dish tightly with greased foil (if thin, use two layers); bake in low oven for 5½ hours. Remove foil, brush turkey with combined remaining port and sugar. Increase temperature to moderate; bake, uncovered, 30 minutes or until browned.

3 Remove turkey from tin; cover with foil to keep warm. Strain juices from tin into jug; remove fat from juices. You will need 3 cups (750ml) pan juices. Heat oil in same baking tin, stir in flour; stir over heat until well browned. Remove from heat, gradually stir in reserved juices; stir over heat until gravy boils and thickens, strain.

4 Serve turkey with gravy.

▪ **sausagemeat stuffing** Heat oil in large frying pan, add onion; cook, stirring, until browned, cool. Transfer onion to medium bowl; stir in remaining ingredients.

turkey with lemon parsley stuffing

4.5kg turkey

50g butter, melted

1 cup (250ml) water

lemon parsley stuffing

125g butter

2 (200g) trimmed celery stalks, chopped finely

8 spring onions, chopped finely

2 cloves garlic, crushed

6 cups (420g) coarse fresh, white breadcrumbs

1 cup coarsely chopped fresh flat-leaf parsley

1 tablespoon finely grated lemon rind

salt and freshly ground black pepper

1 egg, beaten lightly

tips The turkey and the stuffing can be prepared several hours ahead. Stuff turkey just before roasting.

preparation time 40 minutes ■ cooking time 3 hours 20 minutes (plus standing time) ■ serves 8

1   Preheat oven to moderate.

2   Discard neck from turkey. Rinse turkey under cold water; pat dry inside and out with absorbent paper. Fill neck cavity loosely with lemon parsley stuffing; secure skin over opening with toothpicks. Fill large cavity loosely with lemon parsley stuffing; reserve remaining stuffing. Tie legs together with kitchen string; tuck wings under.

3   Place turkey on oiled wire rack in a large flameproof baking dish. Brush turkey all over with half the butter. Rub a little salt into skin. Pour the water into the dish. Cover dish tightly with greased foil; roast in moderate oven for 2 hours. Uncover turkey; brush with remaining butter. Roast, uncovered, in a moderate oven for a further 1 hour or until browned all over and cooked through, brushing with pan juices every 20 minutes. (To test if turkey is cooked, insert a skewer into the thigh; if juices are clear, it is ready.) Remove turkey from dish, cover turkey; stand for 20 minutes while preparing gravy and finishing vegetables.

4   Increase oven temperature to very hot. Lightly oil 12 mini-muffin tins. Place 1 tablespoon of reserved lemon parsley stuffing in each tin. Bake in very hot oven for 10 minutes or until they are browned and crisp.

5   Serve turkey with gravy and seasonal vegetables.

■ **lemon parsley stuffing** Melt the butter in a large frying pan; cook celery, stirring, until softened. Add onion and garlic, cook, stirring, until fragrant. Combine onion mixture in a large bowl with remaining ingredients.

boned turkey breast with couscous stuffing

½ cup (80g) sultanas

½ cup (125ml) lemon juice

4.5kg boned turkey breast

1 cup (250ml) chicken stock

¼ cup (60ml) olive oil

1 cup (200g) couscous

¼ cup (40g) toasted green pumpkin seeds

¼ cup (35g) toasted slivered almonds

¼ cup (35g) toasted pecans, chopped coarsely

¼ cup coarsely chopped fresh flat-leaf parsley

¼ cup coarsely chopped fresh coriander

2 eggs, beaten lightly

1 cup (250ml) water

½ cup (125ml) dry white wine

⅓ cup (50g) plain flour

2 cups (500ml) chicken stock, extra

3 cups (750ml) water, extra

paprika rub

1 teaspoon fennel seeds

1 teaspoon sweet paprika

½ teaspoon ground ginger

2 teaspoons salt

2 cloves garlic, quartered

2 tablespoons olive oil

preparation time 1 hour ■ cooking time 2 hours ■ serves 8–12 (depending on your menu)

1 Soak sultanas in small bowl in half of the juice. Make paprika rub.

2 Preheat oven to moderate.

3 Place turkey flat on board, skin-side down; cover with cling film. Using rolling pin or meat mallet, flatten turkey meat to an even thickness all over.

4 Combine stock, oil and remaining juice in medium saucepan; bring to a boil. Remove from heat; stir in couscous. Cover; stand about 5 minutes or until liquid is absorbed, fluffing with fork occasionally. Transfer couscous mixture to large bowl; stir in sultana mixture, pumpkinseeds, nuts, herbs and egg.

5 With pointed end of turkey breast facing away from you, place couscous stuffing horizontally along centre of turkey meat. Bring the pointed end of breast over stuffing, securing to the neck skin flap with toothpicks. Working from the centre out, continue securing sides of turkey together with toothpicks (you will have a rectangular roll of turkey in front of you). Tie securely with kitchen string at 4cm intervals.

6 Place turkey roll on oiled wire rack in large shallow flameproof baking dish; add the water and wine to dish. Rub turkey roll with paprika rub; cover dish tightly with two layers of greased foil. Roast in moderate oven 1 hour. Uncover; roast in moderate oven about 45 minutes or until turkey roll is cooked though. Transfer turkey roll to large serving platter; cover to keep warm.

7 Place dish with juice over heat, add flour; cook, stirring, until mixture bubbles and is well browned. Gradually stir in the extra stock and the extra water; bring to a boil. Reduce heat; simmer, stirring, until gravy boils and thickens. Strain gravy into large jug; serve with turkey.

■ paprika rub Using mortar and pestle, crush ingredients until smooth.

pomegranate-glazed turkey
with cornbread stuffing

4kg turkey

20g butter

6 shallots (150g)

1 large apple (200g), cut into 6 wedges

1 tablespoon fresh sage leaves

20 black peppercorns

2 cups (500ml) water

1 cup (250ml) chicken stock

½ cup (125ml) brandy

50g butter, melted

½ cup (125ml) pomegranate molasses

2 tablespoons plain flour

macerated fruit

¼ cup (35g) coarsely chopped dried apricots

¼ cup (35g) currants

⅓ cup (80ml) brandy

tips The cornbread stuffing can be made a day ahead.

preparation time 1 hour 30 minutes ▪ cooking time 3 hours 30 minutes (plus cooling and standing time) ▪ serves 8–12 (depending on your menu)

1 Two days before, make macerated fruit.

2 On the day of roasting the turkey, preheat oven to moderate.

3 Discard neck from turkey. Rinse turkey under cold water; pat dry inside and out with absorbent paper.

4 Heat butter in large saucepan; cook whole shallots and apple, stirring, until browned lightly. Cool 10 minutes; stir in sage and peppercorns. Tuck wings under turkey; fill large cavity loosely with stuffing; tie legs together with kitchen string.

5 Place turkey on oiled wire rack in large shallow flameproof baking dish; pour the water, stock and brandy into dish. Brush all over with melted butter; cover dish tightly with two layers of greased foil. Roast in moderate oven 2 hours 10 minutes.

6 Meanwhile, make cornbread stuffing.

7 Uncover turkey; brush with half of the molasses. Roast, uncovered, in moderate oven about 20 minutes or until browned all over and cooked through, brushing frequently with remaining molasses. Remove from dish, cover; stand 20 minutes.

8 Pour juice from dish into large jug; skim 1 tablespoon of the fat from juice, return to same dish. Skim and discard remaining fat from juice. Add flour to dish; cook, stirring, until mixture bubbles and is well browned. Gradually stir in juice; bring to a boil, stirring, until gravy boils and thickens. Strain gravy into same jug; serve turkey with cornbread stuffing and gravy.

▪ **macerated fruit** Combine ingredients in small glass jar, cover; stand at room temperature for two days.

cornbread stuffing

350g chorizo, chopped finely

1 medium brown onion (150g),
chopped coarsely

2 shallots (50g), chopped coarsely

1 large apple (200g), chopped
coarsely

1 tablespoon fresh sage leaves, torn

2 cups (500ml) apple juice

3½ cups (340g) coarsely chopped
stale cornbread

⅔ cup (180g) macerated fruit

cornbread stuffing Line
7cm x 21cm loaf tin with baking
parchment, extending it 5cm over
long sides. Cook chorizo in large
frying pan, stirring, until browned
lightly. Add onion and shallot;
cook, stirring, until onion softens.
Add apple; cook, stirring, until
browned lightly. Remove from
heat; stir in sage, juice, cornbread
and macerated fruit. Place stuffing
in prepared tin in oven alongside
turkey; cook, uncovered, in
moderate oven during last
30 minutes of turkey roasting time.

asian-spiced turkey
with cranberry & peach chutney

4kg turkey

2 tablespoons sichuan peppercorns

2 star anise

1 tablespoon coriander seeds

1 tablespoon cumin seeds

2 teaspoons salt

2 teaspoons dried chilli flakes

1 teaspoon ground ginger

1 teaspoon five-spice powder

⅓ cup (80ml) olive oil

cranberry & peach chutney

7 large peaches (1.5kg)

1 cup (250ml) cider vinegar

¼ cup (60ml) lemon juice

1 cup (150g) dried cranberries

1 small brown onion (80g), chopped finely

½ teaspoon ground cinnamon

½ teaspoon ground cloves

½ teaspoon ground ginger

preparation time 25 minutes ■ **cooking time 2 hours** ■ **serves 8–12 (depending on your menu)**

1 Discard neck from turkey. Rinse turkey under cold water; pat dry inside and out with absorbent paper. Using kitchen scissors, cut along each side of turkey's backbone; discard backbone. Turn turkey skin-side up; using heel of hand, press down on breastbone to flatten turkey.

2 Using mortar and pestle, crush peppercorns, star anise, seeds and salt until crushed coarsely. Dry-fry peppercorn mixture with chilli, ginger and five-spice, in small frying pan, until fragrant. Remove from heat; stir in oil. Rub all over turkey.

3 Place turkey in a preheated moderate oven for about 2 hours or until cooked through. (To test if turkey is cooked, insert a skewer into the thigh; if juices are clear, it is ready.)

4 Meanwhile, make cranberry and peach chutney.

5 Serve turkey with chutney.

■ **cranberry & peach chutney** Place peaches in large bowl, cover with boiling water for 30 seconds; drain, peel, seed. Chop peaches coarsely, combine in medium saucepan with remaining ingredients; bring to a boil. Reduce heat; simmer, uncovered, stirring occasionally, about 1¼ hours or until chutney thickens.

tips Chutney can be made up to three months ahead and stored in sterilised jars ■ You can ask your butcher to butterfly the turkey for you if you wish.

4 duck breast fillets (800g),
trimmed
2 fresh long red chillies,
sliced thinly
8 chicken drumsticks (1.2kg)
2 x 500g poussins, quartered
4 quails (800g), halved
⅓ cup (80ml) kecap manis
(Indonesian sweet soy sauce)
¼ cup (90g) honey
300g cherry tomatoes on
the vine
100g baby spinach leaves

lemon dressing
1 teaspoon ground cumin
2 teaspoons ground coriander
½ cup (125ml) olive oil
¾ cup (180ml) lemon juice

lemon dressing
Dry-fry cumin and coriander
in small heated frying
pan, stirring, until fragrant.
Combine spice mixture in
small jug with oil and juice.

chargrilled poultry platter with lemon dressing

preparation time 20 minutes (plus refrigeration time)
cooking time 30 minutes **serves 8**

1 Make lemon dressing.
2 Combine duck in medium bowl with ¼ cup of the dressing
and half of the chilli; toss duck to coat in chilli marinade.
Combine chicken, poussins and quail in large bowl with
remaining dressing; toss to coat in lemon marinade. Cover
each bowl; refrigerate 3 hours or overnight.
3 Drain duck over small bowl; reserve chilli marinade. Drain
chicken, poussins and quail over medium bowl; reserve lemon
marinade. Cook chicken, poussins and quail, in batches, on
heated oiled grill plate (or grill) until cooked through. During
cooking, brush chicken with reserved lemon marinade,
poussins with ¼ cup of the kecap manis, and quail with
honey. Brush duck with reserved chilli marinade; cook as
desired.
4 Cook tomatoes on same heated oiled grill plate about
5 minutes or until just softened.
5 Cut duck into thick slices. Place spinach on large serving
platter; arrange poultry and tomatoes on platter. Sprinkle
duck with remaining chilli; drizzle poussins with remaining
kecap manis.

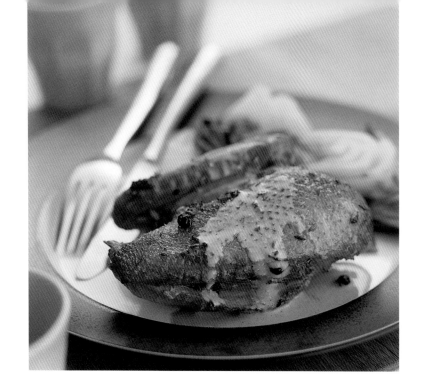

tips A duck wing portion consists of the wing and part of the breast.

garlic roasted duck

2 tablespoons fish sauce

4 cloves garlic, crushed

1 cup (250ml) red wine vinegar

1 large brown onion (200g), coarsely chopped

2 teaspoons juniper berries, bruised

2 teaspoons fennel seeds

4 duck wing portions (1.5kg)

2 tablespoons plain yogurt

preparation time 30 minutes ■ cooking time 50 minutes ■ serves 4

1 Combine fish sauce, garlic, vinegar, onion, berries and seeds in medium bowl. Place duck in single layer in shallow dish; pour over vinegar mixture. Cover dish; refrigerate for 3 hours or overnight.

2 Preheat oven to moderate. Remove duck from marinade; reserve marinade.

3 Place duck, skin-side up, on wire rack over baking dish; bake, uncovered, in moderate oven about 45 minutes or until tender.

4 Place reserved marinade in small saucepan; simmer, uncovered, about 5 minutes or until slightly thickened, strain. Stir yogurt into sauce; serve with duck.

perfect roasts

Roasts are a relatively simple affair, but a few shared tips and tricks will guarantee lip-smacking results.

◼ Remove any silver sinew from beef fillet to prevent shrinkage and toughening

◼ Select a baking dish large enough to fit the roast; make sure the meat does not extend over the sides.

◼ A rack in a baking dish helps good circulation of heat around the meat.

◼ The meat should have reached room temperature before cooking.

◼ Meat can be cooked in an oven bag to prevent spatter and retain moisture; roasting times may need to be reduced, so follow instructions on packaging.

◼ When tying a roast, wet the kitchen string first. As the string dries (from the heat of the oven) it will shrink, holding the meat firm.

◼ Before heating the oven, check that the oven racks are in position.

◼ Very large cuts of meat will need to be turned halfway through roasting.

◼ The best way to tell if a roast is done is to use a meat thermometer. Insert the thermometer into the thickest part of the joint. Be careful not to touch any bone as this will give you an inaccurate reading. The reading should be 60°C for rare, 70°C for medium and 75°C for well-done.

◼ Rest the roast, covered in foil, for 10 to 15 minutes before carving, so that the juices 'settle'.

◼ Carve meat across the grain to ensure tenderness. While carving, hold meat with tongs rather than a fork to prevent juice loss. The best type of knife to use for carving is one with a straight edge, rather than a serrated edge.

■ Fill chicken or turkey cavity loosely with stuffing just before roasting; it will swell during cooking. Secure cavity closed with toothpicks or small skewers. Leftover stuffing can be moistened with a little stock and cooked in lightly oiled mini muffin tins, or formed into a roll and wrapped in lightly oiled foil. Bake the extra stuffing with the roast for the last 20 minutes of cooking time.

■ Before roasting a chicken or a turkey, wash it well in cold water, especially inside the cavity. Pat dry inside and out with paper towelling.

■ Do not freeze an uncooked, stuffed chicken or turkey. Bird and stuffing can be frozen separately, then thawed before filling with stuffing.

■ Baste a roast chicken or turkey only occasionally – frequent basting will result in a pale coloured bird.

■ If using a frozen turkey, allow up to three days to thaw in refrigerator.

■ Tuck wing tips under the body of chicken; tie legs together with string to help bird keep its shape during roasting.

■ To test if roast is cooked, prick the thigh flesh where it meets the body with a metal skewer; if the juice that runs out is clear, it's cooked.

■ To thaw turkey, cut a small corner off the bag in which it is frozen, place turkey in dish. Stand turkey on slight angle so liquid will drain out of the bag as bird defrosts. Discard the liquid from the dish as it accumulates.

■ If keeping a cooked chicken overnight, remove any stuffing from the cavity and refrigerate separately.

honey-glazed pork with sage

2.5kg boned loin of pork

2 teaspoons vegetable oil

1 tablespoon salt

2 cloves garlic, crushed

1 tablespoon finely chopped fresh sage

⅓ cup (90g) honey, warmed

1 tablespoon red wine vinegar

2 cups (500ml) chicken stock

2 tablespoons cornflour

2 tablespoons water

tips Ask your butcher to remove the rind completely from the pork loin and score it.

preparation time 30 minutes ■ cooking time 2 hours 30 minutes ■ serves 8

1 Preheat oven to very hot. Lay pork rind, fat-side down, on wire rack in large flameproof baking dish; rub oil and salt into it. Bake, uncovered, in very hot oven about 30 minutes or until the crackling is crisp and browned; cool. Discard fat from baking dish.

2 Lay pork, fat-side down, on board; sprinkle with half of the garlic and half of the sage. Roll pork to enclose sage and garlic; secure with kitchen string at 2cm intervals.

3 Place pork on wire rack in large flameproof baking dish. Reduce oven temperature to moderately hot; bake pork, uncovered, 30 minutes. Cover pork with foil, reduce oven temperature to moderate; bake 1 hour.

4 Combine honey, vinegar and remaining sage and garlic in small bowl. Remove foil from pork, brush pork with half of the honey mixture. Bake pork, uncovered, 30 minutes or until browned and cooked through, brushing occasionally with remaining honey mixture. Remove pork from dish; cover with foil.

5 Strain pan juices from baking dish into heatproof jug; remove fat from pan juices (you will need ⅔ cup of pan juices). Add stock to baking dish with pan juices. Stir in combined cornflour and water; stir until sauce boils and thickens. Serve pork slices with sauce and crackling.

rack of pork with apple sauce

coarse salt

1.3kg pork rack (6 cutlets)

1.25kg firm-fleshed potatoes

750g squash, chopped coarsely

1 tablespoon olive oil

apple sauce

3 large green apples (600g)

¼ cup (60ml) water

4 fresh sage leaves

1 teaspoon sugar

preparation time 30 minutes ■ cooking time 1 hour
30 minutes ■ serves 6

1 Preheat oven to very hot. Rub salt evenly into rind of pork.
Cover bones with foil to prevent burning. Place pork, rind-side
up, in large baking dish; bake, uncovered, in very hot oven
about 35 minutes or until rind is blistered and browned.
2 Place potatoes and squash in separate baking dish, drizzle
with oil. Reduce oven temperature to moderate; bake pork
and vegetables, uncovered, about 40 minutes or until pork is
cooked through. Remove pork from dish; cover with foil
to keep warm.
3 Increase oven temperature to very hot; bake vegetables
for 15 minutes or until browned and tender. Serve pork with
vegetables and apple sauce.

■ apple sauce Peel and core apples; cut into thick slices.
Combine apple, the water and sage in medium saucepan;
simmer, uncovered, about 10 minutes or until apple is soft.
Remove from heat, stir in sugar.

herbed beef fillet with horseradish cream sauce

1 tablespoon finely grated lemon rind

⅓ cup (80ml) lemon juice

1 teaspoon dried chilli flakes

3 cloves garlic, crushed

¼ cup coarsely chopped fresh
flat-leaf parsley

¼ cup loosely packed fresh
oregano leaves

¼ cup coarsely chopped fresh basil

¼ cup loosely packed fresh
marjoram leaves

⅓ cup (80ml) olive oil

2kg piece beef tenderloin

horseradish cream sauce

1 tablespoon olive oil

2 cloves garlic, crushed

2 teaspoons plain flour

½ cup (125ml) dry white wine

½ cup (140g) horseradish cream

600ml cream

preparation time 15 minutes ■ cooking time 40 minutes ■ serves 8

1 Preheat oven to moderately hot.

2 Combine rind, juice, chilli, garlic, herbs and oil in large bowl, add beef; roll beef to coat in herb mixture. Place beef on oiled wire rack in large shallow baking dish. Roast, uncovered, in moderately hot oven about 40 minutes or until cooked as desired. Cover beef; stand 10 minutes.

3 Meanwhile, make horseradish cream sauce.

4 Serve sliced beef with sauce.

■ **horseradish cream sauce** Heat oil in small frying pan; cook garlic and flour, stirring, until mixtures bubbles and browns lightly. Gradually stir in wine; bring to a boil, stirring. Reduce heat; simmer, uncovered, until liquid reduces by half. Stir in horseradish and cream; simmer, stirring, about 5 minutes or until sauce thickens slightly.

spiced beef with chilli jam

1 tablespoon cumin seeds

1 tablespoon coriander seeds

1 teaspoon cardamom seeds

750g beef eye fillet

chilli jam

2 tablespoons olive oil

2 medium red peppers (400g), chopped

2 small tomatoes (260g), chopped

3 small brown onions (300g), chopped

4 red thai chillies, deseeded, chopped

3 cloves garlic, crushed

½ cup (125ml) white wine vinegar

½ cup (110g) caster sugar

¼ cup (50g) brown sugar

1 tablespoon balsamic vinegar

preparation time 20 minutes ■ cooking time 45 minutes ■ serves 4

1 Place seeds in a dry frying pan; stir over low heat until fragrant. Grind or blend spices until crushed.

2 Roll beef in spices, cover; refrigerate beef 3 hours or overnight.

3 Preheat oven to moderate. Place beef in oiled baking dish; bake, uncovered, in moderate oven about 45 minutes or until cooked as desired. Stand, covered, 10 minutes before carving.

4 Serve beef with chilli jam.

■ chilli jam Heat oil in large saucepan, add pepper, tomato, onion, chilli and garlic; cook, stirring, over low heat, about 20 minutes or until pepper is soft. Add white wine vinegar and caster sugar; stir over heat, without boiling, until sugar dissolves. Simmer, uncovered, about 15 minutes or until mixture is thick. Stir in brown sugar and balsamic vinegar; blend or process mixture until roughly chopped. Spoon into hot sterilised jar, seal while hot; cool, refrigerate.

middle-eastern lamb
with olive couscous stuffing

2kg leg of lamb, butterflied

1 tablespoon olive oil

⅓ cup (80ml) orange juice

½ teaspoon ground cinnamon

¼ cup (90g) honey

2 cloves garlic, crushed

1½ tablespoons cornflour

2 cups (500ml) beef stock

olive couscous stuffing

½ cup (100g) couscous

½ cup (125ml) boiling water

20g butter

1 small white onion (80g), chopped finely

1 teaspoon ground cumin

2 tablespoons flaked almonds, toasted

1 small apple (130g), peeled, cored,
chopped coarsely

1 tablespoon brown sugar

¼ cup (40g) coarsely chopped pitted
black olives

tips Ask your butcher to
butterfly the leg of lamb for you.

preparation time 30 minutes ■ cooking time 1 hour 30 minutes ■ serves 6

1 Preheat oven to moderate.

2 Place lamb on board, pound with meat mallet until lamb is an even thickness. Place olive couscous stuffing in centre of lamb; roll up from short side to enclose the stuffing.

3 Secure lamb with skewers, tie with kitchen string at 2cm intervals. Place lamb on wire rack in baking dish, brush with oil. Bake, uncovered, in moderate oven 1 hour.

4 Combine juice, cinnamon, honey and garlic in small bowl; brush a little juice mixture over lamb. Return lamb to moderate oven for 30 minutes or until tender; baste with remaining juice mixture several times during cooking. Remove lamb from dish; stand, covered, 10 minutes before carving.

5 Meanwhile, blend cornflour with a little of the stock in small bowl; stir into juices in baking dish with remaining stock. Stir over heat until mixture boils and thickens; strain. Serve with lamb.

■ olive couscous stuffing Combine couscous and the water in heatproof bowl; stand, covered, 5 minutes or until all the liquid has been absorbed. Meanwhile, heat butter in small frying pan, add onion; cook, stirring, until soft. Add cumin, nuts, apple, sugar and olives; cook, stirring, about 3 minutes or until apple is softened slightly. Stir in couscous; cool.

boned shoulder of lamb with coriander hazelnut pesto

preparation time 20 minutes ■ cooking time 1 hour 45 minutes ■ serves 6

⅓ cup (50g) unroasted hazelnuts

½ cup firmly packed fresh coriander leaves

⅓ cup firmly packed fresh basil leaves

1 tablespoon grated fresh ginger

5 cloves garlic, crushed

2 tablespoons lime juice

2 teaspoons fish sauce

1 teaspoon brown sugar

2 tablespoons olive oil

1.7kg lamb shoulder, boned

tips Ask the butcher to bone the lamb shoulder for you.

1 Preheat oven to moderately hot. Spread nuts in a single layer on oven tray; toast, uncovered, in moderately hot oven about 5 minutes or until skins begin to flake. Rub hazelnuts in soft cloth to remove skins; cool.

2 Reduce oven temperature to moderate. Blend or process nuts, herbs, ginger, garlic, juice, sauce and sugar until pureed. With motor operating, pour in oil; process until pesto thickens.

3 Spread lamb with half of the pesto. Roll from short side to enclose pesto; secure lamb with skewers, tie with kitchen string at 2cm intervals.

4 Place lamb on wire rack in large baking dish. Spread remaining pesto onto outside of lamb.

5 Bake, uncovered, in moderate oven about 1¾ hours or until cooked as desired. Stand lamb, covered, 10 minutes before carving.

fig & orange glazed ham

8kg cooked leg ham
60 whole cloves (approx.)

fig & orange glaze
1 cup (320g) fig jam
2 tablespoons dijon mustard
⅓ cup (80ml) orange juice
2 tablespoons brandy

**preparation time 20 minutes ■ cooking time
1 hour 15 minutes ■ serves 16**

1 Cut a circle in rind of ham about 10cm from shank end. To remove rind, run your thumb around edges of rind just under skin. Start pulling rind from widest edge of ham; continue to pull rind carefully away from fat up to cut at shank end. Use reserved rind to cover the cut surface of ham to keep it moist during storage.

2 Preheat oven to moderate. Using a sharp knife, score across fat at about 3cm intervals, cutting just through surface of fat. Do not cut deeply into fat, or it will spread apart during cooking. Score in opposite direction to make a diamond pattern; stud with cloves.

4 Place ham on wire rack in large baking dish; cover shank with foil. Brush ham with half of the fig and orange glaze; bake, uncovered, in moderate oven about 1¼ hours or until browned, brushing often with remaining glaze during cooking.

■ **fig & orange glaze** Combine jam, mustard, juice and brandy in small saucepan; stir over low heat, without boiling, until jam melts.

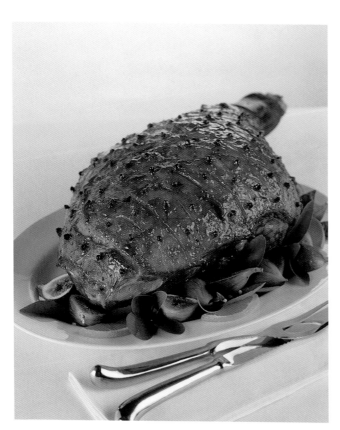

asian-style baked ham

7kg cooked leg of ham
1 cup (250ml) soy sauce
¾ cup (180ml) dry sherry
⅓ cup (75g) firmly packed
brown sugar
⅓ cup (120g) honey
2 teaspoons red food colouring
4 cloves garlic, crushed
2 teaspoons five-spice powder
60 cloves (approx.)

tips As an alternative to the
Asian flavours used above, a glaze
of orange, ginger and maple syrup
also goes beautifully with this
ham. Combine 1 cup maple syrup,
1 cup fresh orange juice, ⅓ cup
orange marmalade, ¼ cup grated
fresh ginger and 2 teaspoons
finely grated orange rind in
small saucepan; bring to a boil.
Reduce heat; simmer, uncovered,
15 minutes then strain before
brushing over ham during baking.

preparation time 15 minutes (plus refrigeration time)
■ cooking time 1 hour 30 minutes ■ serves 8–12
(depending on your menu)

1 Cut through rind about 10cm from shank end of leg in
decorative pattern; run thumb around edge of rind just under
skin to remove rind. Start pulling rind from shank end to
widest edge of ham; discard rind.
2 Using sharp knife, make shallow cuts in one direction
diagonally across fat at 3cm intervals, then shallow-cut in
opposite direction, forming diamonds. Do not cut through top
fat or fat will spread apart during cooking.
3 Combine soy, sherry, sugar, honey, colouring, garlic and
five-spice in small bowl. Place ham on wire rack in large
baking dish; brush ham with soy mixture. Centre a clove in
each diamond shape, cover; refrigerate overnight.
4 Preheat oven to moderate.
5 Place ham on wire rack in large baking dish; pour
marinade into small jug. Cover ham with greased foil; bake
in moderate oven 1 hour. Uncover; bake in moderate oven
about 30 minutes or until ham is lightly caramelised, brushing
frequently with marinade during cooking.

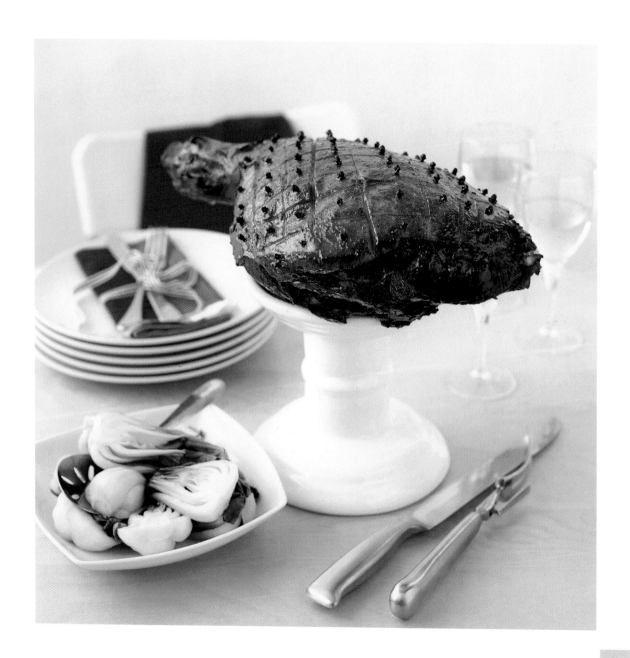

straight to the sauce . . .

A good sauce can turn a plain roast into something sublime. These recipes will ensure your roasts are unforgettable.

gravy

makes 2 cups (500ml)

1 small brown onion (80g), chopped finely
2 tablespoons plain flour
½ cup (125ml) dry red wine
1½ cups (375ml) chicken or beef stock

1 Remove roast from baking dish, cover to keep warm. Reserve 2 tablespoons of juices in baking dish; discard remaining juice.
2 Add onion to dish; cook, stirring, until soft. Stir in flour; cook, stirring, about 5 minutes or until browned. Pour in wine and stock; cook over high heat, stirring, until gravy boils and thickens. Strain gravy before serving.

tips To adapt this gravy into peppercorn or mushroom gravy, place strained gravy in small saucepan; add 1 tablespoon drained canned green peppercorns or 100g finely sliced cooked button mushrooms. Cook, stirring, for 2 minutes.

devilled sauce

makes 2 cups (500ml)

1 tablespoon olive oil
1 medium brown onion (150g), chopped finely
2 cloves garlic, crushed
1 teaspoon hot paprika
¼ cup (50g) firmly packed brown sugar
⅓ cup (80ml) cider vinegar
1 teaspoon Tabasco sauce
1 tablespoon Worcestershire sauce
2 cups (500ml) beef stock
1 tablespoon cornflour
1 tablespoon water

1 Heat oil in medium frying pan, add onion and garlic; cook, stirring, until onion is soft. Stir in paprika, sugar and vinegar; cook, stirring, without boiling, until sugar dissolves.
2 Add sauces and stock; simmer, uncovered, about 15 minutes or until reduced to 2 cups. Stir in blended cornflour and water; stir until sauce boils and thickens.

traditional mint sauce

makes 1¼ cups (310ml)

1 cup (250ml) cider vinegar

¼ cup (60ml) boiling water

¼ cup finely chopped fresh mint leaves

1 tablespoon brown sugar

1 teaspoon salt

¼ teaspoon ground black pepper

1   Combine ingredients in small bowl; stand 30 minutes before serving.

apple sauce

makes 1 cup (250ml)

2 small apples (260g)

2 tablespoons sugar

½ cup (125ml) water

pinch ground cinnamon

1   Peel apples; cut into quarters. Remove core; slice apple.

2   Combine apple, sugar, water and cinnamon in small pan, cover; bring to a boil. Reduce heat; simmer, covered, about 5 minutes or until apple is pulpy. Whisk until sauce is smooth.

salt-crusted ocean trout
with thai-flavours hollandaise

2kg cooking salt

3 egg whites

2.4kg whole ocean trout

thai-flavours hollandaise

10cm stick (20g) fresh lemon grass

2 tablespoons water

½ cup (125ml) white wine vinegar

1 tablespoon lemon juice

1 teaspoon black peppercorns

1 tablespoon finely chopped fresh
lemon grass

6 egg yolks

250g butter, melted

2 tablespoons lime juice

4 fresh kaffir lime leaves, shredded
finely

tip Cooking salt is coarser than
table salt, but not as large-flaked
as sea salt: it is sold packaged in
bags in most supermarkets. You'll
need a very large (approximately
30cm x 40cm) baking dish in
order to fit in the whole fish.

preparation time 20 minutes ▓ cooking time 1 hour 15 minutes ▓ serves 8

1 Preheat oven to moderately hot.

2 Combine salt with egg whites in medium bowl (mixture will resemble wet sand).
Spread about half of the salt mixture evenly over base of shallow 30cm x 40cm
baking dish; place fish on salt mixture then cover completely (except for tail) with
remaining salt mixture. Cook fish in moderately hot oven 1 hour.

3 Meanwhile, make thai-flavours hollandaise.

4 Remove fish from oven; break salt crust with heavy knife, taking care not to
cut into fish. Discard salt crust; transfer fish to large serving platter.

5 Carefully remove skin from fish; flake fish into large pieces. Serve fish with
the hollandaise sauce.

▓ Thai-flavours hollandaise Bruise lemon grass stick with side of heavy
knife. Combine lemon grass stick with the water, vinegar, juice and peppercorns
in small saucepan; bring to a boil. Reduce heat; simmer, uncovered, until mixture
reduces to 2 tablespoons. Discard lemon grass stick; stir in chopped lemon grass;
cool 10 minutes. Combine vinegar mixture with egg yolks in medium heatproof
bowl over medium saucepan of simmering water; whisk mixture constantly about
5 minutes or until thickened. Gradually add butter in thin, steady stream, whisking
constantly until mixture thickens. Whisk in juice and lime leaves.

slow-roasted salmon with chili sauce

750g piece salmon fillet, boned,
with skin on
1 tablespoon finely shredded
kaffir lime leaves
¼ cup (55g) caster sugar
2 tablespoons lime juice
2 tablespoons water
1 fresh red thai chilli, deseeded,
chopped finely
1 tablespoon coarsely chopped
fresh coriander

preparation time 10 minutes ■ **cooking time 35 minutes** ■ **serves 4**

1 Preheat oven to very low. Cook fish on heated oiled grill plate until browned both sides. Place fish in large oiled baking dish, sprinkle with lime leaves; bake, covered tightly, in very low oven about 30 minutes or until cooked as desired.
2 Meanwhile, combine sugar, juice and the water in small saucepan; stir over heat, without boiling, until sugar dissolves. Simmer, uncovered, without stirring, 2 minutes; cool slightly, stir in chilli and coriander.
3 Serve fish drizzled with chilli sauce.

roasted pesto salmon

preparation time 20 minutes ■ cooking time 45 minutes
■ serves 8

1 cup loosely packed fresh basil leaves

2 cloves garlic, chopped coarsely

2 tablespoons toasted pine nuts

2 tablespoons lemon juice

¼ cup (60ml) olive oil

1.5kg piece salmon fillet, skin on

2 tablespoons olive oil, extra

2 large red peppers (700g), chopped coarsely

1 large red onion (300g), chopped coarsely

1 Preheat oven to moderately low.

2 Blend or process basil, garlic, nuts and juice until
combined. With motor operating, gradually add oil in thin,
steady stream until pesto thickens slightly.

3 Place fish, skin-side down, on piece of lightly oiled foil
large enough to completely enclose fish; coat fish with half
of the pesto. Gather corners of foil together above fish; twist
to enclose securely. Place parcel on oven tray; roast
in moderately low oven about 45 minutes or until cooked
as desired.

4 Meanwhile, heat extra oil in large frying pan; cook pepper
and onion, stirring, until onion softens.

5 Place fish parcel on serving platter, unwrap; top with onion
mixture, drizzle with remaining pesto.

tips If the pesto is a little too thick for
your liking, thin it down with a little olive oil
before drizzling over the salmon.

vegetables

warm potato salad with caperberries

2kg firm-fleshed potatoes, unpeeled, diced into 2cm pieces

1 tablespoon dijon mustard

2 tablespoons red wine vinegar

½ cup (125ml) extra virgin olive oil

1 small white onion (80g), sliced thinly

¼ cup firmly packed fresh flat-leaf parsley leaves

2 tablespoons fresh dill sprigs

1 cup (200g) cornichons, halved lengthways

½ cup (80g) drained large caperberries, rinsed

preparation time 10 minutes ■ cooking time 15 minutes ■ serves 8

1 Boil, steam or microwave potatoes until just tender; drain.

2 Meanwhile, whisk mustard, vinegar and oil in large bowl until combined. Add hot potatoes to bowl with onion, herbs, cornichons and caperberries; toss gently to combine.

perfect roast potatoes

preparation time 15 minutes
cooking time 55 minutes ■ serves 8

12 medium desirée potatoes (2.5kg),
halved lengthways
⅓ cup (80ml) olive oil

1 Preheat oven to hot. Oil shallow
baking tin.
2 Boil, steam or microwave potatoes
5 minutes; drain. Pat dry with absorbent
paper; cool for 10 minutes.
3 Rake rounded sides of potato gently
with tines of fork; place potatoes,
cut-side down, in single layer, in
prepared tin. Brush with oil; roast,
uncovered, in hot oven about
50 minutes or until potatoes are
browned lightly and crisp.

mediterranean
potato mash

preparation time 25 minutes ▧ cooking time
20 minutes ▧ serves 8

2.5kg red-skinned potatoes, chopped coarsely

100g butter, softened

1½ cups (375ml) hot milk

½ cup (75g) drained sun-dried tomatoes, chopped coarsely

¼ cup coarsely chopped fresh flat-leaf parsley

balsamic dressing

¼ cup (60ml) balsamic vinegar

2 tablespoons olive oil

1 Boil, steam or microwave potatoes until tender; drain.

2 Meanwhile, make balsamic dressing.

3 Mash potatoes in large bowl with butter and milk until
smooth. Stir in tomato and parsley.

4 Serve mash drizzled with dressing.

balsamic dressing Place ingredients in screw-top jar;
shake well.

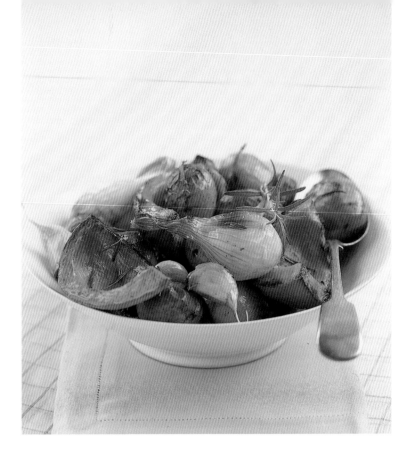

garlic & rosemary roasted vegetables

3 small round squash or
baby turnips (1.2kg)
1.5kg baby new potatoes
800g baby onions, trimmed
8 cloves garlic, unpeeled
2 tablespoons olive oil
¼ cup fresh rosemary

preparation time 10 minutes ▣ **cooking time 1 hour 30 minutes** ▣ **serves 8**

1 Preheat oven to moderate. Cut squash into quarters; remove and discard seeds. Cut each quarter in half.
2 Combine squash, potatoes, onions, garlic, oil and half of the rosemary in large baking dish; bake in moderate oven about 1½ hours or until vegetables are browned and tender. Serve roasted vegetables sprinkled with remaining rosemary.

roasted garlic celeriac

preparation time 10 minutes ■
cooking time 1 hour ■ serves 4

1 large celeriac (1.5kg)
2 tablespoons olive oil
1 medium bulb garlic (70g)
⅓ cup coarsely chopped fresh
flat-leaf parsley
⅓ cup (95g) low-fat plain
yogurt

1 Preheat oven to moderate. Peel
celeriac, cut into 3cm chunks; combine
with oil in large bowl.
2 Place celeriac and unpeeled garlic
bulb on baking-paper-lined oven
tray; bake in moderate oven, turning
occasionally, about 1 hour or until
celeriac is tender and golden brown.
3 Cut garlic bulb in half horizontally,
squeeze garlic pulp from each clove
over celeriac; toss together with parsley.
Serve celeriac topped with yogurt.

balsamic-glazed baby onions

preparation time 10 minutes ■
cooking time 15 minutes ■ serves 8

1 tablespoon balsamic vinegar
1 tablespoon wholegrain mustard
¼ cup (90g) honey
2 tablespoons vegetable oil
500g baby onions, halved

1 Combine vinegar, mustard and honey in small saucepan; bring to a boil. Reduce heat; simmer, uncovered, about 5 minutes or until glaze thickens.
2 Heat oil in large frying pan; cook onion, brushing constantly with glaze, stirring, until browned and cooked as desired.

leeks in vinaigrette

preparation time 20 minutes ■ cooking time 35 minutes ■ serves 8

4 medium leeks (1.4kg)
50g butter, chopped
⅓ cup (80ml) dry white wine
3 cups (750ml) chicken stock

raspberry vinaigrette
150g raspberries
¼ cup (60ml) raspberry vinegar
2 tablespoons olive oil

1 Preheat oven to moderate. Discard root end; trim green section to leave 14cm leek. Remove outer layer of each leek; cut outer layer lengthways into thin strips. Soften strips in saucepan of boiling water; drain.
2 Halve leeks crossways; quarter each piece lengthways. Tie each quarter in the centre with a few leek strips.
3 Combine butter, wine and stock in large baking dish; place leeks in stock mixture. Cook, covered, in moderate oven about 25 minutes or until leeks are tender.
4 Meanwhile, make vinaigrette; drizzle over leeks.

■ raspberry vinaigrette Push berries through sieve into small bowl; discard seeds. Whisk in vinegar and oil.

broccoli polonaise

A 'polonaise', the French interpretation of a classic Polish way of presenting cooked vegetables such as cauliflower, broccoli, asparagus and the like, is a topping of chopped or sieved hard-boiled egg, buttered breadcrumbs and chopped parsley.

preparation time 10 minutes ■ cooking time 10 minutes
■ serves 8

60g butter
1 cup (70g) stale breadcrumbs
4 hard-boiled eggs, chopped finely
¼ cup finely chopped fresh flat-leaf parsley
750g tender-stem broccoli
60g butter, melted

1 Melt butter in large frying pan; cook breadcrumbs, stirring, until browned and crisp. Combine breadcrumbs in small bowl with egg and parsley.
2 Boil, steam or microwave broccoli until just tender; drain.
3 Top broccoli with polonaise mixture then drizzle with the melted butter.

peas with caraway & parmesan

preparation time 35 minutes ▪
cooking time 5 minutes ▪ serves 8

60g butter
1 teaspoon caraway seeds
2 teaspoons finely grated lemon rind
1 small red onion (100g), sliced thinly
4 cups (640g) peas
⅓ cup coarsely chopped fresh flat-leaf parsley
½ cup (40g) finely grated parmesan cheese

1 Melt butter in large frying pan; cook seeds, rind and onion, stirring, until onion softens.
2 Add peas; cook, stirring, until peas are just tender. Stir in parsley; sprinkle with cheese.

baby carrots with orange maple syrup

preparation time 35 minutes ▪ cooking time 20 minutes ▪ serves 8

1.6kg baby carrots
30g butter
2 teaspoons finely grated orange rind
2 tablespoons orange juice
2 tablespoons maple syrup

1 Boil, steam or microwave carrots until just tender.
2 Melt butter in large frying pan; stir rind, juice and syrup in pan until mixture boils. Reduce heat; simmer, uncovered, until syrup mixture thickens slightly. Add drained carrots to pan, stirring gently to coat in orange maple syrup.

peas & beans with hazelnuts

1½ cups (240g) peas

300g fine green beans, trimmed

300g sugar snap peas, trimmed

30g butter

⅓ cup (35g) roasted hazelnuts,
chopped coarsely

1 clove garlic, crushed

salt and freshly ground black pepper

preparation time 15 minutes ▥ **cooking time 12 minutes**
▥ **serves 8**

1 Boil or steam the peas and beans until almost tender; add
the sugar snap peas, cook for a further 30 seconds or until
just tender; drain well.

2 Melt butter in a large frying pan; cook nuts until browned.
Remove nuts from pan with a slotted spoon. Add garlic then
vegetables to pan; toss until combined. Season to taste with
salt and pepper.

3 Serve vegetables topped with nuts.

tips This recipe can
prepared a day ahead;
cook just before serving.

sesame patty-pan squash
& sugar snap peas

16 yellow patty-pan squash (480g)

300g sugar snap peas, trimmed

2 teaspoons sesame oil

1 tablespoon soy sauce

1 tablespoon toasted sesame seeds

preparation time 5 minutes ▓ **cooking time 10 minutes** ▓ **serves 8**

1 Boil, steam or microwave squash and peas, separately, until tender; drain.

2 Place vegetables in large bowl with remaining ingredients; toss gently to combine.

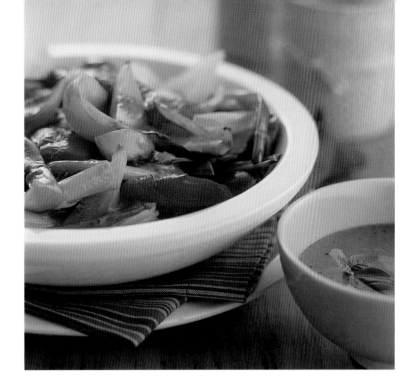

2 medium red peppers (400g)

2 medium green peppers (400g)

2 medium yellow peppers (400g)

10 spring onions

8 cloves garlic

4 small white onions (400g), quartered

1 tablespoon olive oil

port & basil dressing

½ cup (125ml) olive oil

¼ cup (60ml) balsamic vinegar

2 cloves garlic

⅓ cup firmly packed fresh basil leaves

1 tablespoon port

1 tablespoon mild chilli sauce

roasted peppers with port & basil dressing

preparation time 10 minutes ■ cooking time 1 hour ■ serves 8

1 Preheat oven to moderate.

2 Quarter peppers; remove and discard seeds and membranes. Combine with remaining ingredients in large baking dish; bake, uncovered, in moderate oven 1 hour.

3 Serve warm pepper mixture with port and basil dressing.

■ **port & basil dressing** Blend or process ingredients until pureed.

roasted vine tomatoes with crispy basil

preparation time 10 minutes ▧ cooking time 10 minutes ▧ serves 8

500g cherry tomatoes on the vine

2 cloves garlic, sliced thinly

1 tablespoon olive oil

2 teaspoons balsamic vinegar

vegetable oil, for deep-frying

⅓ cup loosely packed fresh basil leaves

1 Preheat oven to moderate. Place tomatoes on oven tray; pour combined garlic, oil and vinegar over tomatoes. Roast, uncovered, in moderate oven about 10 minutes or until tomatoes soften.

2 Meanwhile, heat vegetable oil in small saucepan; deep-fry basil, in batches, until crisp. Serve tomatoes sprinkled with basil.

baby beetroot with caper vinaigrette

preparation time 10 minutes ▧ cooking time 20 minutes ▧ serves 8

1kg baby beetroot

1 tablespoon drained baby capers, rinsed

2 tablespoons white wine vinegar

2 tablespoons olive oil

1 teaspoon dijon mustard

1 Remove stems from beetroot; cook beetroot in large saucepan of boiling water, uncovered, about 20 minutes or until tender. Drain; cool 10 minutes. Peel beetroot.

2 Place beetroot in large bowl with remaining ingredients; toss gently to combine.

tips You need approximately two bunches of baby beetroot for this recipe.

leftovers

turkey rillettes

100g butter

⅓ cup cream

¼ teaspoon hot paprika

2 cups (320g) coarsely chopped cooked turkey meat

½ small red onion, coarsely chopped

¼ cup loosely packed fresh flat-leaf parsley leaves

preparation time 15 minutes ▪ **cooking time 5 minutes** ▪ **serves 4**

1 Melt butter with cream and paprika in small saucepan, stirring over low heat, until combined.

2 Blend or process cooked turkey meat, onion and flat-leaf parsley, pulsing, while adding butter mixture in thin, steady stream.

3 Place rillette mixture in four ½-cup (125ml) dishes, cover; refrigerate until required. Serve with pickled onions, olives and thinly sliced toasted french bread stick.

vietnamese turkey salad

150g mangetout, trimmed

½ cucumber, deseeded and cut into matchsticks

1 medium carrot cut into matchsticks

1 small red pepper, thinly sliced

100g mangetout tendrils

½ cup loosely packed fresh mint leaves

½ cup loosely packed fresh coriander leaves

2 cups (320g) thinly sliced turkey meat

2 tablespoons groundnut oil

2 tablespoons lime juice

1 tablespoon brown sugar

1 tablespoon fish sauce

2 tablespoons coarsely chopped unsalted roasted peanuts

preparation time 20 minutes ▪ cooking time 2 minutes ▪ serves 4

1 Boil, steam or microwave mangetout until just tender; drain. Immediately rinse under cold water; drain.

2 Slice mangetout thinly lengthways; place in large bowl with cucumber, carrot, red pepper, mangetout tendrils, mint, coriander and turkey meat.

3 Place groundnut oil, lime juice, brown sugar and fish sauce in screw-top jar; shake well.

4 Drizzle dressing over salad; toss gently to combine, sprinkle with the chopped peanuts.

ham & egg slice

2 teaspoons olive oil

2 medium brown onions, thinly sliced

2 cloves garlic, crushed

2 cups (360g) finely chopped cooked ham

6 eggs

300ml cream

½ cup finely grated parmesan cheese

¼ cup finely chopped fresh basil

preparation time 15 minutes ■ cooking time 35 minutes ■ serves 8

1 Preheat oven to moderately low. Oil and line base of 20cm x 30cm shallow baking tin.

2 Heat olive oil in medium frying pan; cook onions and garlic, stirring, until onion softens. Cool for 5 minutes.

3 Combine onion mixture in large bowl with ham, eggs, cream, parmesan cheese and basil; pour mixture into prepared tin.

4 Bake, uncovered, in moderately low oven about 30 minutes or until set.

salmon, pea & mint linguine

375g linguine (or any long flat pasta)

1 medium brown onion, finely chopped

1 clove garlic, crushed

½ cup chicken stock

½ cup water

¼ cup dry white wine

1 cup (120g) frozen peas

2 cups (400g) flaked cooked salmon

⅓ cup coarsely chopped fresh mint

preparation time 10 minutes ■ **cooking time 15 minutes** ■ **serves 4**

1 Cook linguine in large saucepan of boiling water, uncovered, until just tender.

2 Meanwhile, cook onion and garlic in oiled large frying pan until onion softens.

3 Add chicken stock, water and wine, reduce heat; simmer, uncovered, until liquid reduces by one third.

4 Add peas, salmon and mint; stir until just heated through. Add to drained pasta; toss gently to combine.

goat's cheese & roast veggie tart

preparation time 15 minutes
■ cooking time 20 minutes ■
serves 4

1 ready-rolled butter puff pastry
sheet
2 cloves garlic, crushed
2 tablespoons fresh oregano leaves
3 cups (500g) coarsely chopped
roasted vegetables
1 medium plum tomato, coarsely
chopped
150g goat's cheese, crumbled

1 Preheat oven to very hot. Line
oven tray with baking parchment.
Place pastry sheet on prepared
tray; spread with crushed garlic,
sprinkle with oregano.
2 Top with roasted vegetables,
tomato and goat's cheese.
3 Bake, uncovered, in very hot
oven about 20 minutes or until
pastry is browned lightly; sprinkle
with 1 tablespoon fresh oregano
leaves.

turkey salad sandwiches

preparation time 15 minutes ■ serves 4

1 cup (150g) finely chopped cooked turkey meat
1 celery stalk, trimmed and finely chopped
30g baby rocket leaves, finely chopped
2 tablespoons toasted slivered almonds, coarsely chopped
¼ cup sour cream
¼ cup whole-egg mayonnaise
1 tablespoon lemon juice
8 slices wholemeal bread

Combine turkey, celery, rocket, almonds, sour cream, mayonnaise and lemon juice
in small bowl. Spread turkey mixture over slices of bread; top with the other slices.

christmas cake cream parfaits

preparation time 20 minutes ▣ **serves 6**

250g mascarpone
2 tablespoons whisky
1 tablespoon icing sugar
½ cup whipping cream
2 cups (300g) crumbled Christmas cake
2½ teaspoons whisky extra
raspberries and sifted icing sugar, optional

1 Combine mascarpone, 2 tablespoons whisky and icing sugar in large bowl.
2 Beat cream in small bowl until soft peaks form; fold cream into mascarpone mixture.
3 Layer 1 cup crumbled Christmas cake in base of six ¾-cup (180ml) glasses; sprinkle ½ teaspoon whisky over cake in each glass. Divide half of the mascarpone mixture among glasses.
4 Repeat process with another 1 cup crumbled Christmas cake, 2 teaspoons whisky and remaining mascarpone mixture. Cover; refrigerate until required.
5 Serve topped with raspberries and sifted icing sugar, if desired.

christmas cake ice-cream terrine

preparation time 15 minutes (plus freezing time) ▣ **serves 6**

450g Christmas cake
2 tablespoons Cointreau
1 tablespoon finely grated orange rind
2 litres good-quality vanilla ice-cream, softened

1 Line 14cm x 21cm loaf tin with cling film. Cut Christmas cake into 1.5cm slices; brush cake slices with Cointreau.
2 Stir orange rind into ice-cream. Spread half of the ice-cream mixture into prepared tin; top with cake slices then remaining ice-cream. Cover with cling film; freeze until firm.
3 Using hot knife, cut terrine into six slices.

fruit cake 'n' eggnog cheesecake

350g fruit cake, cut into 1cm slices

750g packaged cream cheese, softened

300g sour cream

1 teaspoon vanilla extract

¼ cup (60ml) brandy

½ teaspoon ground nutmeg

2 cups (440g) caster sugar

3 eggs

1 cup (250ml) water

1 medium pink grapefruit (425g),
segmented

1 large orange (300g), segmented

150g strawberries, halved

100g red seedless grapes

1 large kiwifruit (100g), cut into 8 wedges

preparation time 25 minutes (plus cooling and refrigeration time)
▨ cooking time 55 minutes ▨ serves 10

1 Preheat oven to moderate. Line base of 22cm springform tin with baking parchment.

2 Cover base of prepared tin with cake slices. Bake, uncovered, in moderate oven about 10 minutes or until browned lightly. Reduce oven temperature to slow.

3 Meanwhile, beat cream cheese, sour cream, extract, brandy, nutmeg and half of the sugar in medium bowl with electric mixer until smooth. Beat in eggs, one at a time, beat only until combined between each addition.

4 Pour mixture into tin. Bake, uncovered, in slow oven about 45 minutes or until just set. Cool cheesecake in oven with door ajar. Cover; refrigerate overnight.

5 Stir remaining sugar and the water in medium heavy-based frying pan over high heat until sugar dissolves; bring to a boil. Reduce heat; simmer, without stirring, uncovered, about 10 minutes or until toffee mixture is golden brown in colour. Remove from heat; stand until bubbles subside.

6 Meanwhile, remove cheesecake from tin, place on serving plate; top with fruit.

7 Working quickly, drizzle toffee over fruit.

desserts

frosted raspberry cream meringues

8 large white muffin paper cases

6 egg whites

pinch cream of tartar

1½ cups (330g) caster sugar

240g raspberries

1 egg white, beaten lightly, extra

2 tablespoons white sugar

300ml whipping cream

2 tablespoons caster sugar, extra

gold cachous

tips The meringues can be made three days ahead; store in an airtight container in a cool, dry place.

preparation time 30 minutes (plus cooling time) ■ cooking time 1 hour ■ serves 8

1 Preheat oven to very low (120°C/100°C fan-assisted). Line two baking trays with slightly flattened paper cases (or trace four 8cm circles onto each of two sheets of baking parchment; turn paper marked side down onto oven trays).

2 Beat the six egg whites and cream of tartar in a medium bowl with an electric mixer until soft peaks form. Gradually add the 1½ cups caster sugar, beating until dissolved between additions.

3 Spoon meringue into a piping bag fitted with large fluted tube. Pipe meringue inside cases (or circles) to form a base; pipe around the edge to form sides.

4 Bake meringues for 1 hour or until dry and crisp; cool in oven with door ajar.

5 Meanwhile, brush half the raspberries individually with a little of the extra egg white. Toss raspberries in white sugar; place on tray lined with baking parchment. Allow to set for 1 hour or until sugar is dry.

6 Lightly crush the remaining raspberries in a bowl with a fork. Beat the cream and extra caster sugar in a small bowl with an electric mixer until soft peaks form; fold in crushed raspberries.

7 Just before serving, fill meringues with raspberry cream; top with frosted raspberries and cachous. Serve on white paper cases, if desired.

very-berry pavlova

6 egg whites

1 cup (220g) caster sugar

1 tablespoon cornflour

600ml whipping cream

⅓ cup (75g) caster sugar, extra

300g fresh blueberries

360g fresh raspberries

250g strawberries, sliced thinly

2 tablespoons icing sugar

mixed berry coulis

120g fresh blueberries

120g fresh raspberries

120g fresh blackberries

¼ cup (55g) caster sugar

preparation time 20 minutes ■ cooking time 25 minutes (plus cooling and refrigeration time) ■ serves 8

1 Preheat oven to moderate. Grease three oven trays, line with baking parchment; mark a 23cm-diameter circle on each piece of paper.

2 Beat egg whites in medium bowl with electric mixer until soft peaks form. Add sugar, 1 tablespoon at a time, beating until sugar dissolves between each addition; beat in cornflour.

3 Spread meringue over circles on prepared trays; bake, uncovered, in moderate oven 10 minutes. Reduce temperature to low; bake 15 minutes. Cool meringues in oven with door ajar.

4 Meanwhile, make mixed berry coulis.

5 Beat cream and extra sugar in small bowl with electric mixer until firm peaks are formed.

6 Place one meringue on serving plate; flatten slightly. Layer with half of the cream mixture then top with half of the combined berries. Repeat layering with a second meringue, remaining cream and three-quarters of remaining berries, reserving remaining berries for garnish. Cover pavlova; refrigerate 3 hours.

7 Top pavlova with reserved berries, dust with sifted icing sugar; serve with coulis.

■ mixed berry coulis Combine ingredients in medium saucepan, simmer, uncovered, over low heat, about 10 minutes or until berries have softened. Push coulis mixture through sieve into medium bowl; cool. Discard seeds.

An Italian lemon-flavoured liqueur,
limoncello was originally made from the juice
and peel of lemons grown along the coast of
Amalfi. You can substitute it in this recipe,
if you wish, with any lemon-flavoured liqueur
or with an orange-flavoured one such as
Cointreau. You will need approximately five
lemons or oranges for this recipe.

90g butter, softened
1 tablespoon finely grated lemon rind
¾ cup (165g) caster sugar
2 eggs
¾ cup (110g) plain flour
½ cup (75g) self-raising flour
⅓ cup (80ml) milk
⅔ cup (150g) coarsely chopped glacé pineapple
⅔ cup (170g) coarsely chopped glacé apricots
⅔ cup (170g) coarsely chopped glacé peaches
¾ cup (110g) coarsely chopped dried pears
¾ cup (110g) toasted shelled pistachios

lemon syrup
½ cup (125ml) lemon juice
1 cup (220g) caster sugar

limoncello cream
300ml whipping cream
2 tablespoons limoncello liqueur

glacé fruit slice
with limoncello cream

preparation time 30 minutes ▦ cooking time 45 minutes (plus
refrigeration time)

1 Preheat oven to moderately low. Line 20cm x 30cm shallow baking
tin with baking parchment, extending paper 3cm over long sides.
2 Beat butter, rind and sugar in small bowl with electric mixer
until light and fluffy. Add eggs, one at a time, beating well between
additions. Mixture may curdle at this stage, but will come together later.
3 Transfer mixture to large bowl; stir in sifted flours, milk, fruit
and nuts. Spread mixture into prepared tin. Bake, uncovered, in
moderately low oven about 45 minutes.
4 Meanwhile, make lemon syrup.
5 Remove slice from oven; pour hot syrup over hot slice in tin.
Cover; refrigerate overnight.
6 Make limoncello cream.
7 Cut slice into small squares; serve with limoncello cream.

▦ lemon syrup Stir ingredients in small saucepan over heat,
without boiling, until sugar dissolves; bring to a boil. Reduce heat;
simmer, uncovered, without stirring, about 10 minutes or until
thickened slightly.

▦ limoncello cream Beat ingredients in small bowl with electric
mixer until soft peaks form.

gourmet chocolate tart

preparation time 40 minutes (plus refrigeration time) ■ cooking time
30 minutes ■ serves 8

2 eggs

2 egg yolks

¼ cup (55g) caster sugar

250g dark eating chocolate, melted

200g butter, melted

tart shell

1½ cups (225g) plain flour

½ cup (110g) caster sugar

140g cold butter, chopped

1 egg, beaten lightly

1 Make tart shell, baking in moderately hot oven as instructed below then reducing oven temperature to moderate.

2 Whisk eggs, egg yolks and sugar in medium heatproof bowl over medium saucepan of simmering water about 15 minutes or until light and fluffy. Gently whisk chocolate and butter into egg mixture.

3 Pour mixture into shell. Bake, uncovered, in moderate oven about 10 minutes or until filling is set; cool 10 minutes. Refrigerate 1 hour. Serve dusted with cocoa powder, if desired.

■ **tart shell** Blend or process flour, sugar and butter until crumbly; add egg, process until ingredients just come together. Knead dough on floured surface until smooth. Wrap in cling film; refrigerate 30 minutes. Grease 24cm-round loose-base flan tin. Roll dough between sheets of baking parchment until large enough to line tin. Line tin with dough; press into side, trim edge, prick base with fork. Cover; refrigerate 30 minutes. Preheat oven to moderately hot. Place tin on oven tray; cover dough with baking parchment, fill with dried beans or rice. Bake, uncovered, 10 minutes. Remove paper and beans carefully; return to oven and bake, uncovered, about 5 minutes or until tart shell browns lightly. Cool to room temperature.

exotic fruit salad

1 litre (4 cups) water

1 cup (270g) grated palm sugar

1 vanilla pod

2cm piece fresh ginger (10g), chopped
finely

3 star anise

1 tablespoon finely grated lime rind

⅓ cup (80ml) lime juice

½ cup coarsely chopped fresh
vietnamese mint

2 large mangoes (1.2kg), chopped
coarsely

3 star fruit (450g), sliced thinly

2 large oranges (600g), segmented

1 large pineapple (2kg), chopped coarsely

1 medium papaya (1kg), chopped coarsely

½ cup (125ml) passionfruit pulp

12 rambutans (500g), halved

12 lychees (300g), halved

tips You need about six medium
passionfruit for this recipe.

preparation time 20 minutes ■ cooking time 15 minutes (plus cooling and
refrigeration time) ■ serves 8

1 Stir the water and sugar in medium saucepan over high heat until sugar
dissolves; bring to a boil. Reduce heat; simmer without stirring, uncovered,
5 minutes. Split vanilla bean in half lengthways; scrape seeds into pan. Add pod,
ginger and star anise; simmer, uncovered, about 10 minutes or until syrup thickens.
Discard pod; cool to room temperature. Stir in rind, juice and mint.

2 Combine remaining ingredients in large bowl. Pour syrup over fruit; stir gently to
combine. Refrigerate fruit salad, covered, until cold.

fruity christmas bombe
with brandy cream sauce

2 litres vanilla ice-cream, softened

⅓ cup (75g) chopped glacé pineapple

⅓ cup (85g) chopped glacé apricots

⅓ cup (70g) red glacé cherries, halved

¼ cup (50g) chopped glacé ginger

1 teaspoon mixed spice

1 teaspoon ground cinnamon

700g packet rich fruit cake

brandy cream sauce

300ml whipping cream

¼ cup (60ml) brandy

2 eggs, separated

½ cup (110g) caster sugar

brandy cream sauce Beat cream and brandy in small bowl with electric mixer until soft peaks form. Beat egg whites in separate small bowl with electric mixer until soft peaks form, gradually add sugar, beating well between additions. Add egg yolks; beat well. Fold cream mixture into egg white mixture.

preparation time 20 minutes (plus freezing time) ■ **serves 8**

1   Oil 1.75-litre (7-cup) pudding basin, line with cling film.

2   Combine ice-cream, fruit, ginger and spices in large bowl. Spoon mixture into prepared basin, cover; freeze about 1 hour or until firm.

3   Split cake in half, cut halves to fit on top of ice-cream in basin, press on gently. Cover; freeze overnight. Serve with brandy cream sauce.

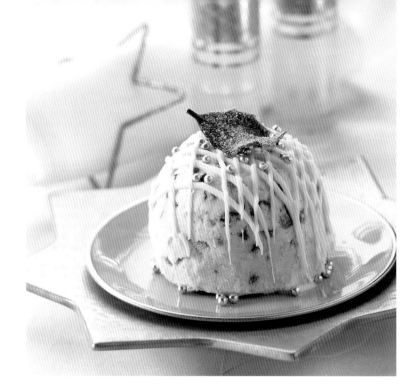

little frozen christmas puddings

2 cups (375g) mixed dried fruit

¼ cup (60g) chopped glacé peaches

¼ cup (60g) chopped glacé apricots

¼ cup (60ml) brandy

¾ cup (110g) macadamias, toasted, chopped finely

1 teaspoon mixed spice

1 teaspoon ground cinnamon

2 litres good quality vanilla ice-cream, softened

150g white eating chocolate, melted

preparation time 20 minutes (plus freezing time) ■ serves 8

1 Combine fruit and brandy in large bowl; cover, let stand overnight.

2 Line bases of eight 1-cup (250ml) freezer-proof moulds (we used tea cups) with baking parchment.

3 Stir nuts, spices and ice-cream into fruit mixture. Divide mixture among prepared moulds, cover; freeze overnight.

4 Turn puddings onto tray, peel away baking parchment. Spoon melted white chocolate into a small plastic bag, then snip off the corner of the bag. Drizzle the melted chocolate over the puddings.

frozen chocolate fruit cake pudding

½ cup (95g) coarsely chopped dried figs

¼ cup (40g) coarsely chopped raisins

¼ cup (50g) coarsely chopped dried prunes

¼ cup (60g) coarsely chopped glacé cherries

4 fresh dates (100g), stoned, chopped coarsely

2 teaspoons finely grated orange rind

½ cup (125ml) brandy

125g butter

½ cup (75g) plain flour

½ cup (110g) firmly packed brown sugar

1 cup (250ml) milk

600ml whipping cream

⅔ cup (220g) chocolate hazelnut spread

1 teaspoon ground nutmeg

1 teaspoon ground cinnamon

4 egg yolks

⅓ cup (50g) toasted hazelnuts, chopped coarsely

200g dark eating chocolate, chopped finely

200g dark eating chocolate, melted, extra

preparation time 40 minutes (plus standing, refrigeration and freezing time)
■ cooking time 10 minutes

1 Combine fruit, rind and brandy in large bowl; mix well. Cover tightly with cling film; store in a cool, dark place overnight or up to a week, stirring every day.

2 Line 17.5cm, 1.75-litre (7-cup) pudding basin with cling film, extending film 5cm over edge of basin.

3 Melt butter in medium saucepan, add flour; stir over heat until bubbling. Remove from heat; stir in sugar then milk and half of the cream. Stir over medium heat until mixture boils and thickens. Transfer to large bowl; stir in spread, spices and yolks. Cover surface of mixture with cling film; refrigerate 1 hour.

4 Stir in fruit mixture, nuts and chopped chocolate. Beat remaining cream in small bowl with electric mixer until soft peaks form, fold into pudding mixture. Spoon mixture into prepared basin, tap basin lightly to remove air bubbles. Cover with foil; freeze 3 hours or overnight.

5 Turn pudding onto tray; remove cling film, return pudding to freezer. Cut a 35cm circle from a piece of paper to use as a guide; cover paper with cling film. Spread melted chocolate over cling film then quickly drape film, chocolate-side down, over pudding. Quickly smooth with hands, avoiding deep pleats in the film. Freeze until firm. Peel away film; trim away excess chocolate. Serve with a selection of fresh and frosted seasonal fruit, if desired.

cakes & puddings

traditional fruit cake

2 cups (300g) currants

2 cups (340g) raisins, chopped coarsely

3 cups (500g) sultanas

½ cup (125ml) dark rum

150g butter

1 cup (200g) firmly packed brown sugar

4 eggs

½ cup (125ml) strawberry jam

1 cup (210g) glacé cherries, chopped

2 cups (340g) mixed peel

1 cup (140g) slivered almonds

2 cups (300g) plain flour

½ cup (75g) self-raising flour

½ teaspoon ground cinnamon

½ teaspoon ground allspice

blanched almonds and extra glacé
cherries, to decorate

¼ cup (60ml) dark rum, extra

preparation time 30 minutes ■ cooking time 3 hours ■ serves 36

1 Combine dried fruit and rum in large bowl, cover; stand overnight.

2 Grease deep 23cm-round cake tin, line base and side with three layers baking parchment, extending paper 5cm above edge of tin.

3 Beat butter and sugar in small bowl with electric mixer until combined. Add eggs, one at a time, beating until just combined between additions; stir in jam. Stir into fruit mixture, then stir in cherries, peel, slivered almonds and sifted dry ingredients.

4 Spread cake mixture into prepared tin; decorate top with blanched almonds and extra glacé cherries, if desired. Bake in low oven about 3 hours.

5 Brush top of hot cake with extra rum, cover tightly with foil; cool in tin.

Lining cake tin

Lining cake tin

Lining cake tin

what you need to know...

Before you begin, quickly read this important information to guarantee
your cake or pudding realises its full and delicious potential.

LINING CAKE TINS

▨ To line the sides of a cake tin, cut three strips of baking parchment long enough
to fit around the tin and 8cm wider than the depth of the tin.

▨ Fold strips lengthways about 2cm from edge and make diagonal cuts about
2cm apart up to the fold. Fit around the curves or corners of the tin, with cut
section resting on the base.

▨ Using base of tin as a guide, cut three paper shapes to cover base of tin;
place paper bases in position.

FILLING CAKE TIN

▨ Spoon small amounts of cake mixture into corners of prepared tin, holding
paper in position. Spread remaining mixture firmly into tin; smooth top with spatula
or damp hand. Hold tin about 15cm above the worksurface; drop tin firmly onto
worksurface to release air bubbles and settle mixture.

TO TEST IF CAKE IS COOKED

▨ After minimum cooking time, feel top of cake with fingertips. If cake feels firm,
gently push a sharp vegetable knife into the thickest part of the cake, as close to
the centre as possible, right through to the base of tin. Gently withdraw knife and
feel the blade; if the blade is simply sticky from fruit, the cake is cooked, but if
there is moist cake mixture on the blade, return the cake to oven for a further
15 minutes before testing again.

WHEN CAKE IS COOKED

■ Make cuts in lining paper level with tin, fold down paper. Cover hot cake with foil, wrap in towel; cool in tin.

TO STORE CAKE

■ When cake has completely cooled, remove from tin. Leaving lining paper intact, wrap in cling film. Place cake in airtight container or plastic freezer bag. Store in a cool place or freeze.

CAKE HINTS

■ The cake mixture can be made ahead – place mixture into prepared tin, cover the surface with cling film and refrigerate for 2 days. Stand mixture about 3 hours to return to room temperature before baking. Cold mixture will take about 30 minutes longer to cook.

TO STORE PUDDINGS

■ If pudding is calico-wrapped, hang pudding for 10 minutes after initial cooking. Remove cloth and allow to cool. Then, for all pudding recipes, wrap cooled pudding in cling film and seal in freezer bag or an airtight container; refrigerate or freeze.

REHEATING PUDDINGS

Three days before you want to use a frozen pudding, place it in the refrigerator to thaw. Remove pudding from refrigerator 12 hours before reheating.

■ **traditional steamed pudding:** Remove cling film, return pudding to steamer and prepare as for cooking method. Steam for 2 hours.

■ **traditional boiled pudding:** Remove cling film and tie a clean, dry, unfloured cloth on pudding. Boil 2 hours as for cooking method. Hang hot pudding 10 minutes, remove cloth. Stand pudding 20 minutes for skin to darken.

■ **pudding in the microwave:** Reheat four single servings at once. Cover with cling film, microwave on HIGH (100%) for up to 1 minute per serving. To reheat whole pudding, cover with cling film, microwave on MEDIUM (50%) about 15 minutes or until hot.

THREE-IN-ONE CHRISTMAS MIX

One quantity of this basic recipe is enough for three of these Christmas recipes – the cake, the pudding (page 94) and the fruit slice (page 96). The mix can be made a month before required, and stored in a the refrigerator. Ideally, the 'chopped' ingredients shown should all be cut to the size of a sultana. Grand Marnier was used in keeping with the citrus content of the mix (you can use any citrus-flavoured liqueur), but it can be substituted with rum, sherry or brandy.

moist christmas cake

preparation time 15 minutes ■ **cooking time 3 hours (plus cooling time)**

½ quantity basic fruit mixture
250g butter, melted, cooled
5 eggs, beaten lightly
2½ cups (375g) plain flour
2 tablespoons Grand Marnier

1 Preheat oven to low. Line base and sides of deep 22cm-square cake tin with one thickness brown paper and two thicknesses baking parchment, extending papers 5cm above sides of tin.
2 Place basic fruit mixture in large bowl. Mix in butter and eggs then sifted flour in two batches.
3 Spread mixture into prepared tin; level top with spatula. Bake, uncovered, in low oven about 3 hours. Brush with liqueur; cover hot cake in tin with foil, cool overnight.

basic fruit mixture

preparation time 45 minutes (plus standing time)

6 cups (1kg) sultanas
2½ cups (375g) currants
2¼ cups (425g) raisins, chopped
1½ cups (250g) stoned dried dates, chopped
1½ cups (250g) stoned prunes, chopped
1¼ cups (250g) glacé cherries, quartered
½ cup (125g) glacé apricots, chopped
½ cup (115g) glacé pineapple, chopped
½ cup (115g) glacé ginger, chopped
¾ cup (120g) mixed peel
3 medium apples (450g), peeled, grated
⅔ cup (240g) fig jam
2 tablespoons finely grated orange rind
¼ cup (60ml) lemon juice
2 cups (440g) firmly packed brown sugar
1 tablespoon mixed spice
1⅓ cups (330ml) Grand Marnier

Mix ingredients in large bowl; cover tightly with cling film. Store mixture in cool, dark place for a month (or longer, if desired) before using; stir mixture every two or three days.

christmas pudding

¼ quantity basic fruit mixture
(see page 92)

250g butter, melted, cooled

3 eggs, beaten lightly

4 cups (280g) stale breadcrumbs

¼ cup (35g) plain flour

tips For tips on how to store
and reheat your pudding, see page
91 ▪ You need a 60cm square of
unbleached calico for the pudding
cloth. If calico has not been used
before, soak overnight in cold water;
next day, boil it for 20 minutes then
rinse in cold water.

preparation time 15 minutes ▪ cooking time 4 hours (plus standing time)

1 Place basic fruit mixture in large bowl. Mix in butter and eggs then breadcrumbs
and the flour.

2 Fill large boiler three-quarters full of hot water, cover; bring to a boil. Have ready
2.5 metres of kitchen string and an extra ½ cup of plain flour. Wearing thick rubber
gloves, put pudding cloth in boiling water; boil 1 minute; squeeze excess water from
cloth. Working quickly, spread hot cloth on bench, rub flour into centre of cloth to
cover an area about 40cm in diameter, leaving flour a little thicker in centre of cloth
where 'skin' on the pudding needs to be thickest.

3 Place pudding mixture in centre of cloth. Gather cloth evenly around mixture,
avoiding any deep pleats; then pat into round shape. Tie cloth tightly with string as
close to mixture as possible. Pull ends of cloth tightly to ensure pudding is as round
and firm as possible. Knot two pairs of corners together to make pudding easier
to remove.

4 Lower pudding into boiling water; tie free ends of string to handles of boiler to
suspend pudding. Cover with tight-fitting lid; boil rapidly for 4 hours, replenishing
water as necessary to maintain level.

5 Untie pudding from handles; place wooden spoon through knotted calico loops
to lift pudding from water. Do not put pudding on bench; suspend from spoon by
placing over rungs of upturned stool or wedging handle in a drawer. Pudding must
be suspended freely. Twist wet ends of cloth around string to avoid them touching
pudding. If pudding has been cooked correctly, cloth will start to dry in patches
within a few minutes; hang 10 minutes.

6 Place pudding on board; cut string, carefully peel back cloth. Turn pudding onto
a plate then carefully peel cloth away completely; cool. Stand at least 20 minutes
or until skin darkens and pudding becomes firm.

fruit mince slice

preparation time 10 minutes
cooking time 25 minutes

2 sheets ready-rolled puff pastry
¼ quantity basic fruit mixture (see page 92)
1 egg white, beaten lightly
1 tablespoon caster sugar

1 Preheat oven to hot. Grease 20cm x
30cm shallow baking tin.
2 Cut one pastry sheet large enough to
cover base of prepared tin. Using fork,
prick pastry all over several times. Place
19cm x 29cm baking tray on top of pastry
to prevent it rising during cooking.
3 Bake pastry in hot oven about
10 minutes or until pastry is browned
lightly and crisp.
4 Remove baking tray; spread fruit mixture
evenly over cooked pastry.
5 Cut remaining pastry sheet large enough
to cover fruit mixture. Brush pastry with
egg white, sprinkle with sugar; carefully
score pastry in crosshatch pattern. Bake,
uncovered, in hot oven about 15 minutes
or until pastry is browned. Serve slice with
custard, if desired

best-ever boiled fruit cake

2⅓ cups (375g) sultanas

2¼ cups (375g) chopped raisins

¾ cup (110g) currants

½ cup (105g) glacé cherries, halved

250g butter, chopped coarsely

1 cup (200g) firmly packed brown sugar

½ cup (125ml) sweet sherry

¼ cup (60ml) water

1 tablespoon treacle

2 teaspoons finely grated orange rind

2 teaspoons finely lemon rind

5 eggs, beaten lightly

1¾ cups (260g) plain flour

⅓ cup (50g) self-raising flour

extra glacé cherries, to decorate

preparation time 30 minutes ▪ cooking time 2 hours 45 minutes ▪ serves 36

1 Combine fruit, butter, sugar, sherry and the water in large saucepan. Stir over heat, without boiling, until butter melts and sugar dissolves. Bring to a boil, then remove from heat. Transfer mixture to large heatproof bowl; cool. *

2 Grease deep 19cm-square cake tin or deep 23cm-round cake tin, line base and sides with three layers baking parchment, extending paper 5cm above edge of tin.

3 Stir treacle, rinds and egg into fruit mixture, then stir in flours. Spread cake mixture into prepared tin; decorate top with extra glacé cherries, if desired. Bake in low oven about 2¾ hours. Cover hot cake tightly with foil; cool in tin.

last-minute fruit cake

1½ cups (240g) sultanas

1 cup (170g) raisins, chopped coarsely

1 cup (150g) currants

½ cup (85g) mixed peel

⅓ cup (70g) glacé cherries, halved

2 tablespoons coarsely chopped
glacé pineapple

2 tablespoons coarsely chopped
glacé apricots

185g butter, chopped

¾ cup (165g) firmly packed brown sugar

⅓ cup (80ml) brandy

⅓ cup (80ml) water

2 teaspoons finely grated orange rind

1 teaspoon finely grated lemon rind

1 tablespoon treacle

3 eggs, beaten lightly

1¼ cups (185g) plain flour

¼ cup (35g) self-raising flour

½ teaspoon bicarbonate of soda

½ cup (80g) blanched almonds

preparation time 20 minutes ■ cooking time 2 hours
(plus cooling time)

1 Line deep 20cm-round cake tin with three thicknesses of
baking parchment, extending paper 5cm above side.
2 Combine fruit, butter, sugar, brandy and the water in
medium saucepan, stir over medium heat until butter is
melted and sugar is dissolved; bring to the boil. Remove from
heat; transfer to large bowl. Cool to room temperature.
3 Preheat oven to low.
4 Stir rinds, treacle and eggs into fruit mixture then sifted
dry ingredients. Spread mixture into prepared tin; decorate
with nuts.
5 Bake in low oven, uncovered, about 2 hours. Cover hot
cake with foil; cool in tin overnight.

tips We used a 600-watt
microwave oven for this recipe.

microwave puddings

preparation time 20 minutes ■ cooking time 19 minutes ■ makes 8

2¾ cups (500g) mixed dried fruit

⅓ cup (80ml) brandy

125g butter

¾ cup (150g) firmly packed dark brown
sugar

2 tablespoons golden syrup

2 eggs

1 large (200g) apple, peeled, grated
coarsely

¾ cup (110g) plain flour

2 teaspoons mixed spice

½ teaspoon bicarbonate of soda

1 Grease eight ¾-cup (180ml) microwave-safe dishes.

2 Combine fruit and brandy in another small microwave-safe bowl; cook, covered,
on HIGH (100%) 1 minute.

3 Beat butter, sugar and syrup in small bowl with electric mixer until combined.
Add eggs, one at a time, beating until just combined between additions. Transfer
mixture to large bowl; stir in fruit mixture, apple and sifted dry ingredients.

4 Divide mixture evenly among prepared dishes, smooth tops.

5 Arrange dishes around edge of microwave turntable; cook, uncovered, on
MEDIUM (50%) 10 minutes. Rotate dishes; cook on MEDIUM (50%) further
8 minutes or until centres of puddings are almost set. Stand puddings 10 minutes;
centres of puddings should be firm. Turn puddings onto serving dishes.

This recipe is gluten-free, contains no dairy products or eggs, and makes one cake or pudding

¼ cups (360g) sultanas
1½ cups (250g) chopped raisins
½ cup (75g) currants
1½ cups (250g) chopped stoned dates
1½ cups (375ml) water
½ cup (125ml) orange juice
2 tablespoons honey
1 cup (200g) firmly packed brown sugar
185g dairy-free margarine
1 cup (125g) soy flour
1 cup (150g) rice flour
1 teaspoon cream of tartar
½ teaspoon bicarbonate of soda
2 teaspoons mixed spice
1 cup (125g) ground almonds

for the cake, grease a deep 19cm-square cake tin, line base and sides with three layers baking parchment, extending paper 5cm above edge of tin. Make cake mixture as above, then spread mixture into prepared tin; bake in low oven about 2½ hours, covering loosely with foil after 1 hour. Cover hot cake tightly with foil; cool in tin.

allergy-free pudding & cake

preparation time 20 minutes ■ cooking time 6 hours ■ serves 10

1 Combine fruit, the water, juice, honey, sugar and margarine in large saucepan. Stir over heat, without boiling, until margarine melts. Transfer mixture to large heatproof bowl; cool.
2 Grease 2.25-litre (9-cup) pudding basin, line base with baking parchment.
3 Stir sifted dry ingredients and ground almonds into fruit mixture. Spoon mixture into prepared basin, cover pudding with greased foil; secure with lid or kitchen string. Place basin in large saucepan with enough boiling water to come halfway up side of basin; simmer, covered, about 6 hours, adding more boiling water as necessary.

four quick toppings for puddings

These Christmas pudding accompaniments are so delectable you might have to make all four! The recipes for butters will freeze successfully for up to 4 weeks, covered tightly. The other recipes are best made just before serving.

cinnamon rum butter

serves 12

250g soft butter
1 cup (200g) firmly packed brown sugar
2 teaspoons ground cinnamon
2 tablespoons dark rum

Beat butter, sugar and cinnamon in small bowl with electric mixer until light and fluffy; add rum, beat until combined. Spoon mixture into piping bag fitted with medium fluted tube. Pipe mixture into twelve 5cm rounds on cling film-lined tray. Refrigerate until firm.

orange liqueur butter

serves 6

125g soft butter
2 teaspoons finely grated orange rind
½ cup (80g) icing sugar
2 tablespoons Irish cream liqueur

Beat butter and rind in small bowl with electric mixer until light and fluffy; gradually add sifted icing sugar, beat until smooth. Add liqueur, beat until combined. Spoon mixture into serving bowl.

easy coffee sauce

serves 8

1 litre vanilla ice-cream
2 tablespoons dry instant coffee
1 tablespoon boiling water

Stand ice-cream at room temperature until melted. Dissolve coffee and boiling water in small bowl; stir into melted ice-cream.

caramel rum custard

serves 6

600ml carton prepared vanilla custard
1 tablespoon dark rum
¾ cup (150g) firmly packed brown sugar
2 teaspoons vanilla essence

Combine custard, rum and sugar in medium saucepan; stir over low heat until sugar is dissolved. Stir in essence. Serve warm or cold.

4½ cups (675g) self-raising flour

3 teaspoons ground ginger

2 teaspoons ground cinnamon

1½ teaspoons ground cloves

1 teaspoon ground nutmeg

185g butter, chopped

1 cup (220g) firmly packed dark
brown sugar

½ cup (180g) treacle

2 eggs, beaten lightly

35cm round or square cake board

assorted sweets

royal icing

2 egg whites

3 cups (480g) icing sugar

royal icing Beat egg whites
in small bowl with electric mixer
until frothy; gradually beat in
sifted icing sugar. Cover icing
with damp cloth while not using.

tips You need thin cardboard or
thick paper to make the patterns.
■ The house can be assembled
three days ahead ■ You can fill
the house with sweets before
putting on the roof.

gingerbread house

preparation time 2 hours 30 minutes (plus refrigeration time) ■ cooking time 45 minutes (plus standing time)

1 Process flour, spices and butter until mixture is crumbly (you may need to process in two batches). Add sugar, treacle and enough egg for mixture to just combine. Turn dough onto floured surface; knead until smooth. Cover; refrigerate 1 hour.

2 Meanwhile, cut paper patterns for gingerbread house: cut two 12cm x 19cm rectangles for roof; two 10.5cm x 16cm rectangles for side walls of house; and two 16cm x 18cm rectangles for front and back walls of house. Trim front and back walls to form two 11cm-high gables.

3 Preheat oven to moderate. Roll dough between sheets of baking parchment until 5mm thick. Peel away top layer of paper; use patterns to cut shapes from dough. Pull away excess dough; slide baking parchment with shapes onto oven tray; bake, uncovered, in moderate oven about 12 minutes or until shapes are just firm (they become crisp after they cool). Re-roll dough scraps into one 5mm-thick piece; cut out trees and chimney.

4 While shapes are still warm and soft, use tip of sharp knife to cut out small windows from side walls of house, then cut out door from front, reserving cut-out door piece. Trim shapes to straighten sides; transfer shapes to wire racks to cool.

5 Make royal icing. Cover board with foil or silver paper.

6 Secure two crossed skewers to back of each roof piece with icing. Allow to dry.

7 Assemble house, securing roof and walls together with icing. If possible, stand house several hours or overnight, supporting sides with four cans, so that it is thoroughly dry before decorating. Decorate board around house with remaining icing to resemble fallen snow.

8 Secure door to house with icing; decorate house with sweets, securing with icing. Secure trees to board and chimney to roof with icing. Dust house with a little sifted icing sugar, if desired.

Bring out this tree with the coffee, suggesting to your guests that they snap off bits of the branches. Or, for an impressive gift, wrap the whole tree in cellophane and deliver it on the day.

christmas nut tree

preparation time 30 minutes (plus refrigeration time)

24cm-round covered cake board
500g dark eating chocolate, melted
1 cup (140g) toasted slivered almonds, chopped finely
½ cup (95g) finely chopped dried figs
100g dark eating chocolate, melted, extra
1 brazil nut
2 teaspoons icing sugar

1 Grease four oven trays; line each with baking parchment. Mark nine crosses, measuring 7cm, 9cm, 11cm, 13cm, 14cm, 15cm, 16cm, 17cm and 18cm on trays, leaving about 3cm space between each cross. Mark an 18cm cross on cake board.

2 Combine chocolate, almonds and figs in medium bowl. Drop teaspoonfuls of the chocolate mixture along all the marked crosses to make branches; refrigerate several hours or overnight.

3 Drop about a teaspoon of the extra melted chocolate into the centre of the 18cm cross on cake board; position the 18cm branch on top, moving it around until the best position is found.

4 Assemble the remaining eight branches in pairs, starting from the largest remaining branch and finishing with the smallest, using about a teaspoon of the extra melted chocolate in the centre of each crossed pair; refrigerate until set.

5 Secure each pair to the next with a little melted chocolate (if the branches look a little uneven, support them underneath with a match box). Secure brazil nut to centre of smallest branch with remaining melted chocolate; refrigerate until chocolate sets between branches. Store tree in refrigerator until required; dust with sifted icing sugar.

christmas crafts & gifts

We used fresh blooms in our stunning door wreath, which can be expensive at this time of year. The wreath should last up to three days, if sprayed twice daily with water. For a more long-lasting wreath, use silk flowers.

1 x grape vine wreath
2 x bunches hydrangeas
1 x bunch assorted foliage in silver
white orchids
dried spanish moss
5 x 30cm lengths 18 gauge wire (optional)
1m fishing line

wreath

1 Leaving the stems on the hydrangeas, carefully feed through the wreath, making sure not to break the stems. Hold in place with the wire.

2 Repeat step 1 using the silver and green foliage.

3 Using fishing line, simply tie the orchids into a cluster on the wreath.

4 Finish by placing spanish moss to hide any imperfections.

tips To save money, you can use the fishing line to tie the flowers in place, rather than the 18 gauge wire ▨ The grape vine already comes in wreath form from your local florist; you can use a willow wreath if you prefer ▨ Orchids are sold as individual blooms.

Every mantlepiece should have a stocking hanging on it at Christmas time. We offer two alternatives here, a contemporary stocking in fresh shades of blue and a more traditional red version.

contemporary stocking

50cm x 120cm main fabric
for stocking leg
25cm piece contrasting fabric
for stocking collar
sewing thread to match

1 Using tracing paper, trace the stocking from the pattern sheet provided. Cut traced pattern in two along dotted line, so you have a rectangular piece (collar) and a stocking leg.

2 Double over main fabric and cut two pieces for the stocking leg, adding an extra 1.5cm for the seam. With right-sides facing, machine stitch around stocking leg. Snip seam, especially around curved areas; press.

3 Using the rectangular pattern (collar) as a guide, increase collar size so that it measures 21cm wide (double the original width); use this to cut 2 pieces from the contrasting fabric, adding an extra 1.5cm for the seam allowance.

4 With right-sides of fabric facing, pin and machine stitch short sides together. Press seams open.

5 Slip collar over stocking, with right sides of collar facing wrong side of stocking and side seams matching. Pin and stitch collar to top of stocking using 1.5cm seam allowance.

6 Fold over bottom edge of collar 1.5cm to form hem; press. Turn stocking right-side out. Fold collar in half and stitch bottom of collar to stocking.

traditional stocking

1 square metre beige or red-coloured felt material

matching cotton

tracing paper

pencil

1   Using tracing paper, trace the stocking from the pattern sheet provided. Cut traced pattern in two along dotted line, so you have a rectangular piece (collar) and a stocking leg.

2   Cut 2 pieces of fabric for the stocking leg, adding an extra 1.5cm for the seam. Machine stitch right sides of fabric together. Snip seam, especially around curved part of stocking. Turn stocking right side out.

3   Using the rectangular pattern (collar) as a guide, increase collar size so that it measures 62cm x 21cm (double the length and width of the original size); add an extra 1.5cm for the seam allowance. Cut 1 piece of fabric for the collar.

4   Pin collar to stocking; machine stitch in place. Turn collar up; machine stitch short sides together allowing 1.5cm for seam allowance.

5   Turn and pin top edge over 1cm to form hem; machine stitch in place.

6   Fold collar in half; decorate with either rickrack or buttons (see right).

DECORATING THE STOCKING

natural stocking

65cm red rickrack

65cm beige rickrack

matching threads

8 red buttons

needle

Machine stitch red and beige rickrack around base of collar. Hand-sew the buttons evenly around the stocking collar.

red stocking

assorted red buttons

matching thread

needle

Randomly hand-sew a mixture of buttons all over the stocking collar.

rickrack red stocking

70cm red rickrack

matching red buttons

matching thread

needle

Hand-sew a line of buttons around the base of the stocking collar. Hand-sew rickrack from the toe to the heel of the stocking.

christmas tree decorations

You will need jewellery wire (26 gauge), beads, jewellery pliers, scissors or special wire cutters. The baubles all begin with a loop for hanging on the tree. Using approx 2cm of the wire indicated, gently bend in half and twist around wire, making an oval loop.

christmas tree

3 x 12cm length wire

2 x 8cm length wire

24 tiny silver beads

34 small glass beads

14 blue crystal beads

10 natural beads

8 round crystal beads

1 large blue crystal bead

1 Using a 12cm wire make a loop (see instructions above); thread on 1 silver and 5 glass beads, put aside.

2 Secure a tiny loop in one 8cm wire (top branch) then thread on half the bead combination, as pictured above. Thread this wire through the last 3 glass beads on the central stem (this becomes the second branch). Bend wire out to form second branch; complete pattern and secure with a tiny loop.

3 Repeat step 2 with 8cm wire on the other side, then thread another 6 glass beads onto the central wire.

4 Using the 12cm wires, repeat step 2 to complete the lower branches of the tree. Finish off central wire with two glass, two silver and a blue bead. Secure with a tiny loop.

blue spiral circle

1 x 30cm length wire

3 tiny silver beads

40 blue crystal beads

40 smaller blue crystal beads

1 pearl bead

1   Using wire make a loop (see instructions at top of page 114); thread all the beads according to the pattern pictured above, finishing with a silver, pearl then another silver bead. Twist wire into small loop to secure around last bead.

2   Bend wire into a spiral shape.

pearl bell

1 x 30cm length wire

1 x 4cm length wire

2 small crystal beads

8 small silver beads

6 small round pearl beads

9 cylindrical pearl beads

6 medium round pearl beads

2 small blue crystal beads

24 glass beads

1   Using 30cm wire, make a loop (see instructions at top of page 114) and thread on two small crystal beads.

2   Thread on beads in sequence as pictured, above.

3   Secure by twisting wire end around the base of the crystal beads. Trim excess wire; shape into a bell. Twist one end of the 4cm wire into a small loop; thread on one silver and one blue crystal bead. Thread wire through cylindrical bead at base of bell; finish off with a blue crystal then silver bead. Secure with a tiny loop.

santa stocking

1 x 26cm length wire

1 x 4cm length wire

36 silver beads

3 blue crystal beads

3 glass beads

1   Using the 26cm wire, make a loop (see instructions at top of page 114) and start threading on all the silver beads. Secure by twisting the end of the wire around the base of the loop at the start of first bead. Trim excess wire.

2   Shape wire into a stocking.

3   Twist 4cm wire tightly between silver beads 5 and 6 (counting from first bead after loop).

4   Thread blue and clear crystals on the 4cm wire and fasten to the other side as in step 3.

christmas cards

purchased pre-made cards or light-weight cardboard
assortment of ribbons (including bows and decoratively shaped
bindings such as flowers)
clear-drying craft glue
double-sided sticky tape
ruler, pencil, scissors
tapestry needle and thread

1 If using cardboard, cut and fold to the desired size (see note, opposite).

2 Cut the ribbons into desired lengths. Using the photographs as a guide only, glue or tape the ribbons onto the cards in your desired design.

3 Use the ruler to very lightly draw pencil lines in a triangular (or tree) shape. Use the needle and thread to sew design onto the card.

note Using pinking shears gives the paper a decorative edge. You can buy these from haberdashery and craft stores, although they can be expensive. A cheaper option, and also available from arts and craft stores, are scissors with various edgings used for paper crafts. When cut on paper, these give myriad different decorative edges.

gift wrapping

selection of different sized boxes in green,
white and lemon
coloured paper
twine
outdoor embellishments such as twigs, seeds, etc
selection of ribbons
scissors, pinking shears
clear-drying craft glue
double-sided sticky tape

1   Using the photographs as a guide only, position the ribbon,
paper, twine, twigs, stems and seeds etc., on the boxes.
2   Once you're happy with the look of your box, tape or glue
the decorations

It's always a delight to receive a home-made gift. Here are a few suggestions for some delicious treats that can be made in advance and given as presents – if you can keep your hands off them yourself, of course!

1 x 19cm-square fruit cake
2 x 500g packets soft icing
icing sugar, for dusting
food colourings
¾ cup (180ml) apricot jam, warmed, sieved
ribbons and decorations

tips to give as gifts, place the cakes on pieces of thick card, measuring about 9cm-square, covered with foil or glossy gift paper ■ gift cakes can be made a month ahead; store in an airtight container at room temperature

little gift cakes

preparation time 1 hour 30 minutes (plus standing time) ■ **makes 9**

1   Cut cake into nine even pieces; cover to keep airtight.

2   Knead icing until smooth on surface dusted with sifted icing sugar. Divide icing into nine even-sized pieces. Tint each piece by kneading in one of the colourings – leave some pieces uncoloured if white icing is desired. Wrap tinted pieces individually in cling film until ready to use.

3   Brush top and sides of cake evenly with jam just before it is ready to be covered with icing. Roll out icing between sheets of baking parchment until large enough to cover top and sides of cake. Lift icing onto cake, then lightly mould icing over cake with dusted hands; trim edges neatly.

4   Repeat with remaining icing and cakes. Icing scraps can be cut to make decorative shapes; secure shapes to cakes with a little more jam. Decorate cakes with ribbons and decorations.

scottish shortbread

250g butter, chopped

⅓ cup (75g) caster sugar

¼ cup (35g) rice flour

2¼ cups (335g) plain flour

2 tablespoons white sugar

gift wrap

cellophane squares

tartan ribbon

preparation time 20 minutes ▓ cooking time 40 minutes ▓ makes 16

1 Preheat oven to low (150°C/130°C fan-assisted).

2 Beat butter and caster sugar in medium bowl with electric mixer until light and fluffy; stir in sifted flours, in two batches. Knead on floured surface until smooth.

3 Divide mixture in half, shape into two 20cm rounds; place on two greased baking trays. Mark rounds into eight wedges, prick with fork, pinch edges; sprinkle with white sugar.

4 Bake about 40 minutes. Stand 5 minutes then cut into wedges; cool on trays.

5 To gift wrap the shortbread, place a quantity of shortbread in the centre of a cellophane square, gather up the cellophane and tie with a ribbon.

tips Shortbread can be made one week ahead and stored in an airtight container.

gourmet rocky road

300g toasted marshmallows with
coconut, chopped coarsely

400g turkish delight, chopped coarsely

¼ cup (40g) roasted almonds,
chopped coarsely

½ cup (75g) roasted shelled pistachios

450g white eating chocolate, melted

gift wrap

white tissue paper

white chiffon ribbon

silver card

preparation time 20 minutes (plus refrigeration time) ■ makes 36 slices

1 Grease two 8cm x 26cm shallow cake tins; line base and sides with baking parchment, extending parchment 5cm above long sides.

2 Combine marshmallows, turkish delight and nuts in large bowl. Working quickly, stir in chocolate; spread mixture into tins, push mixture down firmly to flatten. Refrigerate until set then cut as desired.

3 To gift wrap the rocky road, cut pieces of tissue paper twice the length of the sweets and wide enough to wrap around them twice. Centre a sweet on a piece of tissue, wrap the tissue round and gather in at either end, securing the ends with pieces of ribbon. Attach gift tags made from heart shapes cut from the silver card.

tips The cherries will last indefinitely ■ Do not allow metal lids to touch the liquid; you can use plastic or glass instead ■ This recipe is best made four to six weeks ahead of using ■ Cherries can be served with cream or ice-cream, and the vodka used in mixed drinks, punch or cocktails.

cherries in vodka

500g fresh cherries, pitted
¾ cup (165g) caster sugar
2 cups (500ml) vodka, approximately

gift wrap
glass storage jars
scraps of gingham fabric
ribbon

preparation time 20 minutes ■ cooking time 25 minutes ■ makes 1 litre (4 cups)

1 Place clean jars on sides in large saucepan; cover completely with hot water. Boil, covered, 20 minutes. Remove jars from water; drain upright on board until dry.
2 Layer cherries and sugar in jars; pour over enough vodka to cover cherries completely. Seal. Stand in cool dark place for at least six weeks before using. Invert jars occasionally to help dissolve the sugar.
3 To gift wrap, cut strips of gingham fabric and wrap around centre of jars, securing in place with clear glue. Decorate with a length of ribbon.

Truffles are a cook's secret: they look so impressive but are actually quite effortless to make. Start making your truffles two days in advance so that you don't have to hurry their preparation. Wrap them in pretty gift boxes (see pages 118–9) lined with tissue paper.

dark chocolate & ginger

preparation time 40 minutes (plus refrigeration time)
■ cooking time 5 minutes ■ makes 30

⅓ cup (80ml) whipping cream
200g dark eating chocolate, chopped coarsely
½ cup (115g) glacé ginger, chopped finely
¼ cup (25g) cocoa powder

1 Combine cream and chocolate in small saucepan; stir over low heat until smooth, stir in ginger. Transfer to small bowl, cover; refrigerate 3 hours or overnight.
2 Working with a quarter of the chocolate mixture at a time (keeping remainder under refrigeration), roll rounded teaspoons into balls; place on tray. Refrigerate truffles until firm.
3 Working quickly, roll balls in cocoa; refrigerate until firm.

white chocolate, lemon, lime & coconut

preparation time 40 minutes (plus refrigeration time)
■ cooking time 5 minutes ■ makes 30

½ cup (125ml) coconut cream
2 teaspoons finely grated lime rind
2 teaspoons finely grated lemon rind
360g white eating chocolate, chopped coarsely
1¼ cups (85g) shredded coconut

1 Combine coconut cream, rinds and chocolate in small saucepan; stir over low heat until smooth. Transfer mixture to small bowl, cover; refrigerate 3 hours or overnight.
2 Working with a quarter of the chocolate mixture at a time (keeping remainder under refrigeration), roll rounded teaspoons into balls; place on tray. Refrigerate truffles until firm.
3 Working quickly, roll truffles in coconut, return to tray; refrigerate until firm.

cranberry, port & dark chocolate

preparation time 40 minutes (plus refrigeration time)
■ cooking time 5 minutes ■ makes 30

¼ cup (60ml) whipping cream
200g dark eating chocolate, chopped coarsely
2 tablespoons port
⅓ cup (50g) dried cranberries, chopped coarsely
300g dark eating chocolate, melted

1 Combine cream and chopped chocolate in small saucepan; stir over low heat until smooth, stir in port and cranberries. Transfer to small bowl, cover; refrigerate 3 hours or overnight.
2 Working with a quarter of the chocolate mixture at a time (keeping remainder under refrigeration), roll rounded teaspoons into balls; place on tray. Freeze truffles until firm.
3 Working quickly, dip truffles in melted chocolate then roll gently in hands to coat evenly, return to tray; refrigerate until firm.

peanut butter & milk chocolate

preparation time 40 minutes (plus refrigeration time)
■ cooking time 5 minutes ■ makes 30

⅓ cup (80ml) whipping cream
200g milk eating chocolate, chopped coarsely
¼ cup (70g) unsalted crunchy peanut butter
¾ cup (110g) crushed peanuts

1 Combine cream and chocolate in small saucepan; stir over low heat until smooth, stir in peanut butter. Transfer to small bowl, cover; refrigerate 3 hours or overnight.
2 Working with a quarter of the chocolate mixture at a time (keeping remainder under refrigeration), roll rounded teaspoons into balls; place on tray. Refrigerate truffles until firm.
3 Working quickly, roll balls in peanuts, return to tray; refrigerate truffles until firm.

index

conversion charts

Measures

The cup and spoon measurements used in this book are metric: one measuring cup holds approximately 250ml; one metric tablespoon holds 20ml; one metric teaspoon holds 5ml.

All cup and spoon measurements are level. The most accurate way of measuring dry ingredients is to weigh them. When measuring liquids, use a clear glass or plastic jug with metric markings. We use large eggs with an average weight of 60g.

Liquid measures

metric	imperial
30ml	1 fl oz
60ml	2 fl oz
100ml	3 fl oz
125ml	4 fl oz
150ml	5 fl oz (¼ pint/1 gill)
190ml	6 fl oz
250ml	8 fl oz
300ml	10 fl oz (½pt)
500ml	16 fl oz
600ml	20 fl oz (1 pint)
1000ml (1 litre)	1¾pints

Dry measures

metric	imperial
15g	½oz
30g	1oz
60g	2oz
90g	3oz
125g	4oz (¼lb)
155g	5oz
185g	6oz
220g	7oz
250g	8oz (½lb)
280g	9oz
315g	10oz
345g	11oz
375g	12oz (¾lb)
410g	13oz
440g	14oz
470g	15oz
500g	16oz (1lb)
750g	24oz (1½lb)
1kg	32oz (2lb)

Length measures

metric	imperial
3mm	⅛in
6mm	¼in
1cm	½in
2cm	¾in
2.5cm	1in
5cm	2in
6cm	2½in
8cm	3in
10cm	4in
13cm	5in
15cm	6in
18cm	7in
20cm	8in
23cm	9in
25cm	10in
28cm	11in
30cm	12in (1ft)

Oven temperatures

These oven temperatures are only a guide for conventional ovens. For fan-assisted ovens, check the manufacturer's manual.

	°C (Celcius)	°F (Fahrenheit)	gas mark
Very low	120	250	½
Low	150	275-300	1-2
Moderately low	170	325	3
Moderate	180	350-375	4-5
Moderately hot	200	400	6
Hot	220	425-450	7-8
Very hot	240	475	9

WARNING This book contains recipes for dishes made with raw or lightly cooked eggs. These should be avoided by vulnerable people such as pregnant and nursing mothers, invalids, the elderly, babies and young children.